THE
EVERYTHING®
GIANT BOOK OF
BRAIN-BOOSTING PUZZLES

Dear Reader,

I discovered the power of puzzles when I created Funster.com, a website devoted to wordplay and games. The many dedicated visitors to Funster.com have proved to me that puzzles can be quite addictive. Fortunately, a growing number of scientific studies tell us that puzzle solving can give our brains a boost. So sometimes, if we're lucky, things that are fun are also good for us.

I like the idea of people getting smarter as they solve puzzles, which is why I'm thrilled with this book. If you want to excel at life's mental tasks, then I challenge you to work your way through these pages. As the world grows more complicated (or is it just me getting older?) it seems that having a sharp brain is more of a necessity. The eighteen types of puzzles here provide a great way to practice using our minds where the stakes are not so high and the solutions are ultimately clear. Have fun!

Charles Timmerman

Welcome to the EVERYTHING® Series!

These handy, accessible books give you all you need to tackle a difficult project, gain a new hobby, comprehend a fascinating topic, prepare for an exam, or even brush up on something you learned back in school but have since forgotten.

You can choose to read an *Everything*® book from cover to cover or just pick out the information you want from our four useful boxes: e-questions, e-facts, e-alerts, and e-ssentials. We give you everything you need to know on the subject, but throw in a lot of fun stuff along the way, too.

We now have more than 400 *Everything*® books in print, spanning such wide-ranging categories as weddings, pregnancy, cooking, music instruction, foreign language, crafts, pets, New Age, and so much more. When you're done reading them all, you can finally say you know *Everything*®!

PUBLISHER Karen Cooper

DIRECTOR OF ACQUISITIONS AND INNOVATION Paula Munier

MANAGING EDITOR, EVERYTHING® SERIES Lisa Laing

COPY CHIEF Casey Ebert

ACQUISITIONS EDITOR Lisa Laing

EDITORIAL ASSISTANT Hillary Thompson

EVERYTHING® SERIES COVER DESIGNER Erin Alexander

LAYOUT DESIGNERS Colleen Cunningham, Elisabeth Lariviere, Ashley Vierra, Denise Wallace

Visit the entire Everything® series at *www.everything.com*

THE
EVERYTHING®
GIANT BOOK OF
BRAIN-BOOSTING
PUZZLES

Improve your mental fitness with more
than 750 challenging puzzles!

Edited by Charles Timmerman

Founder of Funster.com

Adams**media**
Avon, Massachusetts

For Ting, whose first dedication was two
years ago. The wait is almost over!

Contains material adapted and abridged from:

The Everything 15-Minute Sudoku Book, by Charles Timmerman, copyright © 2006, by F+W Media, Inc., 1-59869-054-X, 978-1-59869-054-5. *The Everything Brain Strain Book*, by Jake Olefsky, copyright © 2005, by F+W Media, Inc., 1-59337-315-5, 978-1-59337-315-3. *The Everything Crossword & Puzzle Book Volume II*, by Charles Timmerman, copyright © 2009, by F+W Media, Inc., 1-60550-047-X, 978-1-60550-047-8. *The Everything Crosswords & Puzzles for Quote Lovers Book*, by Charles Timmerman, copyright © 2008, by F+W Media, Inc., 1-59869-718-8, 978-1-59869-718-6. *The Everything Cryptograms Book*, by Nikki Katz, copyright © 2005, by F+W Media, Inc., 1-59337-319-8, 978-1-59337-319-1. *The Everything Easy Kakuro Book*, by Charles Timmerman, copyright © 2006, by F+W Media, Inc., 1-59869-056-6, 978-1-59869-056-9. *The Everything Giant Book of Crosswords*, by Charles Timmerman, copyright © 2008, by F+W Media, Inc., 1-59869-716-1, 978-1-59869-716-2. *The Everything Memory Booster Puzzles Book*, by Charles Timmerman, copyright © 2008, by F+W Media, Inc., 1-59869-383-2, 978-1-59869-383-6. *The Everything Pencil Puzzles Book*, by Charles Timmerman, copyright © 2006, by F+W Media, Inc., 1-59337-584-0, 978-1-59337-584-3. *The Everything Word Games Challenge Book*, by Charles Timmerman, copyright © 2005, by F+W Media, Inc., 1-59337-312-0, 978-1-59337-312-2. *The Everything Word Scramble Book*, by Charles Timmerman, copyright © 2007, by F+W Media, Inc., 1-59869-240-2, 978-1-59869-240-2. *The Everything Word Search Book*, by Charles Timmerman, copyright © 2006, by F+W Media, Inc., 1-59337-431-3, 978-1-59337-431-0.

An Everything® Series Book.
Everything® and everything.com® are registered trademarks of F+W Media, Inc.

Published by Adams Media, a division of F+W Media, Inc.
57 Littlefield Street, Avon, MA 02322 U.S.A.
www.adamsmedia.com

ISBN 10: 1-4405-0341-9
ISBN 13: 978-1-4405-0341-2

Printed in the United States of America.

J   I   H   G   F   E   D   C   B   A

This book is available at quantity discounts for bulk purchases.
For information, please call 1-800-289-0963.

Contents

Acknowledgments

I would like to thank the more than half a million people who have visited my website, Funster.com, to play word games and puzzles. You are the inspiration for this book. I'm appreciative of everyone at Adams Media for making this book possible. In particular, Hillary Thompson did a great job pulling everything together and making my job easy. As always, it was a joy to work with my editor Lisa Laing who always keeps me busy. I've been fortunate to have Jacky Sach as my agent; her skill and dedication have benefited me enormously. And a very special thanks to Suzanne and Calla for keeping me on my toes with my brain boosted!

Introduction

IN THIS DAY AND age, being smart is more important than being strong. This book will exercise your brain, and research suggests that this can make you smarter. As every child instinctively knows, play helps prepare us for the real world. The puzzles in this book are like that; they are fun but at the same time they give our brains a boost for tasks that really matter.

Think of mental fitness as being similar to physical fitness. With physical exercise it is important to work all the muscle groups. This book has eighteen different types of puzzles with words, numbers, and logic to provide a whole-brain workout. These puzzles are made to engage your brain, not to melt it down. It's like with physical fitness where repetitions of simple exercises can be very beneficial.

This book isn't only about getting our brains in shape. The goal here is to also have fun—the reason most people do puzzles. The best motivation to keeping any exercise program going is to do something that we enjoy. Hopefully you will find the challenges in these pages engaging; the benefits of mental exercise will be a happy byproduct.

One of the remarkable things about the brain is that it can attempt to understand itself. Scientists studying the brain have made tremendous progress in recent years. One thing they have learned is that brains in more stimulating environments will have an increased number of synapses with more complex connections. This leads to more cognitive ability and greater resilience to the effects of aging. It is common sense when you think about it: use it or lose it. This book will keep your brain moving.

Many people believe that memory loss is inevitable as we age. Research indicates that this doesn't have to be the case. In a study published in the Journal of the American Medical Association, 2,802 participants age 65 and older received cognitive training for two hours per week for five weeks. A significant number of the participants improved their memory and cognitive abilities, and this improvement even persisted for two years after the training.

Another study published in The New England Journal of Medicine found that people could reduce their risk of Alzheimer's disease by adding one mentally stimulating activity per week. Adding more activities, like working a crossword puzzle every day, was even better.

Sometimes our brains simply need a mental diversion from the challenges of a regular day. The puzzles in these pages are great for taking a relaxing break. They will keep your mental gears turning but with a shift in focus. After a session of puzzle solving, we return to earth with a fresh perspective. Often that is when insights come quickly and real-world problems are solved.

These puzzles will provide numerous "aha!" moments when the light bulb turns on in your head and a solution becomes clear. Each of these moments builds confidence in the mind's amazing abilities. And perhaps that is the biggest brain boost of all.

Chapter 1
Word Search Puzzles

All of these word search puzzles are in the traditional format. Words are hidden in a grid of letters in any direction: horizontal, vertical, diagonal, forward, or backward. Words can overlap. For example, the letters at the end of the word "MAST" could be used as the start of the word "STERN." Only the letters A to Z are used, and any spaces in an entry are removed. For example, "TROPICAL FISH" would be found in the grid as "TROPICALFISH."

Holidays

```
E D C Y S H A N A H S A H H S O R K Z U
F A R Y A A Y A D E L L I T S A B L Y S
O S E A L D N F A T H E R S D A Y Y A T
U A T D S A S T E A R T H D A Y Y A D D
R R S L A C V T A F L A G D A Y A D S Y
T A A A I L H I N L R K Z R C C D S N A
H Y E I N Y U I T I U W B D J H G E I D
O A Y R T Y A N N S A C C S R U N N K S
F D A O P S A D A E E S I O K S I I W T
J S D M A A R D S R S F L A W U X T A N
U E G E T R M A S U N E N L D K O N H E
L K O M R G K A M R B E N R A A B E E R
Y W H Y I I T N Y A E M W E E N Y L I A
A A D A C D Z E G D D H U Y W T Z A D P
A F N D K R Z U T P A A T L E Y N V A D
Z Y U R S A G J K Q X Y N O O A E A S N
N U O O D M Y A D R O B R A M C R A L A
A G R B A Y A D S L O O F L I R P A R R
W G G A Y R Y A D S T N E D I S E R P G
K L I L N A O Y A M E D O C N I C B D A
```

ALL SAINTS DAY
APRIL FOOLS DAY
ARBOR DAY
BASTILLE DAY
BOXING DAY
CHINESE NEW YEAR
CHUSUK
CINCO DE MAYO
COLUMBUS DAY

DASARA
EARTH DAY
EASTER
FATHERS DAY
FLAG DAY
FOURTH OF JULY
GRANDPARENTS DAY
GROUNDHOG DAY
GUY FAWKES DAY

KWANZAA
LABOR DAY
LANTERN FESTIVAL
LUNAR NEW YEAR
MARDI GRAS
MAY DAY
MEMORIAL DAY
MOTHERS DAY
PRESIDENTS DAY

RAMADAN
ROSH HASHANAH
SADIE HAWKINS DAY
SAINT PATRICKS DAY
SANTA LUCIA DAY
VALENTINES DAY

Solution on page 304

Classical Music

```
R L I P H L K I J T H E F T R B F P O X
E X N A U A O P N O E B D O H F L R A A
R I N R K Q G F S S O T T U K E T Z C P
B O A H C S M U R D T C N C L S M W R E
O N R Y I O P I U I U R H I E R J E P M
L C R E N R V V A D W A U A U P E E F N
A P A Q O D V E N R R T M M V Q R T E P
C Q N U M Q O O R M T W N R E C G Y N K
O K G A R C C S O T F S E E U N E Y V I
V K E R A M H N Y Y U B E S M M T Q P O
G E M T H E Y O U M M R S H E E V A G T
O J E E L Q B R R A P I E L C R V K L R
V R N T I O S D H A O H F L Z R O O L E
G X T L H W R C A N L D O M Q T O C M C
P L F F P R E S O P M O C N T R D T S N
P A S S A G E M E L O D Y F Y E N N P O
H D B W J S T R I N G D M I H C W H A C
Z C I U W P E N S E M B L E A N C S R B
Q N Y Q K Z V S O N A T A O V O P A Q G
D T G B H P X S Z I N K L S V C P N W R
```

ARRANGEMENT	DRUMS	ORCHESTRA	SONATA
BAND	ENSEMBLE	OVERTURE	STRING
CHAMBER	HARMONY	PASSAGE	SYMPHONY
CHORAL	INSTRUMENTAL	PERCUSSION	THEME
COMPOSER	INTERLUDE	PHILHARMONIC	VOCAL
CONCERT	MAESTRO	QUARTET	WIND
CONCERTO	MELODY	QUINTET	
CONDUCTOR	MOVEMENT	SCORE	

Solution on page 304

Actors

```
D D A L N A L A E Y E N R A C T R A Z H
C H I C O M A R X S E H C E M A N O D Y
B J A M E S D E A N E Y E S U B Y R A G
J Y D N A C N H O J Y E A L P A C I N O
E N Y A W N H O J G K M L S E S O G Q A
T Q P E T E R F O N D A G C N R K V A R
Y O E E L B A G K R A L C O N Y K C V R
N U M R Z A A R F G Q R T I B H H Q O W
E X L M R K D C X F E T I S V E O C I A
L E T B I O M L T R U N O P V E K J D D
L A C G R X L Y A B A R E Y T H C L A N
A L A E N Y U F D N C M C K U O I X N O
Y A R N A W N E L G A H O D E Y R C A F
D N Y E A Y R N N Y A L S P Z L E N Y Y
O A G A C K V I E S N O A A R X L H K R
O R R U S N B R E R N N Q P H A V Y R N
W K A T E R E P O O C Y R A G R H F O E
N I N R M C O M A I C R A G Y D N A Y H
B N T Y A K C A S U C N H O J Q U E D I
U O Q F J V J O H N N Y D E P P X D O V
```

AL PACINO
ALAN ALDA
ALAN ARKIN
ALAN LADD
ANDY GARCIA
ART CARNEY
BING CROSBY
CARY GRANT
CHEVY CHASE

CHICO MARX
CLARK GABLE
DAN AYKROYD
DON AMECHE
ERROL FLYNN
GARY BUSEY
GARY COOPER
GENE AUTRY
GENE KELLY

HARPO MARX
HENRY FONDA
JAMES CAAN
JAMES DEAN
JOHN CANDY
JOHN CLEESE
JOHN CUSACK
JOHN WAYNE
JOHNNY DEPP

PETER FONDA
RED BUTTONS
RIP TORN
ROCK HUDSON
TOM MIX
WOODY ALLEN
YUL BRYNNER

Solution on page 304

Careers

```
P R P B E N Z C B Q I H D T H M R R Q R
H O O P C A P X I M T W L D S O E P E N
X T G N P M J N W A I T E R T K O Y U R
P C G A M K C I W M T S D C A S W R F O
N O I W R R G A N E H Q A B T A S E K H
I Y T O H W F P U H P R A U N C E V E U
C O S E L O Q A K A R N E O T T M Z E A
I U I M G I E C P N P E D G N L V E N X
S M C W A D C M Z I T F H I A F E N I F
U P A N A I U E A C Z N A C J N I R G I
M E M M O I D J M K A P E D T H A J N R
A N R K F E T L N A E T Y Y E U Q M E E
A D A N R R G R G I N R E P F N B S R M
J Z H Q W E M R E R E I H S A C T P H A
T I P C E K L Q U S R E G N I S I I I N
B Q V O N L P C V S S T E A C H E R S B
C H E M I S T R N U R O L I A T D N J T
F U J R T M N U Q U X B G V A D I T O E
Y W W J M L V G X L V F M O B X Q C K R
```

ACTOR	CLERK	MECHANIC	SURGEON
AUTHOR	DENTIST	MUSICIAN	TAILOR
BAKER	DOCTOR	NURSE	TEACHER
BUTCHER	ENGINEER	PAINTER	WAITER
BUTLER	FIREMAN	PHARMACIST	WAITRESS
CAPTAIN	JUDGE	POLICEMAN	WORKMAN
CASHIER	LAWYER	POSTMAN	
CHEF	MAID	SHOEMAKER	
CHEMIST	MANAGER	SINGER	

Solution on page 304

On the Baseball Field

```
V O L X K U J O S U J Z G H D D Q L J Q
A T G G T M H Q O H I E M G P J B B J S
S Z W J F E Z H N V A L L U K G B U D Y
R V O K F V I M E O E L X W R L M I S I
N D X G O J N N Y U M A L D K P A U I W
I E C N G T W F G S R B Y P I M H I T S
E I F B U G O A S E M E F R O S E S A B
Z V A W C R E D T O Y V E N X M S J E I
J L O P U L E T O B G R D X G G Y N I J
K X E L R H A M S V P U Q V Y V W X U K
A X I O G B X L O C R C I N F I E L D R
E G J E W P P E F H G R A N D S L A M P
Y A S H O R T S T O P L B E D G S I U R
M P T R I P L E P W L A L L F T Y E E E
S I K A Y O Y L O A S B E G R O G T L H
T T L L H Y A R B E U I M I N N U U G C
E C A W B T H T B O F A K M A I V L N T
A H W X E T I A D T E E A H S E N V I A
L E S O F P L K U T T N C V M O M N S C
Y R F G S L H O X V X N V X D D X Y I G
```

BALK	DOUBLE	MAJOR LEAGUE	STEAL
BASEBALL	FOUL	OUTFIELD	STRIKE
BASES	GLOVE	PITCHER	TEAM
BATTER	GRAND SLAM	PLATE	THROW
CATCHER	HITS	RUNS	TRIPLE
CHANGEUP	HOME RUN	SHORTSTOP	UMPIRE
CURVE BALL	INFIELD	SINGLE	WALK
DIAMOND	INNING	SPIT BALL	

Solution on page 305

Transportation

```
N S G L N U R D U N O L F T S U Z G B R
F T I R E E L I B O M O T U A S E W A Y
C U S T O M S D P C R F M P H F P R G Y
K G S N M L I R E V R I T I C M E C G A
A V U W S E R A T P U A G R B Y O M A L
B H I D Q E T C E D A H I I U N T A G E
O S T S E H C Y U V W R C L N C I K E D
W H C Q L W Y E O A I Y T E R R K E I B
H I A N C G X L Y T C T C U P O N F O U
B P S Y Y N I L L L E T O L R M A A D R
O E E B C I G O E Q I K A M A E T D I E
A W U S R R W R L O U N C R O W X B G G
G S E E O E Y T N G E R T I X C M K M N
U A L C T E P A S S P O R T T R O O Z E
I D S I O T A R R I V A L I G W A L E S
T A Q O M S W U B W I N D S H I E L D S
H J U O L H U T R N M S T A T I O N S A
S N W Z E I A H A Y T E N I G N E T U P
P S T E D X N X K N I A R T J H R T B H
C G L P I M Y E E E A B S B P I D G L P
```

AIRPLANE

ARRIVAL

AUTOMOBILE

BAGGAGE

BICYCLE

BOAT

BRAKE

BUS

CONNECTION

CUSTOMS

DELAY

DEPARTURE

ENGINE

GASOLINE

HIGHWAY

LOCOMOTIVE

MOTORCYCLE

PASSENGER

PASSPORT

RAILROAD

SHIP

STATION

STEERING WHEEL

SUITCASE

TAXI

TICKET

TIRE

TRAIN

TRAM

TROLLEY CAR

TRUCK

WHEEL

WINDSHIELD

Solution on page 305

Novels

```
H P S E S I R O S L A N U S E H T O B V
O E V T I G L I S M H D N U L I B N A Y
F R A Q H O N U C O I A F O J T R A T A
H N Y R L E G I W L M J R J E X A C T I
U K A I T A G A Y E A D D N U E V L L D
M M T M M O R R L D O U D R V C E O E N
A A R E R D F B A F Y E D O O O N V F I
N E H A S E I D T P R A L I N L E E I O
B T R E F S G H A I E N L T U R W H E T
O G N I I L E N S R I S H I A S W T L E
N D N V F F A T I N K E O G S S O R D G
D A N I L E H M E G R N T F H A R E E A
A I I I V E L M I O E I E A W I L D A S
G J E E N O O A A N M H N S F R D N R S
E S N I R W L D P E A E T P S E A U T A
A U G W E I V A H T I W M O O R A T H P
D H E G N A R O K R O W K C O L C A H A
T L L R S M R A O T L L E W E R A F A G
R Q N O C L A F E S E T L A M E H T A M
P R E I D L O S D O O G E H T E M W D U
```

A CLOCKWORK ORANGE	DUNE	LOVING	THE GOOD SOLDIER
A FAREWELL TO ARMS	HEART OF DARKNESS	OF HUMAN BONDAGE	THE GRAPES OF WRATH
A PASSAGE TO INDIA	HOWARDS END	ON THE ROAD	THE MAGUS
A ROOM WITH A VIEW	I CLAUDIUS	PALE FIRE	THE MALTESE FALCON
ANIMAL FARM	INVISIBLE MAN	RAGTIME	THE SUN ALSO RISES
AS I LAY DYING	LOLITA	SHANE	UNDER THE VOLCANO
BATTLEFIELD EARTH	LORD JIM	TENDER IS THE NIGHT	WOMEN IN LOVE
BRAVE NEW WORLD	LORD OF THE FLIES	THE GINGER MAN	

Solution on page 305

Candy

```
J G N M I N T D P W E P O R D M U G N C
Z Q X P T C K S H E U C J U J U B E S E
F C P P T I E W I L P H I C E H E A D J
A H P R H O R L Q N O P A R M G L V Q L
M O F A M B T T T R Y N E Y O T D X X W
R C X L D C D U E T D D D R W C E U O B
G O L I R L T H T Y I N N A M L I P F B
V L O N V Q O R C T A R T A P I O L U S
N A L E O U A O E C I E B P C P N T O M
A T L E N S R E N M R F A T C D T T U W
E E I D A N F O U T C D R O U E R G N O
B Y P V F F T G A Y E O R U R N G A R L
Y F O W O T E F C I D N U S I N A A H L
L F P T O L F L D A B N C G I T B E N A
L A Q C B Y S N O A R O A W H T T O P M
E T U B D S A D L Z T A E C U D B I F H
J M U Q I C H L Z C E H M N K N R Y C S
P B B K Y S S K H V C N A E O C S O I R
U O S U G A R P L U M E G B L E O E P A
A N O U G A T K C K P O V E P G W R V M
```

BONBON	COUGH DROP	LOLLIPOP	PRALINE
BUBBLE GUM	FUDGE	LOZENGE	ROCK CANDY
BUTTERSCOTCH	GUMDROP	MARSHMALLOW	SALTWATER TAFFY
CANDIED APPLE	HARD CANDY	MINT	SUGARPLUM
CANDY CORN	HOREHOUND	NOUGAT	TAFFY
CARAMEL	JELLY BEAN	PEANUT BAR	TOFFEE
CHEWING GUM	JUJUBE	PEANUT BRITTLE	TUTTI FRUITTI
CHOCOLATE	KISS	PEPPERMINT	
COTTON CANDY	LICORICE	POPCORN BALLS	

Solution on page 305

Lawyers

```
F F G Q W J Y R D I R S M L I V I C E Z
N P V R E N I A T E R E L A A D V I C E
P O G W E I W C T T F V V I C E T I C U
W M B R N G L K I I I B Z I T C V I B F
W K G D I I D U C W U Z W T D I U R Z E
A L I V E E S U C R Q Q E W N E G S A E
W C K N J G V L J L Q H C J H W N A E S
T B T J H H A A F Q D L I A J L C C T X
G D W I P W G T N E T U C E S O R P E E
P D B Y B J Z A Q C H R A E W S S R C E
E V Q K B K I J F B E C Z S O M E A A L
X X L A N I M I R C W G N C T C G B S I
A M A Z J M L Q J L P A Y E T M R E E F
U W R O B B D R T Y T M Z U B C A D E J
A B R X I P Y E N R O T T A O L H I U U
T W A D S N B T E Z T V L U D E C S S R
Y Z I P Y R X S K N K A N N O I T C A Y
V W G K I L A G E L I S N O M M U S B A
P K N E O S Q F D R E L O U M W D Y F Z
N F F P D Y I C T L V V T G B I P I O S
```

ACCUSE	CHARGES	GRIEVANCE	SIDEBAR
ACQUIT	CITE	INDICT	SUE
ACTION	CIVIL	JUDGE	SUIT
ADVICE	CLIENT	JURY	SUMMON
ARRAIGN	COUNSEL	LAW	SWEAR
ATTORNEY	CRIMINAL	LEGAL	TRIAL
BENCH	EVIDENCE	LITIGATE	
BRIEF	FEES	PROSECUTE	
CASE	FILE	RETAINER	

Solution on page 306

Greek Gods

```
G E V J S O E H O Y L C P Q N I K E S B
W T S N P T Q W B N J D Q B N Q Y P T U
G I S E Y S S N M D W N A H I G E R K X
P M C Q R S B I V U C P S U S Y N O I D
T V P R U A C S C M H M T A R E H P B A
B S G L E V Q S N R S E D A H Q O Y R K
A E Y U T T E A O S U E Z R Y S E N A P
R H N T H M E D P S U V G S E A T I S W
K E C Q R E I M U T Z C I I I K A H U V
A I R E S T E E S H M D J N Q C W L H
Z I H I E U H T J D E O F X Y N E T O E
Z U E S N P T S I T N S U R U E H E E S
X E O G R Y I S R A S E L U C R E H A P
A R P O Y S E A E E N O H P E S R E P E
E Z M H E H H S R A O L L O P A A T S R
L Y T M Y Y R E H S H S I R E V T B U A
T C E L P R H E Z O I P F E Q A H R T S
Q N R N M T B L C K K R E H G V E W O R
A S O O E E M F E K K U I H Q A N Q N O
W S P A X D G S S A E R O B X V A G I M
```

AEOLUS	EOS	HERCULES	NIKE
AETHER	ERINYES	HERMES	NOTUS
APHRODITE	ERIS	HESPERA	PAN
APOLLO	EROS	HESTIA	PERSEPHONE
ARES	EURUS	HYGEIA	POSEIDON
ARTEMIS	HADES	HYPNOS	ZEPHYR
ATHENA	HEBE	IRIS	ZEUS
BOREAS	HECATE	MORPHEUS	
DEMETER	HEPHAESTUS	MORS	
DIONYSUS	HERA	NEMESIS	

Solution on page 306

Dinosaurs

```
E A N U R O G N A T H U S Z X R S S C Q
W U N O D O R U E L P O I L N U U U A V
S M S S U R U A S O E T A L P A L R L A
A U U T O O A I S Y L I N I D S T U S I
N L H T R R R T N O D O N Y C O A A U S
A O L C T E N N W D H S O G I L O S D U
S R D O U A P I I P F T C A U L C O I R
I X A O S S B T T T C X M V R A A N L U
N W O J N A O U O H H K K C Y F Z N C A
R C I L E A U N R S O O V P U R T A O S
O W L C R P U R I R P L C D D A E R T O
S A H C K L A G U E A O E H G W U Y P M
E Z D T J R A T I S D S N S E D Q T Y L
M C O E L O P H Y S I S A D T I R C R A
O S U R U A S O L Y K N A U Y E R B C H
R S U R U A S O N I E T E P R L S U E T
E A R U A S A N Y L L E A E L U U X S H
B U J B R A C H I O S A U R U S S S L P
I C S M E T R I O R H Y N C H U S M F O
R H A M P H O R H Y N C H U S E S A B G
```

ALLOSAURUS

ANKYLOSAURUS

ANUROGNATHUS

BRACHIOSAURUS

COELOPHYSIS

CRYPTOCLIDUS

CYNODONT

DEINOSUCHUS

DINILYSIA

DWARFALLOSAUR

EUSTREPTOSPONDYLUS

IBEROMESORNIS

IGUANODON

LEAELLYNASAURA

LIOPLEURODON

METRIORHYNCHUS

MUTTABURRASAURUS

OPHTHALMOSAURUS

ORNITHOCHEIRUS

ORNITHOLESTES

PETEINOSAURUS

PLATEOSAURUS

QUETZACOATLUS

RHAMPHORHYNCHUS

TAPEJARA

TYRANNOSAURUS

Solution on page 306

Electronics

```
A L T E R N A T O R N R F T R G O D O D
G U L P K R A P S O R U E R I S M E S N
T Q A G G H R R T U S H D G C M D N C U
T Q N U E E F T O E R O E I R O E R I O
B E L A P N U G R T R E L O H A E R L R
R P N M E B E O A G I L S T S G H Q L G
R E U G H L T R N L A C A I R T E C O R
E J K S A C E I A T V C A A S P A C S O
M R U A U M N C O T E A H P O T O T C T
R P E D E T R R T L O C N C A M O R O U
O L N I H R T O E R E R S O P C E R P B
F I A G F E B C T L O O A E S S E B E I
S D I N L I T T K A R L N R N C A R T R
N L Y T I R T C I T L S Y E M T O E M T
A A U N O M I C C U A U D T T A K P E S
R O E D A R R E E T C N S E I C T D E I
T H E N T M L E O R O R R N O C O U R D
Y A L E R E O R T C E Y I S I N V X R L
C I T A T S O R T C E L E C A C O I L E
D R R O T A L U G E R E G A T L O V I G
```

ALTERNATOR
ANODE
ARMATURE
BATTERY
CAPACITOR
CATHODE
CHARGER
CIRCUIT BREAKER
COIL
COMPENSATOR
CONDENSER

DISTRIBUTOR
DYNAMO
ELECTRODE
ELECTROLYTIC
ELECTROSCOPE
ELECTROSTATIC
FUSE
GALVANOSCOPE
GENERATOR
GROUND
INDUCTOR

INSULATOR
JUMPER
LIGHTNING ROD
MAGNET
OSCILLATOR
OSCILLOSCOPE
OUTLET
PLUG
PUSH BUTTON
RECTIFIER
RELAY

RESISTOR
RHEOSTAT
SOCKET
SPARK PLUG
TERMINAL
TIMER
TRANSFORMER
TRICKLE CHARGER
VOLTAGE REGULATOR

Solution on page 306

Sea

```
A A E W A Y I P N I Y L M S V Z V B R L
M Q I F H T O P I A B F N C V C X Y E Y
L W T V U K I E N V F N Z O Y P C V P Z
L U U Q W S O D E C B E X A A J Q O P A
E T K D W I U V E Q E U D S C H J S I V
S B T C D S X G L S J R S T H N L K L W
S P M U T O Z D A C A T Y J T A W E C I
E O S T I Z C I L O J Z N D C T A T U N
V R L T W N L K B F W A U I A O V C I D
X T O E N X Z R R D R V T O H J E H Y J
Y M O R C K A W N A J U B M H K S B G A
A A P Z T T D Y M A A R E N O O H C S M
S W W S S X R A H N Y E L L A G H F N M
B M I L D K T A M G S E T E T L K E N E
J Y Y M D A M S D E N R K S G N B R C R
A H J U C P A H E D F I A A A A N R V B
C J B L R R N I R M O M D E L R Y Y X R
B G Z E J N Q P P G R S C B E Q X O S I
N B W V O W Q N I D E O E T O K X K V G
C K A X Q Y C E A N N M S M G W L V V S
```

AFT	DINGHY	NAUTICAL	STERN
BOAT	DOCK	OCEAN	TIDE
BOW	FERRY	PORT	VESSEL
BRIG	FORE	SAIL	VOYAGE
CATAMARAN	GALLEY	SCHOONER	WAVES
CLIPPER	KETCH	SHIP	WINDJAMMER
COAST	LAKE	SLOOP	YACHT
CUTTER	MAST	STARBOARD	YAWL

Solution on page 307

Green Words

```
Q B N A V N U I D S Q B Y I P C F Y L F
T F V N U G P C A R D P E A K J E S S C
F C Z V M Y J E H J E O T L K Q B B T L
O R R M J J Y N A B R K A K G E P M R P
W I N T E R Y H P C C L E D R O L U O V
R X K C S P T W N A E L E E M N S H P B
E P D W C U R B B F L Y T A Y I S T A J
V D Z I T B A K L Y E F I Y I O X Y Y Y
E X M F L A P F E H C L X F E N M O O R
P D B E V J D K G T F N J B L N W Q P W
T A X S R F Z W A P E P P E R E S U O H
M A P G D W T O L T S V N C N E W W W G
X M Z V N B L M L P J A O A V T L E B E
V O R G Q I O K I W S L L I E G D A E S
G T A P L S T W V C D H L A R B X N S F
R W G U F V W T L Y D O Y O D H T C A P
K V C B M D V B U I H W C P O G L H X L
S S B J X B M Y U P N E C R F A E T B U
O D Q V G C T P E S R G N C T Y A N S A
A L V B W N G E R M J R E P M P G G C A
```

BACK	EYED	ONION	SEA
BAY	GROCER	PARTY	TEA
BEAN	HORN	PEA	THUMB
BELT	HOUSE	PEACE	VILLAGE
BERET	KELLY	PEPPER	WINTER
BOWLING	LAND	PUTTING	
CARD	MAIL	ROOM	
EVER	OLIVE	SALAD	

Solution on page 307

Chapter 2
Forget Me Nots

The puzzles in this chapter present a simple challenge: remember lists of random items. This might sound difficult at first, but it will become easy and fun when you use the link system. The idea behind the link system is to make a mental chain out of the list of items to be remembered. This is done by associating each item in the list with the next item in some memorable way. For a link to work best, the items should interact with each other. For example, suppose you want to link KNEE and HOUSE. You could imagine a giant's knee crashing into your house. Or you could link HAT and FERRY by picturing someone wearing a ferry-shaped hat. We remember unusual things, so let your imagination run wild! Perhaps you will discover secrets about how your memory works.

Forget Me Not Challenge 1

- chest
- chocolate
- scissors
- screw
- table
- cushion
- cord
- bucket
- roof
- lock

Forget Me Not Challenge 2

- book
- penguin
- bridge
- luggage
- token
- mountain
- sneaker
- computer
- blanket
- mug

Forget Me Not Challenge 3

- wheel
- plate
- neck
- kettle
- heart
- bird
- bottle
- train
- pocket
- key

Forget Me Not Challenge 4

- yacht
- wine
- fingerprint
- tulip
- granite
- vampire
- sneeze
- horn
- queen
- diamond

Forget Me Not Challenge 1

_____ _____
_____ _____
_____ _____
_____ _____
_____ _____

Forget Me Not Challenge 2

_____ _____
_____ _____
_____ _____
_____ _____
_____ _____

Forget Me Not Challenge 3

_____ _____
_____ _____
_____ _____
_____ _____

Forget Me Not Challenge 4

_____ _____
_____ _____
_____ _____
_____ _____

Forget Me Not Challenge 5

- worm
- hat
- head
- shelf
- hook
- stick
- fish
- band
- leg
- nut

Forget Me Not Challenge 6

- spleen
- tape
- piano
- mosquito
- notebook
- bicycle
- sand
- paint
- snow
- oil

Forget Me Not Challenge 7

- hospital
- army
- stomach
- fly
- floor
- jewel
- snake
- sock
- umbrella
- leaf

Forget Me Not Challenge 8

- Chihuahua
- pager
- scalpel
- oregano
- monocle
- globe
- sneaker
- paperclip
- newspaper
- blueberry

Forget Me Not Challenge 5

_____   _____

_____   _____

_____   _____

_____   _____

_____   _____

Forget Me Not Challenge 6

_____   _____

_____   _____

_____   _____

_____   _____

_____   _____

Forget Me Not Challenge 7

_____   _____

_____   _____

_____   _____

_____   _____

_____   _____

Forget Me Not Challenge 8

_____   _____

_____   _____

_____   _____

_____   _____

_____   _____

Forget Me Not Challenge 9

- needle
- shoe
- stamp
- map
- tooth

- baby
- wing
- moon
- engine
- ship

Forget Me Not Challenge 10

- text
- bacteria
- frosting
- hose
- blender

- pillow
- orchid
- bulldozer
- possum
- pottery

Forget Me Not Challenge 11

- hair
- cloud
- bell
- pig
- toe

- boy
- monkey
- ring
- office
- pipe

Forget Me Not Challenge 12

- mouse
- tack
- rock
- basketball
- cloud

- pear
- cellar
- ornament
- leaf
- skin

Forget Me Not Challenge 9

_____   _____

_____   _____

_____   _____

_____   _____

_____   _____

Forget Me Not Challenge 10

_____   _____

_____   _____

_____   _____

_____   _____

_____   _____

Forget Me Not Challenge 11

_____   _____

_____   _____

_____   _____

_____   _____

_____   _____

Forget Me Not Challenge 12

_____   _____

_____   _____

_____   _____

_____   _____

_____   _____

Forget Me Not Challenge 13

- window
- sun
- button
- bee
- bed

- curtain
- dress
- collar
- bone
- horse

Forget Me Not Challenge 14

- cave
- tricycle
- heat
- stapler
- concrete

- hairspray
- oboe
- mascara
- nostril
- church

Forget Me Not Challenge 15

- throat
- foot
- drawer
- camera
- sheep

- book
- knife
- pencil
- stem
- library

Forget Me Not Challenge 16

- pyramid
- lily
- crab
- bracket
- poetry

- egg
- adventure
- orangutan
- mortgage
- coffee

Forget Me Not Challenge 13

_____   _____
_____   _____
_____   _____
_____   _____
_____   _____

Forget Me Not Challenge 14

_____   _____
_____   _____
_____   _____
_____   _____
_____   _____

Forget Me Not Challenge 15

_____   _____
_____   _____
_____   _____
_____   _____
_____   _____

Forget Me Not Challenge 16

_____   _____
_____   _____
_____   _____
_____   _____
_____   _____

Forget Me Not Challenge 17

- net
- pen
- arch
- finger
- receipt

- dog
- wire
- brick
- horn
- tree

Forget Me Not Challenge 18

- net
- flag
- mail
- vodka
- skunk

- vacuum
- canyon
- casket
- tent
- skillet

Forget Me Not Challenge 19

- sail
- ear
- card
- cake
- comb

- line
- skin
- nail
- tail
- flag

Forget Me Not Challenge 20

- grapefruit
- tarantula
- highway
- whistle
- puzzle

- calendar
- pond
- watch
- rope
- garage

Forget Me Not Challenge 17

_____   _____

_____   _____

_____   _____

_____   _____

_____   _____

Forget Me Not Challenge 18

_____   _____

_____   _____

_____   _____

_____   _____

_____   _____

Forget Me Not Challenge 19

_____   _____

_____   _____

_____   _____

_____   _____

_____   _____

Forget Me Not Challenge 20

_____   _____

_____   _____

_____   _____

_____   _____

_____   _____

Forget Me Not Challenge 21

- cow
- hammer
- church
- box
- match

- lip
- school
- cart
- muscle
- bulb

Forget Me Not Challenge 22

- tugboat
- presents
- cactus
- wolf
- oven

- pie
- banjo
- pantry
- puddle
- knife

Forget Me Not Challenge 23

- bag
- pot
- hand
- knee
- bridge

- ball
- picture
- coat
- thread
- boat

Forget Me Not Challenge 24

- vacation
- memo
- cape
- riddle
- hair

- secret
- hurricane
- lobster
- magazine
- sink

Forget Me Not Challenge 21

_____   _____

_____   _____

_____   _____

_____   _____

_____   _____

Forget Me Not Challenge 22

_____   _____

_____   _____

_____   _____

_____   _____

_____   _____

Forget Me Not Challenge 23

_____   _____

_____   _____

_____   _____

_____   _____

_____   _____

Forget Me Not Challenge 24

_____   _____

_____   _____

_____   _____

_____   _____

_____   _____

Forget Me Not Challenge 25

- berry
- spoon
- mouth
- chin
- ticket
- spring
- store
- bath
- house
- cat

Forget Me Not Challenge 26

- wall
- ant
- blade
- rail
- cheese
- garden
- clock
- town
- cup
- drain

Forget Me Not Challenge 27

- whistle
- brain
- shirt
- sponge
- rat
- eye
- arm
- carriage
- star
- feather

Forget Me Not Challenge 28

- basket
- thumb
- face
- skirt
- oven
- brush
- glove
- door
- tongue
- root

Forget Me Not Challenge 25

_____ _____

_____ _____

_____ _____

_____ _____

_____ _____

Forget Me Not Challenge 26

_____ _____

_____ _____

_____ _____

_____ _____

_____ _____

Forget Me Not Challenge 27

_____ _____

_____ _____

_____ _____

_____ _____

Forget Me Not Challenge 28

_____ _____

_____ _____

_____ _____

_____ _____

_____ _____

Chapter 3
Triplet Puzzles

Determine the common word that can be combined with each of the three given words. For example, consider these three words: trap, prize, and out. The common word is door, which makes the answers trapdoor, door prize, and outdoor. Compounds can be open (high school), closed (schoolhouse) or hyphenated (school-age).

Triplet 1

1. check
2. smart   _OUT_
3. stretch

Triplet 2

1. stand
2. boxer   _KICK_
3. side

Triplet 3

1. sell
2. fall   _____
3. cake

Triplet 4

1. white
2. brain   _____
3. cloth

Triplet 5

1. processor   _WORD_
2. cross
3. pass

Triplet 6

1. sweet
2. attack   _____
3. break

Triplet 7

1. bitter
2. heart   _sweet_
3. tooth

Triplet 8

1. mine
2. force   _FIELD_
3. trip

Triplet 9

1. proof
2. effect   _____
3. bite

Triplet 10

1. walk
2. base   _BOARD_
3. bulletin

Triplet 11

1. down   _CLOSED?_
2. game
3. case

Triplet 12

1. pit
2. gap   _STOP_
3. watch

Solution on page 308

Triplet 13

1. black
2. cast   _OUT_
3. break

Triplet 14

1. fountain
2. pal   _PEN_
3. bull

Triplet 15

1. stem
2. phone   _CELL_
3. cancer

Triplet 16

FLAG

1. white
2. winner
3. stick

Triplet 17

1. bed
2. Christmas
3. keeper

Triplet 18

1. back
2. first   _HAND_
3. held

Triplet 19

1. bottom
2. blue
3. dumb

Triplet 20

1. easy
2. man
3. high

Triplet 21

1. chair   _WHEEL_
2. big
3. cart

Triplet 22

1. score
2. wheeler   _FOUR_
3. eyes

Triplet 23

1. dance   _FLOOR_
2. plan
3. ground

Triplet 24

1. basket
2. point
3. corn

Solution on page 308

Triplet 25

1. blow
2. roar
3. clean

Triplet 26

1. book
2. pay _CHECK_
3. mate

Triplet 27

1. black
2. room _BOARD_
3. surf

Triplet 28

1. brain
2. cloth _____
3. white

Triplet 29

1. bad
2. wash _MOUTH_
3. loud

Triplet 30

1. moon
2. dew _HONEY_
3. bee

Triplet 31

1. coat
2. gate _____
3. cotton

Triplet 32

1. neck
2. spring _____
3. heart

Triplet 33

1. rain
2. kick _____
3. gum

Triplet 34

1. bull's
2. witness _____
3. ball

Triplet 35

1. paste
2. sweet _____
3. pick

Triplet 36

1. hot
2. wood _____
3. bull

Solution on pages 308–309

Triplet 37

1. cease
2. cracker _____
3. wild

Triplet 38

1. bean
2. table _____
3. break

Triplet 39

1. mark
2. locked _____
3. Ice

Triplet 40

1. vault
2. fishing POLE
3. north

Triplet 41

1. flag
2. shape SHIP
3. space

Triplet 42

IRON

1. trip
2. horse _____
3. grid

Triplet 43

1. loader
2. care _____
3. hand

Triplet 44

1. strangle
2. up _____
3. house

Triplet 45

1. guard
2. busy _____
3. some

Triplet 46

1. home
2. bench _____
3. patch

Triplet 47

1. needle
2. view _____
3. pin

Triplet 48

1. flash
2. board _____
3. post

Solution on page 309

Triplet 49

1. stir
2. small   _FRY_
3. French

Triplet 50

1. happy
2. glass   _HOUR_
3. rush

Triplet 51

1. dipper
2. chicken   _LITTLE_
3. league

Triplet 52

1. blood
2. main   _____
3. line

Triplet 53

1. common
2. cuts   _COLD_
3. shoulder

Triplet 54   _BAND_

1. brass
2. worm   _____
3. wedding

Triplet 55

1. boiler
2. glass   _____
3. paper

Triplet 56

1. backer
2. clothes   _____
3. border

Triplet 57

1. station
2. home   _____
3. data

Triplet 58

1. home
2. turner   _____
3. boy

Triplet 59

1. ground
2. pack   _____
3. horse

Triplet 60

1. ladder
2. foot   _____
3. mother

Solution on pages 309–310

Triplet 61

1. office
2. soap   *BOX* _____
3. mail

Triplet 62

1. combat
2. end _____
3. comfort

Triplet 63

1. ground
2. mate _____
3. word

Triplet 64

1. six
2. back   *PACK* _____
3. rat

Triplet 65

1. box
2. junk _____
3. black

Triplet 66

1. marker
2. keeper _____
3. year

Triplet 67

1. fish
2. super _____
3. dust

Triplet 68

1. scarlet
2. head   *LETTER* _____
3. love

Triplet 69

1. laughing
2. Wood   *STOCK* _____
3. broker

Triplet 70

1. coming
2. motor _____
3. maker

Triplet 71

1. bath
2. mate _____
3. class

Triplet 72

1. cover
2. saw _____
3. storm

Solution on page 310

Triplet 73

1. saver
2. wild
3. style

LIFE

Triplet 74

1. wolf
2. battle
3. baby

GRAY

Triplet 75

1. count
2. melt
3. stairs

Triplet 76

1. bulb
2. news
3. back

Triplet 77

1. copy
2. finish
3. journalism

PHOTO

Triplet 78

1. melon
2. dish
3. proof

WATER

Triplet 79

1. lame
2. soup
3. sitting

DUCK

Triplet 80

1. flower
2. scout
3. Friday

Triplet 81

1. lifter
2. barber
3. window

SHOP

Triplet 82

1. parallel
2. way
3. trailer

Triplet 83

1. table
2. zone
3. bitter

Triplet 84

1. tooth
2. up
3. paint

Solution on page 310

Triplet 85

1. butter
2. cake   _CUP_
3. suction

Triplet 86

1. clip
2. back   _PAPER_
3. news

Triplet 87

1. ache
2. artichoke   _HEART_
3. worm

Triplet 88

1. good
2. power   _____
3. living

Triplet 89

1. dance
2. button   _____
3. pork

Triplet 90

1. drift   _WOOD_
2. chuck
3. red

Triplet 91

1. cake   _LIGHT_
2. stop
3. wave

Triplet 92

1. book
2. key   _____
3. worthy

Triplet 93

1. bulb   _LIGHT_
2. flash
3. moon

Triplet 94

1. round
2. check   _____
3. stage

Triplet 95

1. keeper
2. under   _SCORE_
3. four

Triplet 96

1. court
2. stick   _____
3. sale

Solution on pages 310–311

Triplet 97

1. tender
2. wear
3. hill

FOOT

Triplet 98

1. minister
2. time
3. rate

PRIME

Triplet 99

1. under
2. card
3. annual

Triplet 100

1. black
2. corn
3. room

Triplet 101

1. shock
2. noon
3. taste

AFTER

Triplet 102

1. double
2. wind
3. examine

CROSS

Triplet 103

1. fair
2. big
3. plan

GAME

Triplet 104

1. internal
2. grinder
3. donor

Triplet 105

1. buzz
2. polish
3. road

Triplet 106

1. phone
2. block
3. blood

Triplet 107

1. battle
2. party
3. drive

Triplet 108

1. run
2. face
3. turn

ABOUT

Solution on page 311

Triplet 109

1. trade
2. rainy   NIGHT
3. light

Triplet 110

1. chicken
2. off   WALK
3. board

Triplet 111

1. made
2. nursing   HOME
3. spun

Triplet 112

1. pink
2. knot   SLIP
3. stream

Triplet 113

1. gas
2. top   TANK
3. think

Triplet 114

1. Christmas
2. top   TREE
3. hugger

Triplet 115

1. goose
2. white   EGG
3. head

Triplet 116

1. ball
2. butter   FLY
3. dragon

Triplet 117

1. dead
2. man
3. hair

Triplet 118

1. hay
2. service
3. hot

Triplet 119

1. grass
2. baby
3. bird

Triplet 120

1. heart
2. lord
3. main

Solution on pages 311–312

Triplet 121

1. rail
2. rage   _ROAD_
3. kill

Triplet 122

1. bold
2. poker   _GAME_
3. card

Triplet 123

1. big
2. gun   _SHOT_
3. long

Triplet 124

1. moth
2. point   _____
3. room

Triplet 125

1. down
2. knee   _____
3. off

Triplet 126

1. gap
2. watch   _____
3. short

Triplet 127

1. draw
2. space   _____
3. horse

Triplet 128

1. show   _WINDOW_
2. sweet   _____
3. shop

Triplet 129

1. mind
2. grand   _____
3. piece

Triplet 130

1. word
2. fair   _____
3. plan

Triplet 131

1. back
2. sand   _____
3. thin

Triplet 132

1. vane
2. fair   _WEATHER_
3. proof

Solution on page 312

Triplet 133

1. hall
2. post _____
3. book

Triplet 134

1. foot
2. book _____
3. key

Triplet 135

1. milk
2. down _____
3. up

Triplet 136

1. sales
2. dark _____
3. fever

Triplet 137

1. lift
2. high _____
3. arm

Triplet 138

1. check
2. needle _____
3. blank

Triplet 139

1. top
2. house _____
3. tag

Triplet 140

1. blue
2. honey _____
3. struck

Triplet 141

1. horse
2. back _____
3. fanny

Triplet 142

1. cast
2. once _____
3. drive

Triplet 143

1. still
2. style _____
3. wild

Triplet 144

1. bars
2. business _____
3. wrench

Solution on page 312

Triplet 145

1. answering
2. secret _____
3. charge

Triplet 146

1. smoke
2. sun _____
3. silk

Triplet 147

1. pet
2. pool _____
3. seat

Triplet 148

1. eye
2. low _____
3. band

Triplet 149

1. name
2. fountain _____PEN_____
3. point

Triplet 150

1. away
2. over _____
3. age

Triplet 151

1. piggy
2. account _____BANK_____
3. note

Triplet 152

1. hawk
2. sore _____
3. socket

Triplet 153

1. market
2. chicken _____
3. live

Triplet 154

1. puppy
2. less _____
3. bird

Triplet 155

1. worm
2. finger _____
3. bearer

Triplet 156

1. block
2. room _____
3. driver

Solution on pages 312–313

Triplet 157

1. iron
2. less   _____
3. some

Triplet 158

1. tail
2. pollution   _____
3. show

Triplet 159

1. shot
2. stick   _____
3. happy

Triplet 160

1. card
2. sandwich   _____
3. soda

Triplet 161

1. back
2. symptoms   _____
3. pen

Triplet 162

1. game
2. cross   _____
3. count

Triplet 163

1. down
2. hole   _____
3. mushroom

Triplet 164

1. hot
2. catcher   _____
3. eared

Triplet 165

1. race
2. switch   _____
3. call

Triplet 166

1. pin
2. body   *hair*
3. dryer

Triplet 167

1. in
2. out   *hole*
3. up

Triplet 168

1. mush
2. mate   _____
3. service

Solution on page 313

Chapter 4
Sudoku Puzzles

Sudoku burst onto the world stage in 2005 and continues to grow in popularity. Perhaps one of the secrets to its success is the puzzle's charming simplicity. Sudoku is played on a 9 × 9 grid. Heavier lines subdivide this grid into nine 3 × 3 boxes. The object is to fill in the grid so that every row, column, and 3 × 3 box contains the numbers one through nine with no repeats. The puzzle begins with some of the numbers already entered. There will always be only one solution for each puzzle.

Sudoku Puzzle 1

1	5	2	9	4	7	3	6	8
3	4	6	2	8	1	9	7	5
8	9	7	5	3	6	2	1	4
4	2	8	1	7	5	6	9	3
9	3	1	4	6	8	5	2	7
6	7	5	3	9	2	4	8	1
5	1	4	7	2	9	8	3	6
7	6	9	8	5	3	1	4	2
2	8	3	6	1	4	7	5	9

Solution on page 314

Sudoku Puzzle 2

9	5	6	8	2	1	4	7	3
4	3	8	5	7	6	1	9	2
1	7	2	9	3	4	5	8	6
2	8	3	1	6	9	7	5	4
6	1	7	2	4	5	8	3	9
5	4	9	7	8	3	6	2	1
7	6	4	3	9	8	2	1	5
8	9	5	6	1	2	3	4	7
3	2	1	4	5	7	9	6	8

Solution on page 314

Sudoku Puzzle 3

2	7	6	5	9	8	3	4	1
8	4	1	2	7	3	6	9	5
5	9	3	4	1	6	8	7	2
7	3	8	3	6	4	5	1	9
6	1	4	9	8	5	7	2	3
9	5	3	7	3	1	4	8	8
1	6	5	8	4	9	2	3	7
3	8	7	1	5	2	9	8	4
4	2	2	8	3	7	1	5	8

Solution on page 314

Sudoku Puzzle 4

3	4	2	8	6	9	7	1	5
8	1	7	5	3	2	9	6	4
5	6	9	1	4	7	8	3	2
9	2	1	4	8	6	3	5	7
6	8	5	7	1	3	4	2	9
4	7	3	2	9	5	6	8	1
7	5	4	6	2	8	1	9	3
2	9	6	3	7	1	5	4	8
1	3	8	9	5	4	2	7	6

Solution on page 314

Sudoku Puzzle 5

6	2	8	7	9	1	3	5	4
1	3	4	8	6	5	7	2	9
7	9	5	4	3	2	8	6	1
5	1	7	9	4	8	6	3	2
9	4	3	5	2	6	1	8	7
2	8	6	3	1	7	9	4	5
8	7	1	2	5	3	4	9	6
3	5	9	6	7	4	2	1	8
4	6	2	1	8	9	5	7	3

Solution on page 314

Sudoku Puzzle 6

1	4	3	2	9	7	5	6	8
5	2	7	4	8	6	9	3	1
6	9	8	1	5	3	4	7	2
7	5	9	3	2	1	8	4	6
4	3	1	5	6	8	2	9	7
8	6	2	9	7	4	3	1	5
9	1	5	6	4	2	7	8	3
3	7	4	8	1	5	6	2	9
2	8	6	7	3	9	1	5	4

Solution on page 314

Sudoku Puzzle 7

3			9		6			1
2								4
	6		4		2		9	
8	1	2				3	5	6
9	5	7				4	1	8
	8		3		7		6	
5								2
7			5		1			9

Solution on page 315

Sudoku Puzzle 8

8				6		5		3
5		1	3					
		2		8			1	
6		3	8					
1		9	7		6	4		2
					1	6		7
	1			5		8		
					8	3		9
3		8		4				5

Solution on page 315

Sudoku Puzzle 9

3			7	4		8		
								5
8		6		3	5	7	2	1
	5					9		4
6								2
9		4					7	
7	8	9	6	2		5		3
5								
		3		5	8			7

Solution on page 315

Sudoku Puzzle 10

6	4	2			9	7	3	
	5			6			4	
9			5			6		2
8	6							
				9				
							5	8
1		5			4			3
	8			5			9	
	9	6	2			5	8	1

Solution on page 315

Sudoku Puzzle 11

6		5	3		8	7		2
1		2				8		9
2	4		9		1		5	3
3	5		6		7		8	4
5		4				3		8
7		1	4		6	9		5

Solution on page 315

Sudoku Puzzle 12

9		3				5	7	
							1	
2	6				7			9
	3		7	8				
8	7		1	5	6		2	3
				4	3		5	
5			6				3	1
	9							
	8	6				7		5

Solution on page 315

Sudoku Puzzle 13

8	1	6	5	7	4	9	3	2
2	3	4	8	1	9	7	6	5
7	9	5	6	3	2	1	4	8
5	6	7	2	4	1	8	9	3
3	4	1	9	8	6	2	5	7
9	2	8	7	5	3	6	1	4
1	7	9	3	2	5	4	8	6
6	8	3	4	9	7	5	2	1
4	5	2	1	6	8	3	7	9

Solution on page 316

Sudoku Puzzle 14

4			7		2			9
5		2				7		1
		7				4	2	
		9	4					5
6	7						1	4
3					1	8		
	1	5				9		
9		6				1		7
7			1		9			6

Solution on page 316

Sudoku Puzzle 15

1	5	7						6
8								
		3	6	7				5
5			1	3		4		
7		1		4		8		9
		8		9	5			1
3				1	4	6		
								4
6						3	9	8

Solution on page 316

Sudoku Puzzle 16

	7		8					
4	8	1	7		9			2
2			1		4		7	
8	9					6		
6								8
		3					2	4
	4		2		6			5
9			5		1	7	8	6
					7		4	

Solution on page 316

Sudoku Puzzle 17

2	3		4	9		5	7	
							9	
					3		2	8
					4			1
	1	4	3	8	7	9	5	
3			1					
4	5		7					
	2							
	9	3		2	5		1	4

Solution on page 316

Sudoku Puzzle 18

7	6		3					8
							5	
	8			1	7	3	9	
3			6		2			5
	9			8			7	
4			9		3			2
	4	1	8	2			3	
	7							
8					4		6	1

Solution on page 316

Sudoku Puzzle 19

7			9		5			6
		6	8		4	9		
4	9						5	8
		3	4		8	6		
		5	1		9	2		
5	2						6	4
		1	5		2	8		
3			7		6			2

Solution on page 317

Sudoku Puzzle 20

	5		1			4		
4	7		8				1	6
		6	4		3			
				5	1	6		2
			2		6			
6		7	3	8				
			5		2	9		
5	8				9		6	3
		3			8		5	

Solution on page 317

Sudoku Puzzle 21

	1	3	7	6	2			
4		6	3	1				8
		2		8				
3						6		2
7		8						5
				7		2		
5				3	4	1		7
			5	9	6	8	4	

Solution on page 317

Sudoku Puzzle 22

	3	5	6	7			1	8
	8	1		3	4			
			5					3
		7	4			1	8	
	9	4			3	7		
5					9			
			8	1		2	5	
1	6			4	5	8	9	

Solution on page 317

Sudoku Puzzle 23

9			4		6			7
2	4						6	9
		7	9		2	4		
1			6		3			2
7			1		5			4
		9	5		1	8		
3	2						7	5
8			7		9			6

Solution on page 317

Sudoku Puzzle 24

	9	1			3		4	
4			8		9			3
3		5		6			7	
	7							
1			7	8	6			5
							6	
	1			3		5		2
6			5		8			4
	5		9			3	8	

Solution on page 317

Sudoku Puzzle 25

2	7	4	8	6	5	3	1	9
3	8	6	9	1	7	2	4	5
1	9	5	2	4	3	8	6	7
5	3	7	4	9	1	6	2	8
9	1	2	3	8	6	7	5	4
6	4	8	7	5	2	1	9	3
4	2	9	1	3	8	5	7	6
8	6	1	5	7	4	9	3	2
7	5	3	6	2	9	4	8	1

Solution on page 318

Sudoku Puzzle 26

4	8	7	6	9	2	1	3	5
3	2	9	4	5	1	7	8	6
1	6	5	3	8	7	9	2	4
5	3	8	2	4	9	6	7	1
2	1	4	7	6	5	8	9	3
9	7	6	1	3	8	4	5	2
6	9	2	8	1	3	5	4	7
8	4	3	5	7	6	2	1	9
7	2	1	9	2	4	3	6	8

Solution on page 318

Sudoku Puzzle 27

Solution on page 318

Sudoku Puzzle 28

1	2	5	4	6	8	3	9	7
7	3	4	9	1	2	8	6	5
8	6	9	3	7	5	4	2	1
5	7	3	8	2	6	9	1	4
6	4	8	1	9	7	2	5	3
9	1	2	5	3	4	7	8	6
2	8	7	6	4	1	5	3	9
3	5	6	7	8	9	1	4	2
4	9	1	2	5	3	6	7	8

Solution on page 318

Chapter 5
Lost and Found

Fit all of the missing letters into the grids. If you put them in the right places, you'll find that every word crosses another, horizontally or vertically.

Lost and Found 1

Missing Letters

A	A	N	R
T	T	K	C
N	L	C	A
C	D	L	O

A	L				P	R		Y
R		I	T	S			R	
	A		E		H		T	
H		E		T	E			
	E	L		E	S			
A		Y	E			I	L	
R	A		N			S		A
			E	P				V
		Y			S	E	A	

N	O	B		L	I	P	S
O		I		A		I	
P	O	S	S	I	B	L	E
	N		C	E	A	S	E
A		U	G	L	Y		
		I		S	E	W	S
L		F	T		R		E
O		O		P	A	S	T	A
W	A	X		I			R

Lost and Found 2

Missing Letters

X	S	L	O
S	S	L	I
I	E	L	A
A	E	L	K

Solution on page 319

Lost and Found 3

Missing Letters

D	T	E	P
R	C	E	S
B	S	I	O
R	E	D	L

			C		T	U		
M			C		T	U		
O		M	U	M			A	
	R					A		H
E		R		W	O		E	
R		A	P	A	R	T		
A	C	C				I	N	G
T	A		E			S		O
	L		M	E	N			
	L							

	S			O	M	B		
S		Y						A
	E			R			A	P
A		H	I	E	V			
				A		F		S
E		F	E		T	I	V	E
	I	R			I	T		E
S	C		R	E	D			
Y		G		D		A	L	

Lost and Found 4

Missing Letters

E	A	P	B
C	O	M	H
E	C	E	C
N	S	F	I

Solution on page 319

Lost and Found 5

Missing Letters

E	O E		B
S	L	I	F
E	N	N	S
E	U	R	R

Lost and Found 5 grid:

A	C	T		H			W	
	H			I		P	E	
P				S	U			
			A				D	D
			V	E	R			I
	T	O	E			A	G	
	I			O		B		S
F	A	R	E	W			L	
	N					E	L	

Lost and Found 6

Missing Letters

U	E	H	L
L	O	S	R
P	S	E	B
S	M	C	T

Lost and Found 6 grid:

	O	T	E			Z	I	
E				A	R	E		E
R		A		P				A
					S	O	N	
			I	T	E			
	E	E				I		S
	A	N	D		B		T	
A				A		L	Y	
	H		E		E			

Solution on page 319

Lost and Found 7

Missing Letters

A	K	T	O
E	H	Z	S
I	A	Y	L
P	A	U	C

M	A	R				S		
I				G	L		D	
D	I	G		R				
D				E		R		
			H	A	B	E	T	
		H				D		S
	J		B		A			I
		T		C	K			
		O	T		S	A		E

Lost and Found 8

Missing Letters

D	A	E	R
S	S	L	I
T	O	O	A
M	R	E	E

	D		E	F	F			
D	I	D		O			I	
R				R	O	A	D	
	L		O					C
G		T	O	R	C	H		R
	G	A			L	I	N	
R		N	E	W				W
I		C			R	E		S
		E	T		K			

Solution on page 320

Lost and Found 9

Missing Letters

R	O	Y	E
N	L	M	Y
D	L	N	D
H	E	D	S

	A	D		U		A	D		
E			U		E				
L				U		O			E
P		B	A	B	L				
	A			L	E				
	F		F		Y			S	
A	T			Y	O			K	
N		A						I	
	E	T					U		P

		B		D		P		H
T				E	F	O	R	
E		L			A	P	O	R
		O	M		T		B	
	O	W		L	A		R	
		T		L	A	T		
O	A	S		S		I		D
O			L	I	S		S	
K	N	E						

Lost and Found 10

Missing Letters

E	T	L	H
I	E	E	R
T	B	B	O
T	V	X	I

Solution on page 320

Lost and Found 11

Missing Letters

L	I	E	T
A	O	I	S
I	O	C	A
R	A	E	M

(Top-right grid)

			L		B		D	
	I	S				T		D
M			V	E	R			
I			E			B		T
S	H			S			S	
T		T			A	X		S
			L	O			O	
		M			M	O	N	G
	L	E	A	K				

(Bottom-left grid)

	R			C	R	E		
H		M					L	
						O	U	R
S		N	S		U		M	
	L		E	U	R			E
O	T	H			S			A
U		I	N	G		D		G
			E	Q				
S		S			G		E	

Lost and Found 12

Missing Letters

P	T	O	R
R	E	A	U
L	P	S	E
S	F	U	P

Solution on page 320

Lost and Found 13

Missing Letters

T	T	E	T
H	C	L	U
A	L	R	G
P	C	S	R

					P	L	O	
	U	B	I	C		I		O
H		A		O			A	W
O	C			S				E
	H	O	S	P	I			
H	O	N	E	S			W	
	I		F			E	A	S
		O	U	P			R	
						I	D	

S				U	P			
		I	L			T		U
A		N		S	A		L	S
R		T	O					K
		E			O	C	U	S
			E	A	T	H		
A		D				E	A	D
L		E	D	G		S		A
	A	D			R			

Lost and Found 14

Missing Letters

H	T	T	E
L	D	F	O
B	I	S	E
N	O	C	E

Solution on page 321

Lost and Found 15

Missing Letters

T	Z	A	D
E	Z	V	L
E	W	E	E
A	E	L	S

J	A				K	I			
			I	N	N		A		
	I	G	N		E		W		
		E	C	R			S	E	
B		T				I			
			A		E	D	G		
B	L	O			A			N	
	S	W				E	S	T	
	E			S					

Lost and Found 16

Missing Letters

N	D	E	F
D	E	A	I
E	R	N	N
A	A	M	K

E		A	F		I	R
X		O				A
	G	I	G		W	I
M		X		M	I	N
I			C	A		E
N		P	L		E	S
		N	E	D		
	E		A		P	G
A	N	Y	O		D	

Solution on page 321

Lost and Found 17

Missing Letters

T	R	E	B
I	I	R	A
C	S	B	A
A	N	S	Y

	I	N	C				S	E
B		U				R		
E	V		L		T	E		R
D				G	R	A		
	D		I	L			L	
P		N		A		W	E	
		C	A		C	E		A
S		E		E			I	G
	O		T					

O	W	L					L	
	H	O			L	E		F
N	O			D	A			
A			J			E	T	
T		B	A	N	G		E	
U			M			N	D	
		D	A	T				T
	Y	E			G			
		W		T	E	M		

Lost and Found 18

Missing Letters

A	E	O	U
P	W	O	A
R	P	A	Y
W	S	S	N

Solution on page 321

Lost and Found 19

Missing Letters

B	**L**	**E**	**L**
A	**D**	**O**	**O**
R	**E**	**O**	**E**
L	**E**	**R**	**R**

B	U	I			S		E	
U			O			C		Y
	E	S	S		D			
	L		S	S	O	M	S	
	S	M	E			T		I
G			S	E		T		Y
	D				A		N	
G			S	P		E		
	Y			Y	I		L	D

Lost and Found 20

Missing Letters

N	**R**	**N**	**A**
R	**E**	**I**	**E**
R	**S**	**Y**	**D**
G	**R**	**N**	**U**

	H	E	R	O				
	E					E		E
O			A	N		W	O	
	I		G		Y			
S	T	I			E	D		S
	A		E	S	S			
A	G	R		E		M	A	T
	E		D		Y		R	
			Y		E		D	

Solution on page 322

Lost and Found 21

Missing Letters

L	S	O	O
R	T	N	F
G	I	Y	I
A	O	U	N

Top-right grid:

C	H	I				C		
A				N		I		O
R		B		A	N		R	Y
	H		W	L		A		S
G		D			A	R	D	
	R		B	S			R	
		E			G	I		N
	O		E	S			W	
	R		W			A	N	

Bottom-left grid:

		R	I	L	L		P	
			O				L	
	S		F			J		W
	T		E		P	E		
	O	P				T		D
	R		L	A	Y		A	
D		E		I	S		U	E
		L			L		I	
F	I		H		O		E	N

Lost and Found 22

Missing Letters

R	S	A	S
A	H	E	Y
T	T	I	S
E	X	O	E

Solution on page 322

Lost and Found 23

Missing Letters

D	A	E	V
Y	M	A	R
I	E	G	A
T	E	O	E

Grid (top right):

	G		P			R		
R	A			M	A	K		S
	S	O	L					
					O	I		
	H	I	K			V		T
R	E	M	E		B	E	R	
E		A		E				
L	E	G		N				
					H	E	R	

Lost and Found 24

Missing Letters

S	K	P	I
M	E	E	R
I	R	M	P
R	D	L	U

Grid (bottom left):

H						O	
I		A		E	A	R	S
	O	M		L	I	D	
		E		A	I		
	W		O	N	G		R
			K		T		A
O		C		O	A	D	S
A	M	A	T				
K		N		S			S

Solution on page 322

Lost and Found 25

Missing Letters

D	N	D	U
T	U	L	L
T	P	E	E
C	U	C	U

O	U	T					G	
U						H	A	
	I	B			R		U	
		E	X			S	E	E
		G		A	S	K		E
	F		N	C	T	I	O	N
		N	U	T				
				R	T	L		
	B	O	S	S				

Lost and Found 26

Missing Letters

S	E	C	E
O	N	E	R
O	B	H	P
O	V	A	T

A	S			C	U		
	E	U			O	U	
E		E	N			R		A
		X		E	R	N	A	L
I	N		O	M			P
C					I	R	S
E		E	T	S			
	S		Y		U		G
				N		S	

Solution on page 323

Lost and Found 27

Missing Letters

C	U	E	D
G	R	N	N
A	R	S	E
D	O	O	A

C				E	P	T	S	
	A		O		R		C	
	T		P	O				R
	H	A	Y			O	N	E
C		C				A	T	S
R		C		B		D		P
I	D				M			O
E		S			S	O	O	
			T	Y				

Lost and Found 28

Missing Letters

O	E	T	C
E	D	H	S
I	T	C	N
A	Y	G	O

			C				
A		N			L	E	S
U		E		R			O
	U	I	D	E			
U		T			T	O	M	S
S				L	A	R	
	I	E	D			K	I	P
	T	R		U	T			A
		R		E	X		

Solution on page 323

Chapter 6
Double Scrambles

Unscramble the letters to form words. Then, unscramble the first letters of the words you made to form a word related to the title. Some groups of letters can be unscrambled to form more than one word. For example, the letters OWEBL can be rearranged to form ELBOW or BELOW. In these cases, part of the challenge is to determine the correct word.

Will They Come Out Tonight?

- HESEP   _S H_
- LSLKI   _S K_
- ATESR   _RATE_
- IAPRL   _A P_
- XALRE   _R E_

_____

Makes a Boat Go

- LEEDG   _L E_
- ORSWD   _S W_
- LAUTD   _A D_
- SNEVE   _S E_
- NXDIE   _I N_

_____

Yes or No

- GNUYO   _____
- BSEAR   _____
- ECXTA   _____
- AWLLO   _____
- EOYMN   _____

_____

Out of This World

- IODRA   _____
- ETHAC   _____
- EASID   _____
- HATSO   _____
- GBAED   _____

_____

Solution on page 324

Take Away

- HRNOT _____
- LLPIS _____
- OIRSN _____
- ABURN _____
- RRMAY _____

_____

How to Get an A

- APSRC _____S_C_____
- DAINR _____D_R_____
- NEUCL _____V_N_____
- UTHMB _____T_H_____
- OUHTY _____Y_O_____

_____

Abracadabra

- CLDOU _____
- RAEDG _____
- GEARE _____
- OMOTR _____
- ILDAE _____

_____

Made with Bread

- NSTUT _____
- EOTRW _____
- ITMID _____
- GTNAE _____
- SSIAO _____

_____

Solution on page 324

Dry Off

- ACEON _____
- TGHIL _____
- PYMTE _____
- ROYRW _____
- RKCTI _____

_____

Room at the Top

- IPCRS _____
- TLEAB _____
- UAEGR _____
- OTCHR _____
- EGMIA _____

_____

Black and White All Over

- TOSOR _____
- ZIPYP _____
- ASYES _____
- ARAEW _____
- EBRDO _____

_____

Pioneer Vehicle

- DWWIO _____
- OWREN _____
- HRGPA _____
- ASMNE _____
- RAOCT _____

_____

Solution on page 324

Slow Mover

- EAMUS _____
- ALBEL _____
- UNTPI _____
- NNYNA _____
- ASMPW _____

_____

Why Are You So Sour?

- MYERR _____
- LNINE _____
- ERVYE _____
- OEPRA _____
- SINEO _____

_____

Not Once, Not Three Times

- OOCRL _____
- HICWT _____
- ORINY _____
- NEMEY _____
- TASEE _____

_____

One Hump or Two?

- ORLVE _____
- RYAMO _____
- ORIHC _____
- EVNET _____
- KENLA _____

_____

Solution on page 325

A Wake-Up Call

- CAHRN   _____
- NONYA   _____
- EAOWK   _____
- UGLAH   _____
- OMOES   _____

_____

That's Funny

- HBYOB   _____
- ILVEO   _____
- RDAIP   _____
- NITUL   _____
- SMCUI   _____

_____

Owns a Pitchfork

- IDSCO   _____
- GALER   _____
- RORER   _____
- ESSUI   _____
- VLCAO   _____

_____

A Thousand

- VLNAA   _____
- EMYRH   _____
- EGESE   _____
- RAAYR   _____
- MDEAR   _____

_____

Solution on page 325

You Like

- IYELD   _____
- CNUOE   _____
- IUCYJ   _____
- WOLEB   _____
- INNTH   _____

_____

Neigh Sayer

- TONEF   _____
- LAEEG   _____
- EHARC   _____
- TBAIH   _____
- ARPHS   _____

_____

Would You Like a Burger with Those?

- ETMSI   _____
- ANFYC   _____
- ITHRS   _____
- TGHIR   _____
- VLSEE   _____

_____

Nonsense

- TMIIL   _____
- YSOUR   _____
- INNRE   _____
- HNIES   _____
- EELVR   _____

_____

Solution on page 325

It May Be Wild

- YEARL   _____
- DNSYA   _____
- CSORE   _____
- GNTAI   _____
- UONNI   _____

_____

They Are Open or Shut

- REAGN   _____
- DRAYI   _____
- AADLS   _____
- ERHTO   _____
- GRANO   _____

_____

See It in a Parade

- IVAOD   _____
- FEHRS   _____
- LKCYU   _____
- TTEEH   _____
- REROD   _____

_____

Purchase at a Nursery

- RLUAN   _____
- AUTBO   _____
- EVOLN   _____
- MEHTE   _____
- POTNI   _____

_____

Solution on page 326

Tie the Knot

- SAROT _____
- MYAEB _____
- THYUO _____
- IAGAN _____
- IONBR _____

_____

Charlie Chaplin Persona

- THCPI _____
- GLANE _____
- RMJOA _____
- HERCA _____
- DMITI _____

_____

Surgeon's Assistant

- RAYEL _____
- NBLOE _____
- LRRUA _____
- UCELN _____
- EPSLE _____

_____

Rocker Site

- YAEDR _____
- RCCUO _____
- EOHUS _____
- PIONT _____
- RACHI _____

_____

Solution on page 326

Grown-Up Kids

- EGRAT   _____
- NILAE   _____
- ERTOH   _____
- FTHEI   _____
- TESPE   _____

_____

Pasta Topper

- NTLUI   _____
- KEEHC   _____
- RESCO   _____
- TFEAR   _____
- TEREN   _____

_____

Fable Finale

- NTAGE   _____
- VRRIE   _____
- MIEVO   _____
- PRAEO   _____
- ALREG   _____

_____

Classroom or Poolroom Item

- LKNET   _____
- NATHU   _____
- EODGL   _____
- ARIES   _____
- ROCHI   _____

_____

Solution on page 326

It's Stuck in the Corner

- NROIM   M _____
- AYARR   A _____
- ENLAP   P _____
- STEAE   T _____
- IPLLS   S _____

_____

Give a Hoot

- PHSAE   _____
- OVILE   _____
- IRTGE   _____
- ASUUL   _____
- ENHOY   _____

_____

Three, They Say

- AZORR   R _____
- RMEAD   _____ D _____
- CEWRK   _____ W _____
- OCICM   C _____
- NTFEO   _____ O _____

_____

Prepare for Surgery

- REMHY   _____
- ERUPP   _____
- OLROC   _____
- ABCON   _____
- EENVS   _____

_____

Solution on page 327

106   THE EVERYTHING GIANT BOOK OF BRAIN-BOOSTING PUZZLES

Tot Watcher

- DDADE _____
- ENVLO _____
- EIDYL _____
- ONSEI _____
- EVNER _____

_____

Syrup Source

- BOLRA _____
- MAARL _____
- XTEAC _____
- PCINA _____
- MIACG _____

_____

Cold Covering

- SERUP _____
- OTAIR _____
- PTMOE _____
- FOLOR _____
- OIBRT _____

_____

Toward Santa's Pole

- IGTHN _____
- NOUCE _____
- CEATH _____
- PHAPY _____
- XALRE _____

_____

Solution on page 327

First-Anniversary Gift

- PTIOL _____
- AOUDL _____
- RAYLO _____
- ECAPE _____
- EDRLE _____

_____

One of the Deadly Sins

- IGRDI _____
- EODNZ _____
- TVENE _____
- PLSEU _____
- EILDA _____

_____

Out of Practice

- ARDPI _____
- ITHSG _____
- TSATE _____
- YHTAC _____
- UIONN _____

_____

Cheese Choice

- FSTFA _____
- SCEAR _____
- IMAGE _____
- WRROY _____
- AKTSE _____

_____

Solution on page 327

Uncle Sam Feature

- ORPNA   _____
- EBYRR   _____
- TIDRY   _____
- RODAI   _____
- LUAEQ   _____

_____

Diametrically Opposite

- IONNO   _____
- AVEIL   _____
- SLSAO   _____
- ALPNT   _____
- ANRCH   _____

_____

'70s Hot Spot

- SIAED   _____
- KLIYS   _____
- DLYLO   _____
- NAOGR   _____
- TARCF   _____

_____

Dining Room Staple

- RCHTO   _____
- VELLE   _____
- ASESY   _____
- DBLEN   _____
- KENLA   _____

_____

Solution on page 328

Worthless Wheels

- CYERM _____
- AUHLG _____
- PEMYT _____
- NVEER _____
- OAISS _____

_____

Some Canines

- LHOET _____
- THIKN _____
- NEOYJ _____
- NKTAH _____
- EGAEL _____

_____

Conversation Starter

- LTGIH _____ L I _____
- DAYHN _____ H A _____
- NARLE _____ L ℇ _____
- YMENE _____ ℇ N _____
- CAOEN _____ O U _____

_____

Rosetta Stone Language

- GERCA _____ G R _____
- ATEEN _____ ℇ A _____
- NIKFE _____ K N _____
- EHIGT _____ ℇ I _____
- NMAOR _____ R D _____

_____

Solution on page 328

Chapter 7

Crossword Puzzles

Studies have shown that doing crossword puzzles is a great way to keep your brain young. Give the puzzles in this chapter your best shot. It's okay if you can't fill in every entry; you will still be getting a good mental workout.

Crossword Puzzle 1

Across

1. Blockhead
5. Mall units
10. Deception
14. Violinist Leopold
15. Seven-time AL batting champ Rod
16. "Jane ___"
17. Analogy words
18. Cosmetician Lauder
19. Pet lovers' org.
20. Tar
22. Most cheeky
24. Beg
27. Mon. follower
28. City on the Rhine
31. Grand Coulee, e.g.
33. Pierces
37. "Holiday ___"
38. In layers
41. Auto racer Fabi
42. Handheld computer, briefly
43. CIA predecessor
44. "___ a chance!"
46. Happy hour hangout
47. "___ tu" (Verdi aria)
48. "Relax, and that's an order!"
50. Gold: prefix
51. Singer Reese
54. Brain scan, for short
55. Threadbare
57. "___ in the Family"
59. Discontinue
61. "Eureka!"
65. Present and future
69. Fit
70. Thomas of "That Girl"
73. Continental coin
74. Bellicose deity
75. Suffix with sect
76. Aborigine of Japan
77. Barber's cry
78. English Channel feeder
79. "Cut it out!"

Down

1. Platform
2. Any of three English rivers
3. "I ___ Song Go Out of My Heart"
4. ___ l'oeil
5. Happening place
6. Consumes
7. Food scrap
8. Chick's sound
9. Saccharine
10. Six-line poem
11. Ballyhoo
12. Circle parts
13. Butcher's stock
21. ___ the good
23. U.S.S.R., now
25. "___ Fideles"
26. ___ es Salaam
28. Two-footed animal
29. Conductor Previn
30. Escargot
32. Household
34. Up, in baseball
35. Lollapalooza
36. Rueful
39. OT book
40. Hairstyles
45. Brusque
49. Common Mkt.
52. Most recent
53. Capone and Capp
56. Trojan hero
58. Green beans
60. Do penance
61. Larger ___ life
62. Aesop's also-ran
63. "Jeopardy!" host Trebek
64. Hawaiian tuber
66. Diamonds, e.g.
67. Brain-teasing Rubik
68. Progresso product
71. Backboard attachment
72. Escape

Solution on page 329

Crossword Puzzle 2

Across

1. "Go back," in word processing
5. "Miracle on 34th Street" store
10. Gator kin
14. One of the Fab Four
15. Birdlike
16. Etna output
17. "___ Blue"
18. Backward-looking
19. Tel ___, Israel
20. Kind of tank
22. Set of advantages
24. Rembrandt van ___
25. Shutterbug's setting
27. Support, with "up"
29. Anticipated
30. Shoulder muscles, for short
34. DI doubled
35. Puts forth, as effort
38. Belafonte song opener
39. Storekeeper's stock: Abbr.
40. Bridle part
41. Acorn, eventually
43. Its cap. is Sydney
44. Retain
46. Win over
48. Fight enders, briefly
49. College application part
51. Film director's cry
52. Legume
54. Prefix with linear
56. Upper limit
57. Italian cheese
60. Signs of spring
63. The Miners of the Western Athletic Conf.
64. Inmate who's never getting out
67. Dirt

69. Buster Brown's dog
70. Desktop pictures
71. "Swan Lake" garb
72. Rob Roy, for one
73. Radium discoverer
74. Like a bug in a rug

Down

1. The WB rival
2. Thumbs-down votes
3. Fool
4. Veteran
5. California county
6. Opposite of sans
7. Op. ___
8. Shostakovich's "Babi ___" Symphony
9. Muzzle

10. Held on to
11. Sitarist Shankar
12. "Metamorphoses" poet
13. Bat's home
21. Laid-back
23. Pea container
25. It's a wrap
26. Begin a journey
27. Evergreens
28. Tears apart
29. Sense
31. Sri ___
32. 1980s–'90s ring champ
33. Scatters, as seed
34. Emcee's need
36. Greek letters
37. Anatomical pouch
42. Shish ___
45. Defensive wall
47. It makes MADD mad

50. Craving
53. Is
55. Baby's woe
56. Code name
57. Dead-end jobs
58. Aural
59. "Let ___!"
60. Actor Santoni
61. Sentence subject, usually
62. In ___ (undisturbed)
65. Post-op stop
66. In favor of
68. Big galoot

Solution on page 329

Crossword Puzzle 3

Across

1. 24-hr. conveniences
5. El ___
8. "Tosca" tune
12. Masterstroke
13. "Yes ___?"
14. Bucephalus, e.g.
15. Turnpike charge
16. QB Flutie
17. Lulus
18. Uncomfortable
20. Central point
21. "Fiddler on the Roof" matchmaker
22. Police dept. employee
23. Jerks
26. Most optimistic
30. Bewitch
31. Scribe
34. Knight club
35. Come to light
37. Coquettish
38. Great white ___
39. Linguist Chomsky
40. Cozily warm
42. Mail order abbr.
43. World records?
45. Numbered works
47. Mil. authority
48. Spoken for
50. Similar to
52. Uses a shortcut
56. Toyota rival
57. "___ my way"
58. Any day now
59. Hitching post
60. Kittens' cries
61. Atmosphere
62. Lump
63. Fingers, for short
64. Some M.I.T. grads

Down

1. Broadway opener
2. Screwdriver, for one
3. Think (over)
4. Spreads out
5. Zagreb resident
6. Occupied, as a lavatory
7. Venetian bigwig
8. Never
9. Buy by Benny
10. "Able was ___ I saw . . ."
11. Internet pop-ups, e.g.
13. Danish city
14. Loudness units
19. Fiesta Bowl site
22. Put on
23. Journalist Alexander
24. 1992 also-ran
25. Like some symmetry
26. Beams
27. Wild West family
28. Listerine alternative
29. Looks after
32. Sgts., e.g.
33. Extinct flightless bird
36. Squarely
38. Ballyhoos
40. Koppel of "Nightline"
41. Subway coins
44. Daub
46. Wild
48. Domesticated
49. Acknowledges
50. Laze
51. "What's gotten ___ you?"
52. ___ Valley, CA
53. A party to
54. ___ synthesizer
55. Aims
56. Witch

Solution on page 329

Crossword Puzzle 4

Across

1. Patronize, as a restaurant
6. "The Purple People Eater" singer Wooley
10. Educator's org.
13. Generals' insignia
14. Puff of a joint
15. Broadway award
16. Fifty minutes past the hour
17. Working without ___
18. Grafted, in heraldry
19. Arnaz of "I Love Lucy"
20. High season, on the Riviera
21. Restaurant patrons
23. Accent
26. Bohemian
27. Rugged ridges
30. Juno, to the Greeks
32. Fertile soil
33. Small deer
35. Florida's Miami-___ County
39. "Do Ya" rock grp.
40. Helmsman
43. Broadway's "Five Guys Named ___"
44. Parts of a min.
46. Alpine stream
47. Moving about
49. Made a hole in one
51. Magician's cry
52. Jutlander
54. Lustrous fabric
57. Brawls
59. Actor Chaney
60. Juan's "another"
64. Years in Spain
65. ". . . unto us ___ is given": Isaiah
67. Loud, as a crowd
68. "___ we forget . . ."

69. "And Then There Were ___"
70. "Beetle Bailey" character
71. The "Superstation"
72. Takes to court
73. Highway curves

Down

1. Founded: Abbr.
2. Suit to ___
3. Beach shades
4. Manet and Monet
5. General of Chinese menu fame
6. Condition
7. Sharpens
8. Barely make, with "out"

9. ___ noire
10. Trio trebled
11. Door
12. Affirmative votes
15. Foursome
20. Triage sites, briefly
22. Bern's river
24. "___ of the D'Urbervilles"
25. Sex researcher Hite
27. Amber brews
28. Patton, to Scott
29. Fair-hiring org.
31. Compass dir.
33. Studies
34. "___ the land of the free . . ."
36. Quantities: Abbr.
37. "I dare you!"
38. Architect Saarinen

41. Inventor's monogram
42. Pink, as a steak
45. Most reasonable
48. Ladies of Spain
50. Mediocre mark
51. Ballpoint, e.g.
52. Star in Cygnus
53. At ___ for words
55. By oneself
56. Softens, with "down"
57. ___ liquor
58. Lacking
61. Rocky peaks
62. Foam at the mouth
63. Loads from lodes
66. Nearly worthless coin
67. Enzyme ending

Solution on page 329

Crossword Puzzle 5

Across

1. Workout sites
5. Stick-in-the-mud
9. Allegation
14. In apple-pie order
15. The same: Lat.
16. Prefix meaning "sacred"
17. "Back in the ___"
18. Biblical verb
19. Hearing-related
20. Chemical cousin
22. Pershing's WWI command
24. Believer's suffix
25. Corkwood
27. Superman foe ___ Luthor
29. French dear
31. Washington's ___ Stadium
33. Rumple
37. Kind of sauce
38. Actress Shearer
40. Swiss capital
41. "___ which will live in infamy": FDR
43. "___ Married an Axe Murderer" (Mike Myers comedy)
44. 1973 Rolling Stones #1 hit
45. "Ciao!"
46. Linoleum layer
48. Byrnes of "77 Sunset Strip"
49. Direction from which el sol rises
50. Mangy mutt
51. A+ or C-
53. 601, in old Rome
55. Avid
57. Cost-of-living stat
60. Cached
62. Delaware tribe
65. Hullabaloo
67. Diehard
69. "All ___ are off!"
71. Arctic abode
72. "Whip It" rock group
73. "The jig ___!"
74. Paint layers
75. Plow pullers
76. Hairdo

Down

1. Wildebeest
2. "___ Can" (Sammy Davis Jr. autobiography)
3. Come together
4. Disco light
5. Beethoven opera
6. Smells
7. Receive
8. Jewish youth org.
9. Rub raw
10. "Charlie's Angels" costar Lucy
11. Ethereal: Prefix
12. Some nest eggs, for short
13. Snakes do it
21. Fictional weaver
23. Antlered animal
26. Wardrobe
28. Marvel Comics group
29. Musical endings
30. Marriott competitor
32. Flunk
34. Goaded
35. Derogatory
36. Germ
37. Bargain event
39. Queue after Q
40. Fruitless
42. Got ready to drive
47. Incited
50. Early second-century year
52. Language of the Koran
54. Mass confusion
56. Animated
57. Trendy
58. ___ stick
59. Seat of Allen County, Kan.
61. Pedestal part
63. Cuban cash
64. Pins and needles holder
66. In demand
68. Annoy
70. Tanning lotion letters

Solution on page 330

Crossword Puzzle 6

Across

1. Skating event
6. ___ the finish
10. 1990s Indian P.M.
13. Cruel sorts
14. Local theater, slangily
15. Party mtg.
16. Actress Patricia et al.
17. Jordanian queen
18. Autobahn auto
19. Crossword worker?
20. Ambition
21. Strapped
23. Even though
26. Hostelries
27. Round lot's 100
30. Classroom drudgery
32. "Deed I Do" singer
33. Go-getter
35. ___-Pei (wrinkly dog)
39. Curved Alaskan knife
40. Save for a rainy day
43. "Die Meistersinger" heroine
44. Uses a shuttle
46. Peat sources
47. Divination deck
49. Boris Godunov, for one
51. Baseball's Hank and Tommie
52. Baccarat alternative
54. Thinly spread
57. Breakfast fare
59. "Aladdin" prince
60. Auto pioneer
64. Had debts
65. Dickens clerk
67. Catch some Z's
68. "___ of the Thousand Days" (1969 film)
69. Cole Porter's "Well, Did You ___?"
70. Boxer Ali
71. D-Day vessel
72. Suvari of "American Beauty"
73. Allude

Down

1. Cornmeal bread
2. A long, long time
3. 1979 revolution site
4. Brush up on
5. "Greetings" org.
6. Bellybutton type
7. A Judd
8. Blood letters
9. Garr of "Mr. Mom"
10. Where Joan of Arc died
11. Much of Chile
12. "Ars amatoria" poet
15. Film festival site
20. Belly muscles
22. Coll. hoops competition
24. Bottom of the barrel
25. Corners
27. Boarded up
28. Granada greeting
29. Stuck, after "in"
31. Sch. in Tulsa
33. Opportunities, so to speak
34. Assn.
36. Deli order
37. Bard's river
38. "Darn it!"
41. TV schedule abbr.
42. Fund-raising grps.
45. Bit of progress
48. Biological rings
50. "My boy"
51. "Exodus" hero ___ Ben Canaan
52. Babes in the woods
53. "___ you glad you did?"
55. Song of joy
56. Beginning
57. Young Arab
58. "Beg pardon . . ."
61. Viking Eriksson
62. Edit out
63. Bandy words
66. "The Three Faces of ___"
67. Camera type, briefly

Solution on page 330

Crossword Puzzle 7

Across

1. Kind of market
5. Bingo relative
9. "The Wizard of Oz" studio
12. Carry on
13. Toothbrush handle?
15. Spelling of "Beverly Hills 90210"
16. Betwixt and between
17. Fertilizer ingredient
18. "___ Brockovich"
19. It's a stunner
21. "7 Faces of Dr. ___"
22. "The King ___"
23. "Note to ___ . . ."
26. Cough syrup amts.
28. Add-ons: abbr.
31. Pod items, old-style
33. ___-Bismol
37. Addis Ababa's land: Abbr.
38. Another, in Andalusia
39. Backward
40. "Can't argue with that"
42. Scarlett O'Hara, e.g.
44. Fast-moving card game
45. Take turns
47. Friend of Masterson
49. Actress Merkel
50. "Lulu," e.g.
51. "Ah, Wilderness!" mother
52. Domino spot
53. Roll
55. Make well
57. Barracks site
60. Spotted, to Tweety
62. Native Israeli
66. Inning sextet
67. Chosen ones
70. "No ___!"
71. Platte River people
72. Like some keys
73. Edible pocket
74. Haul
75. Mason, e.g.: Abbr.
76. Sunnis, e.g.

Down

1. Greek group, for short
2. Priest of the East
3. Auspices
4. Dangerous mosquito
5. ___-Tiki
6. Verdi's "___ tu"
7. One of the major leagues: Abbr.
8. Pharmaceutical ointment
9. Eve's opposite
10. Electrical network
11. Certain iPod
14. Abbr. in a closely held business
15. Service groups
20. Auction vehicle, often
24. Leave alone
25. Hack's customer
27. Letter abbr.
28. Prefix with dollars
29. Barber's need
30. "On the Beach" author
32. They're underfoot
34. Animate
35. Lopez of pop
36. Available
39. Cliffside dwelling
41. Like harp seals
43. Pirate's punishment
46. ___ chi
48. Exemplars of twinship
51. List shortener
54. Champagne glass part
56. Reindeer herders
57. Heave-ho
58. Golf, for one
59. Tuck away
61. Hit the road
63. Cheese with a rind
64. Campus mil. org.
65. Like ___ out of hell
68. Barracks bed
69. "Don't give up!"

Solution on page 330

Crossword Puzzle 8

Across

1. Beyond tipsy
4. Charles barker
8. Infield cover
12. Assayers' samples
14. Checked out
15. Blackthorn fruit
16. Home, informally
17. Other: Fr.
18. Airline launched in 1948
19. Dimethyl sulfate and others
21. "Fear Street" series author
23. Trencherman
26. Aliens, briefly
27. Daytime fare
30. Brooks of "Blazing Saddles"
32. Barn dances
36. Prepare, as a salad
37. Opening word
39. Hawaii's Mauna ___
40. "Baloney!"
41. Fold, spindle or mutilate
42. 50 Cent piece
43. Bother
44. Bass, e.g.
45. Comes to mind
47. Heart
48. Takes a chance
50. Blazed a trail
51. Carryalls
52. The law, to Mr. Bumble
54. Words repeated at the start of the "Sailor's Song"
56. Former Greek P.M. Papandreou
60. Singer Brewer
64. Have a bias
65. What's here
68. Dribble
69. Highway division
70. Lessens
71. Gen. Robt. ___
72. Go downhill fast?
73. Counterfeit
74. A.A.R.P. members

Down

1. Hermitic
2. Cholers
3. Makeup, e.g.
4. Track-and-field org.
5. Concorde, e.g.
6. Guam, e.g.: abbr.
7. An Astaire
8. African bloodsucker
9. Sheryl Crow's "___ Wanna Do"
10. Colorful horse
11. Brazilian soccer legend
13. Brews
14. Play group
20. Dorm VIPs
22. Sore throat cause, briefly
24. Food Network name
25. ___ gestae
27. Prized violin, briefly
28. Alley Oop's girl
29. Autumn bloomer
31. Rio Grande city
33. "Adam Bede" author
34. Mr. Moto portrayer
35. Benefits
37. Mediterranean isl.
38. More, in Madrid
41. En ___ (all together)
46. Band performance
47. Unrefined
49. Took in
51. "Fore" site
53. Fills up
55. Jeanne d'Arc et al.
56. "___ well that ends well"
57. "Hud" Oscar winner
58. Hamlet, e.g.
59. Bygone ruler
61. Congers and kin
62. Amphilochus, in Greek myth
63. Bronx Zoo houseful
66. Tikkanen of hockey
67. Theological sch.

Solution on page 330

Crossword Puzzle 9

Across

1. Panama and porkpie
5. Addis ___
10. Helgenberger of "CSI"
14. Seuss's "Horton Hears ___"
15. Fray
16. "Aba ___ Honeymoon"
17. Catch but good
18. Hobbit's home
19. Leveler
20. Go-getter
22. Lower
24. Armed forces VIP
26. Govt. lender
27. Fashions
30. Panama, e.g.
32. Manchurian border river
36. Even if, briefly
37. Compared to
39. Presidential middle name
41. Dict. offerings
43. "SNL" alum Cheri
45. Burst of wind
46. Lessee
48. Sisters
50. Like Gen. Powell
51. Plant with bell-shaped flowers
52. ___ Croix, Que.
53. A long time
55. "The Simpsons" bartender
57. Bears' lairs
59. Is faithful
63. "___ Weapon"
67. Athens's home
68. Hokey
70. Prefix with spherical
71. Inside info
72. Jam ingredients
73. Final, e.g.
74. Phoenician port
75. Oater transport
76. Big Indian

Down

1. Bridge holding
2. Off
3. Watered down
4. Comfort giver
5. Bad lighting?
6. "Humph!"
7. Dedicated
8. Forlorn
9. First Hebrew letter
10. Store stock: Abbr.
11. Sighs of relief
12. Stadium stats
13. School of whales
21. Atomizer's output
23. "Big Mouth" Martha
25. Chew the fat
27. ___ Helens
28. "Now I remember!"
29. "Holy Sonnets" poet
31. With regard to
33. Calc. prerequisite
34. 1944 Preminger classic
35. Big name at Indy
38. All the rage
39. Cacophony
40. Baseball's Ed and Mel
42. Give in to gravity
44. Had second thoughts about
47. Iditarod destination
49. New Year's Eve word
52. Show to the door
54. Purim honoree
56. SeaWorld attractions
58. "Family Ties" mother
59. Call to a mate
60. New Look designer
61. Clinton's birthplace
62. Lady of Sp.
64. Prefix with -gon
65. Key of Beethoven's Symphony No. 7: Abbr.
66. Bean town?
67. Go with, with "for"
69. Creamy quaff

Solution on page 331

Crossword Puzzle 10

Across

1. North Sea feeder
5. Figure skater Thomas
9. "The Rum ___ Tugger" ("Cats" tune)
12. Some spies
14. Biblical name meaning "hairy"
15. First-class
16. Cousin of a raccoon
17. Utmost extent
19. Blank filler: abbr.
20. Some brews
22. Districts
23. Shop worker
25. Wrinkle
26. "Beats me"
28. Expunge
29. Put through a sieve
30. Gave birth in a stable
32. D.J.'s stack
33. Bullwinkle foe
34. Horror director Craven
37. Touches up
39. Sparkle
41. Fervid
43. Symbol of discipline
44. Undertakes
45. Lazy
47. Rainbowlike
48. Works the land
49. The Crystals' "___ a Rebel"
52. Draw on a board
54. Miss America topper
56. Spare parts?
57. The Untouchables, e.g.
58. Descendant
59. Outer: prefix
60. Hawk
61. Bear with us at night

Down

1. Disco standard
2. Anon
3. Some bands
4. Like Gen. Schwarzkopf
5. Al ___ (firm)
6. C4H8O2, e.g.
7. Scornful cries
8. Birth control option, briefly
9. Pawed
10. Discomfort
11. Reagan attorney general
13. Stored, as fodder
15. Concurred
18. Country/rock singer Steve
21. Pier grp.
24. "To Autumn," e.g.
25. Animation frames
26. AEC successor
27. Suffix with human
28. Oration station
30. Helvetica, for one
31. Old California fort
33. Propensity
34. Terrier type
35. Ambient music pioneer
36. Benchmark: Abbr.
37. Detroit duds
38. Gettysburg general
39. Some trick-or-treaters
40. "___ Liaisons Dangereuses"
41. Of a main line
42. Take back
43. Allen of "Home Improvement"
44. Quebec peninsula
45. Grainy, in a way
46. Vogue
48. Notability
50. Oscar Wilde poem "The Garden of ___"
51. Yemen's capital
53. "Punk'd" airer
55. Hosp. area

Solution on page 331

Crossword Puzzle 11

Across

1. Thesis defense, often
5. Smell ___
9. Haile Selassie worshiper
14. Grabber's cry
15. Crunchy munchie
16. "Save me ___"
17. Barbara of "Mission: Impossible"
18. Service expert?
19. Too much, in music
20. "Entertaining Mr. ___" (Joe Orton play)
22. French soul
24. Turn down, as lights
25. Wetland flora
27. Surgery ctrs.
29. "Private Parts" author
31. "___ a pity"
33. First Hebrew letter: var.
37. "Am ___ believe . . . ?"
38. Some pitchers
40. Attack ad, maybe
41. "Now you ___ now . . ."
43. Airport abbr.
44. Break off
45. Draw ___ in the sand
46. "Touched by an Angel" co-star
48. Avg.
49. Clark of the Daily Planet
50. ___-mo (instant replay feature)
51. Schools for engrs.
53. Carry-___ (small pieces of luggage)
55. Nick name?
57. Little shaver
60. ___ grass
62. Dog star
65. The last Oldsmobile made
67. ___ were

69. "Eh"
71. Where to see "The Last Supper"
72. "Song of the South" title
73. Not exo-
74. English Channel feeder
75. Arab capital
76. Heedless

Down

1. Fed. fiscal agency
2. Narrow inlets
3. Deep blue
4. "The Raven" maiden
5. Finished
6. Fought the clock
7. The Red Baron, for one

8. When said three times, a WWII film
9. Critic, at times
10. ___ rule
11. E-mail, say
12. Jacques of "Mon Oncle"
13. Bit to split
21. Freshen
23. Criminal patterns, for short
26. Sound investments?
28. "___ difference!"
29. Inscribed stone
30. Front-wheel alignment
32. Apropos of
34. Most trifling
35. Positions for Goren
36. Mr. Rogers
37. Writer Dinesen

39. Clayey deposit
40. Gets wind of
42. A fan of
47. "Ol' Blue Eyes"
50. F.I.C.A. funds it
52. Dissed, in a way
54. Everybody's opposite
56. "Star Trek" extra
57. Skedaddles
58. What George couldn't tell
59. Hero's place
61. Notebook projections
63. "The Last Days of Pompeii" heroine
64. Are, in Argentina
66. Appeared in print
68. Mme., in Madrid
70. Gut reaction?

Solution on page 331

ASDFGHJKL

Crossword Puzzle 12

Across

1. Hail Mary, e.g.
5. Archaeological find
9. "Not on ___!" ("No way!")
13. ___ O's (Post cereal)
14. Plaintiff
15. City on the Aire
16. Manor man
17. Charter
18. Do-___
19. "To reiterate . . ."
21. Lao-tzu follower
23. Call, as a game
24. Fat, in France
26. Chain letters?
27. Be-bopper
28. Not just "a"
30. Canner's supply
34. Diamond corners
37. Chutzpah
39. Never, in Nuremberg
40. Some native New Yorkers
41. Actor Alejandro
42. Auto option
44. "Go on . . ."
45. Nice notions
47. Diamond groups
48. Some deer
50. D.C. setting
51. Bear lair
52. Antiquity, in antiquity
54. Petitions
56. Amaze
59. Toots
62. Ballerina Makarova
64. Done in
65. Expressionist Nolde
67. Miniature sci-fi vehicles
68. Cartoon mirages
69. Dispense, with "out"
70. First president of South Korea
71. 100-lb. units
72. Brain passage
73. Beach, basically

Down

1. Kind of bear
2. Came into being
3. Line of type
4. Poor blokes
5. Concert souvenir
6. "A Dog of Flanders" author
7. Debussy subject
8. Cy Young winner Saberhagen
9. Forward pass
10. Resting places
11. Cut, maybe
12. "The Waste Land" poet's monogram
15. Minnesota's state bird
20. 1999 U.S. Open champ
22. Citrus quaffs
25. D and C, in D.C.
27. Average grade
29. "Airplane!" star Robert
31. "Back ___ hour" (shop sign)
32. Awful
33. Theological schools: Abbr.
34. Den denizen
35. Florence flooder
36. Competing team
37. Engendered
38. Most rational
43. Architect Maya ___
46. "___ Dinah" (Frankie Avalon hit)
49. One thing after another
51. He'll give you a hand
53. Contact, e.g.
55. Band together
56. Hi from Ho
57. Spread
58. Let up
59. Beanery side
60. Future's opposite
61. Circular opening?
63. Car loan figs.
64. Assn.
66. Big Apple attraction, with "the"

Solution on page 331

124   THE EVERYTHING GIANT BOOK OF BRAIN-BOOSTING PUZZLES

Crossword Puzzle 13

Across

1. Whopper juniors?
5. Gardener's aid
10. Hearty hello
14. Actress Petty
15. Upholstery fabric
16. "Z" actor Montand
17. Bare-bones subj.?
18. Circles overhead
19. Tabloid fodder
20. Deejay Casey
22. Bishop's domain
24. Falls off
27. '80s defense prog.
28. Record biz initials
31. Fields of comedy
33. Dadaist collection
37. Offshoot
38. Headed for overtime
39. Stirred up
41. Carpe ___
43. Dictator's aide
45. Madly in love
46. Fillet
48. Deaden
50. Beach acquisition
51. Carpentry groove
52. Army base near
    Petersburg, Va.
53. A little work
54. Mail HQ
56. They may be cast
58. Like tactile hair
62. Cabbies
66. Moist
67. Nutty as a fruitcake
70. "Believe" singer
71. "Famous" cookie maker
72. 1973 #1 Rolling Stones
    hit
73. Soprano Te Kanawa
74. Karaoke need
75. Do a double take, e.g.
76. ___ souci

Down

1. Antiaircraft fire
2. Isle of Mull neighbor
3. Victoria's Secret
   selections
4. Put in place
5. Archaic verb ending
6. 1950 film noir classic
7. Richly adorn
8. Kay Thompson creation
9. Fix, as a golf green
10. Stevenson fiend
11. National competitor
12. "Able was ___ . . ."
13. D-Day vessel
21. Diamond target
23. "See ya!"
25. Sang-froid
26. Let it be, editorially
28. Highway safety org.
29. Reacted to a tearjerker
30. Amorphous creature
32. Birth cert., e.g.
34. Fix, as a fight
35. Word with hot or home
36. Popeye's creator
39. "Arise, fair sun, and
    kill the envious moon"
    speaker
40. "Drat!"
42. Stylish, in the '60s
44. Empty, in math
47. Egg drinks
49. One of Alcott's "little
    women"
52. As an example
55. Kind of bear
57. Gridiron stat
58. Final Four game
59. "Star Wars" creature
60. Big Board abbr.
61. Eastern discipline
63. ___ Pet (novelty item)
64. "Show Boat" composer
65. Hindu honorifics
66. Hoover, e.g.
68. Snap
69. So far

Solution on page 332

Crossword Puzzle 14

Across

1. Samantha of "The Collector"
6. Tarot suit
10. ___ buco (veal dish)
14. Dry white wine
15. Introduction to culture?
16. Crack, in a way
17. Beeper calls
18. It may be pitched
19. "Pal Joey" lyricist
20. France's patron saint
22. Singer?
24. Complex dwelling
26. Common Market: Abbr.
27. Acid, so to speak
28. Talk up
31. G, in the key of C
33. Remote button
35. Proverb ending?
36. Business biggie
38. Bubbling over
42. Fountain name
44. "The Island of the Day Before" author
45. John ___ Garner
46. "Frasier" dog
47. Board
49. Part of U.S.N.A.: Abbr.
50. Pinch hitter
52. "___ 'nuff!"
53. "Beloved" writer Morrison
54. Sportscaster Cross
57. Asta, to Nick and Nora
59. Benefit
61. Kind of diver
63. Vast extents
66. Ballet attire
67. "The Untouchables" extras
70. Time and ___
72. Halley's sci.
73. Go for
74. Andrea Bocelli, for one
75. Will of "Jeremiah Johnson"
76. Ht.
77. "Ready, ___!"

Down

1. Dubious "gift"
2. Egg on
3. "Eleni" author Nicholas
4. Means of access
5. Plant exudation
6. "Wheels"
7. Actor Tognazzi
8. Plain writing
9. Kitchen gizmo
10. ___ Rios, Jamaica
11. "We ___ Overcome"
12. Agra attire
13. Withdrew, with "out"
21. Spanish ayes
23. Vast amounts
25. Clan carving
28. "Women and Love" author
29. Sale site
30. Entreated
32. Spikes
34. Pugilists' org.
36. Commuters' woes
37. ___ Ark
39. ___ account (never)
40. Words of confidence
41. Dolly ___ of "Hello, Dolly!"
43. Baron's superior: abbr.
48. Darks or whites
51. Retro car
53. Snicker
54. Lapel label
55. Don't waste
56. Sporty Chevy
58. Indian tongue
60. "Endymion" poet
62. Contented sound
64. Gasp
65. Toil wearily
68. Just make, with "out"
69. It's east of Calif.
71. Not to

Solution on page 332

Chapter 8

Diagramless

The diagramless crossword puzzle adds a bit of extra fun to your puzzling task. Not only do you have to know the answers to the clues, but you have to place them in the proper squares on the grid. Start with 1-across and work in pencil. These puzzles have regular crossword puzzle symmetry.

Diagramless 1

Across

1. Russian-built fighter
4. Apt. features
7. Unclose, poetically
8. Hiking paths
11. ___ Beta Kappa
14. Deep distress
15. Baby bird of prey
16. ___ Schwarz (toy store)
17. Fast fliers: Abbr.
19. Medieval poem
20. Anti-fraud agcy.
21. "___ a real nowhere man . . ."
22. Missing a deadline
24. Dockers' org.
26. President pro ___
27. Musical notes
28. Victrola company
30. Money
34. Hill-building insect
35. Chapel words
36. Floral welcome
37. Connery of film
39. Banquet hosts: Abbr.
40. Golfer Se Ri ___
41. Girl's pronoun
43. Believer
44. Movie-rating org.
46. Beatnik's exclamation
48. Airport overseer: Abbr.
49. Day: Sp.
52. General region
54. Harbor boat
55. Motor
57. New Orleans summer hrs.
60. God, in Roma
61. Parts of a play
62. Homer Simpson expletive
63. Boundary
64. "Eureka!" is one

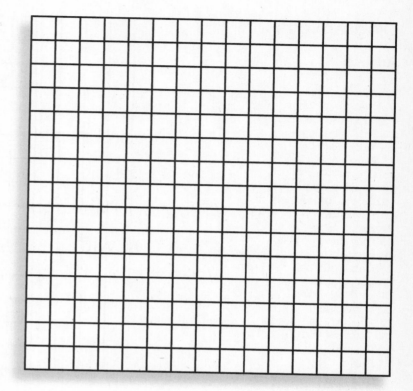

Down

1. Cut the lawn
2. Nasdaq debut: Abbr.
3. Thousands, to a hood
4. Button material
5. Maid's cloth
6. Window ledge
8. Head, in France
9. Poetic meadow
10. Subway entrance device
11. Fizzling-out sound
12. Despise
13. Org. overseeing quadrennial games
18. California mount
23. HBO competitor
24. "Play ___ it lays"
25. Fishing cord
26. Southwest art center
28. Relative of hoarfrost

29. Atlanta-based public health agcy.
31. Type of skiing
32. Airplane assignment
33. Go on foot
38. Govt. code breakers
42. Pluto's realm
44. Hawaii's "Valley Isle"
45. When doubled, a Samoan port
46. Having hair like horses
47. Mars's Greek counterpart
48. 1-800-FLOWERS rival
50. Corporation abbr.
51. Onetime Time film critic James
53. Electrical letters
56. Place for the night
58. Beetle
59. Your, in the Bible

1-across starts in the 1st square from the left.

Solution on page 333

Diagramless 2

Across

1. Li'l Abner creator
5. Astronomical hunter
7. "Gunsmoke" network
10. The Titanic, e.g.
11. Yes, in Paris
12. Blaze remnant
15. Baseball VIPs
16. Naval noncom: Abbr.
19. Outdoor parking area
21. Kipling lad
24. French nobleman
25. Early afternoon hour
26. Kids with curfews
28. Massachusetts's motto start
30. Pod inhabitant
31. Van Gogh home
32. Comfy spot
36. Peer Gynt's creator
39. Computer in "2001"
40. Drove too fast
44. Bag carrier
45. Wind direction: Abbr.
46. Kwik-E-Mart owner on "The Simpsons"
47. Bygone airline
48. Chicago White ___
49. Morse code sound
50. Stanley Cup grp.
53. "___ a Rock": Simon and Garfunkel
55. Gaming cube
56. Strand
61. Topic for Dr. Ruth
62. "Tiny" Albee character
63. Every twelve mos.

Down

1. Rank above maj.
2. "Exodus" protagonist
3. Sewing-basket item
4. "The Murders in the Rue Morgue" writer
6. Org. for gun owners

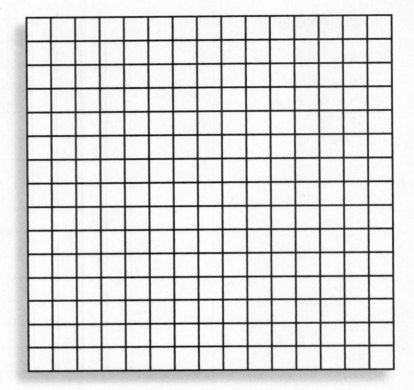

7. Machine tooth
8. Bleacher creature?
9. Ebert's former partner
13. Feeds the pigs
14. Beehive product
16. B followers
17. Bit of wordplay
18. ROTC relative
20. Instructs
22. Suffix with Paul
23. Editorial submissions: Abbr.
26. Mai ___ (drink)
27. Makes a goof
29. Extreme shoe width
33. "Gimme ___!" (start of a Rutgers cheer)
34. Capital of Vietnam
35. "The Downeaster ___" (Billy Joel song)
36. Hairy TV cousin

37. Gift decoration
38. Bleachers
41. Paper holder
42. MPG raters
43. "That's obvious!" in teen talk
51. Hotfoot it, old-style
52. Superman foe ___ Luthor
54. CEO's degree, maybe
57. Ron of "Tarzan"
58. Atmosphere
59. A quarter of M
60. Attention-getting word

1-across starts in the 1st square from the left.

Solution on page 333

Diagramless 3

Across

1. Favorable vote
4. Soft shoe, for short
7. Tommy follower?
8. Hogs' home
9. Enzyme suffixes
11. '50s nuclear trial
13. PC linking acronym
15. Suffix with drunk or tank
17. Wagering place: Abbr.
20. Napoleonic general
21. Beauregard's boss
22. British big shot
23. Never, in Nuremberg
24. Outfield material
25. Collarless shirts
26. "___ it something I said?"
27. Electrically charged atom
28. Brother of Curly and Shemp
30. Gold measures: Abbr.
31. Anecdote collection
32. Boise is its cap.
33. L-P link
34. Lamb's dad
37. "At once!"
40. Average mark
41. Above, in poetry
42. Rocky outcropping
43. Snake that squeezes its prey
44. High, arcing shot
45. Collar, as a crook
46. Grain bristle
47. One hundred yrs.
48. A whole slew
52. Director Vittorio De ___
55. Lincoln or Vigoda
56. Took the bait
57. Try for apples
58. Wrong: Pref.

Down

1. Irish island
2. Interjections from Rocky

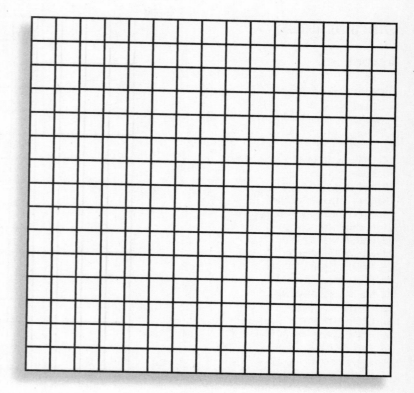

3. High season, on the Riviera
4. Wyo. clock setting
5. Taxonomic suffix
6. Songwriter Coleman et al.
10. Hair stylist's shop
11. Suffix with lemon or lime
12. Sound of music
13. Luke Skywalker's sister
14. Yeses at sea
16. One side in checkers
18. Sock front
19. Kids' ammo
20. Wind dir.
24. Cubs slugger Sammy
25. 4:00 social
27. "___ be my pleasure!"
28. Hair on a horse's neck
29. Yoko of music
30. Set of tools

33. Intends
34. Acting job
35. "___ Flux" (Charlize Theron movie)
36. Hazel's boss, to Hazel
37. Train stop: Abbr.
38. Ode title opening
39. Wall St. traders
40. Dairy animal
43. ___-relief
47. Lions and tigers
49. Auto for hire
50. Blood-type group
51. Cotillion girl
53. Apple competitor
54. LI doubled

1-across starts in the 4th square from the left.

Solution on page 333

Diagramless 4

Across

1. Silent acknowledgment
4. "Either you do it, ___ will!"
5. Capital of Yemen
9. Elderly
12. Meeting: Abbr.
14. "The Giving Tree" author Silverstein
15. Actor ___ Ray
16. Hereditary
18. Miss Trueheart of "Dick Tracy"
19. Mlle.'s Spanish counterpart
21. Number-crunching pro
23. Kasparov's game
24. Mythical world lifter
28. Bear's abode
29. Highest-quality
32. Vietnamese festival
33. Long and slender
35. UK record label
36. Pharmacist's weight
38. Bygone car
39. She preceded Mamie
40. Swiss mountain
41. No longer fresh
43. "Soap" Family
45. Canoe paddle
47. Blue Jay or Oriole
48. Datebook entry: Abbr.
51. Noisy insect
55. Maximum
56. College grad
57. Pyramid scheme, for one
61. Uneaten morsel
62. Leak slowly
63. Hair coloring
64. ___ jiffy (quickly)

Down

1. Calculator figs.
2. It's north of Calif.
3. Malign, in slang
5. ID with two hyphens
6. "I have an idea!"

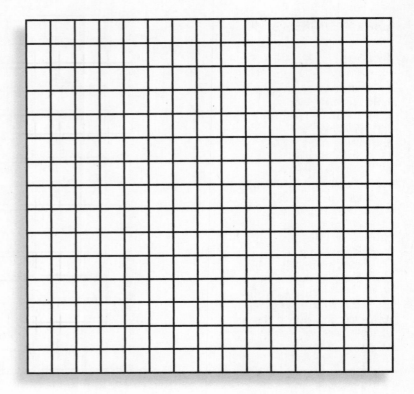

7. Amount after expenses
8. Oscar winner Guinness
9. Guadalajara "Rah!"
10. Mormon grp.
11. "Uno" + "uno"
13. Rests for a moment
15. Rat chaser?
17. "Illmatic" rapper
19. Clippers
20. Milk curdler
22. Game show host Sajak
23. 450, in old Rome
25. Inc., in Britain
26. Fill with fizz
27. Less up-to-date
29. Stinging insect
30. Letters after els
31. ___ boom bah
34. Campground letters

37. Army cops: Abbr.
39. Arthur who played Maude
42. Mississippi senator Trent
43. Slight amount
44. Sigher's word
46. Some DVD players
48. Start of a Latin 101 trio
49. ___ favor: please (Sp.)
50. Seattle clock setting: Abbr.
52. ___ de la Cit
53. Feed lines to
54. Unit of elec. current
58. 401, in old Rome
59. Author Rand
60. "Oh, give ___ home . . ."

1-across starts in the 1st square from the left.

Solution on page 333

Diagramless 5

Across

1. Downs' opposite
4. China's Mao ___-tung
7. Water cannon target
11. Elevations: Abbr.
12. Jefferson's Monticello, e.g.
13. Atlantic Coast states, with "the"
15. Bit of sunshine
16. WWII transport
17. Tooth pro's deg.
20. ___ Diego, CA
22. Three, on a sundial
23. Imbibe slowly
24. Sept. preceder
25. Emergency PC key
26. More statuesque
28. Slower, in mus.
29. Attached with glue
32. Wire diameter measure
35. Angry feeling
36. Sleep phenom.
38. "Put ___ Happy Face"
39. Pavement material
40. ___'wester
41. Highway: Abbr.
42. Prosecutors, for short
44. Captain Hook's assistant
46. Daylong marches
50. Coupe or convertible
51. Actress Lombard
52. Vienna is its cap.
53. Metal in pewter

Down

1. Ending for press
2. Detectives, for short
3. Drunkard
4. Dissertation
5. Radio interference
6. Double-curve letter
8. Small mountain lake
9. Airport posting: Abbr.
10. Spanish king

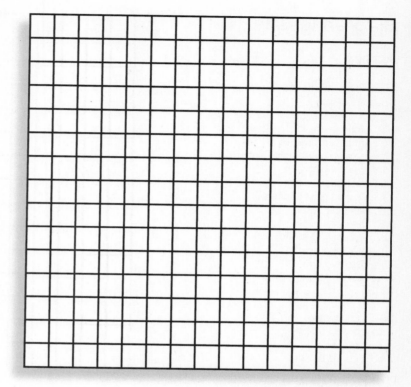

14. Football scores: Abbr.
16. Be deceitful
18. Dah's partner
19. Not dense
20. Seek damages from
21. Part of USDA: Abbr.
24. Changes
27. All fired up?
29. Actress Zadora
30. Departure's opposite: Abbr.
31. ___ gratias: Thanks to God
32. "The Island of Dr. ___"
33. Buries
34. New Guinea port
37. Juilliard subj.
39. Ivan, for one
42. Santa's mo.
43. One ___ time (individually)
45. Universal Studios' former parent co.
47. Stew vessel

48. ___ Lilly and Company
49. Japanese money

1-across starts in the 9th square from the left.

Solution on page 334

Diagramless 6

Across

1. Somalian fashion model
5. Library device
7. Corp. takeover
10. Dutch master Jan
11. EarthLink alternative
12. ___-mo (instant replay feature)
15. Gives a thumbs-up
16. Poisonous snake
19. Late columnist Landers
21. Brain-scan letters
24. Dove's sound
25. Stephen of "Michael Collins"
26. Navel type
28. Existence: Lat.
30. Krazy ___ of the comics
31. En ___: as a group
32. Fell behind slightly
36. Pro hoopster
39. Doo-wop syllable
40. Poker pair
44. Propelled a canoe
45. Lunch meat
46. 19th letter of the Greek alphabet
47. Pinup's leg
48. Hans of Dadaism
49. Cause friction
50. Find a sum
53. ___-Man (arcade game)
55. Scooby-___ (cartoon dog)
56. On ___ (winning)
61. G-man: Abbr.
62. "Gay" French city
63. Topers

Down

1. Driver's lic. and such
2. Small rug
3. Ended a fast
4. Jacqueline Kennedy ___ Bouvier
6. MD's helpers
7. ___ -Tzu: Taoist philosopher
8. ___ choy (Chinese green)

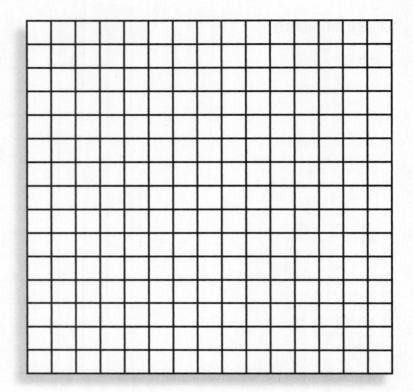

9. Mary-Kate and Ashley
13. Escapades
14. ___ a time (individually)
16. Highest card
17. Morse code message
18. Opposite of neg.
20. Boris's partner
22. "___ for Evidence" (Grafton novel)
23. "That's incredible!"
26. "___ Mine" (George Harrison book)
27. West Coast wine valley
29. Gen. Robert ___
33. Run-of-the-mill: Abbr.
34. Like some wits or cheeses
35. Florida port
36. Yuletide beverage
37. Lamb's cry
38. Naval fleet
41. Basketball position: Abbr.
42. Water: Fr.

43. Long sandwich
51. "Man's best friend"
52. Decimal point
54. Beanie
57. ___ Tafari (Haile Selassie)
58. Tijuana gold
59. Disappoint, with "down"
60. Brown with a Band of Renown

1-across starts in the 1st square from the left.

Solution on page 334

Diagramless 7

Across

1. Noah creation
4. "Otherwise . . ."
7. Lawyers' grp.
10. Property
11. Anchorman Rather
12. Leaky radiator sound
13. Georgia and Ukraine, once: Abbr.
14. Greek dawn goddess
17. Calendar abbreviation
19. Is the owner of
21. Helpers for profs
23. Was in possession of
24. "Are you a man ___ mouse?"
25. Loveseat
27. Kung ___ shrimp
28. ___ Lingus: Irish carrier
29. ACLU concerns: Abbr.
32. Knights' horses
35. Feedbag grain
36. "The best things in life ___ free"
37. Michigan's ___ Canals
38. Sugar: Suffix
39. Sure-footed work animal
40. Capone and Pacino
42. Catches sight of
44. Doctors' group: Abbr.
47. "Evil Woman" rock group
48. New York's ___ Island
51. Football great Dawson
52. Crude carriers
53. Dishonorable one

Down

1. One hundred percent
2. Alphabetic run
3. Lock opener
4. Hospital areas: Abbr.
5. Second notes of the scale
6. Lighten, as a burden
7. Commercials, e.g.
8. Go from pub to pub
9. Cochise portrayer Michael

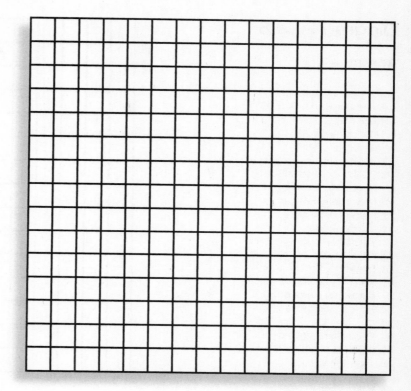

13. But: Lat.
15. Extra play periods, for short
16. Ms. enclosure
17. "___ a Moon Out Tonight"
18. Middle East inits.
20. ___ Paulo, Brazil
22. Says
26. Golf ball support
29. Australian hopper, for short
30. Grad's cap attachment
31. "The Spectator" essayist
32. Former jrs.
33. 1950 Edmond O'Brien classic thriller
34. Note after fa
36. ___ in "Able"
41. Fully satisfy
43. Extremely long time
45. Sea: Fr.
46. Question's opposite: Abbr.

48. Assn.
49. Aunt in Madrid
50. City official: Abbr.

1-across starts in the 5th square from the left.

Solution on page 334

Diagramless 8

Across

1. Cyclops had one
4. Letter between pi and sigma
7. Actor Max ___ Sydow
8. Down for the count
9. Penny-___ poker
11. Doctor, at times
13. Cookbook abbreviation
15. Muscles to crunch
17. NHL legend Bobby
20. Friend's opposite
21. ___ de Janeiro
22. Where Switz. is
23. Bit of energy
24. "Nightline" host Koppel
25. WWII transports
26. Derek and Jackson
27. "The ___ Squad"
28. ___ Simbel
30. Word after jet or time
31. Omaha's state: Abbr.
32. Tape speed abbr.
33. Shipping unit: Abbr.
34. Kitten's sound
37. Breadth
40. Sp. woman
41. Like "to be": Abbr.
42. Op. ___ (footnote abbr.)
43. Bray starter
44. Mary ___ cosmetics
45. "Survivor" shelter
46. How to address a Fr. lady
47. Happened upon
48. Lots and lots
52. ___good example
55. "___ Yankee Doodle dandy"
56. "___ know you?"
57. Physique, briefly
58. 100 cts.

Down

1. Gabor and Peron
2. Hither and ___

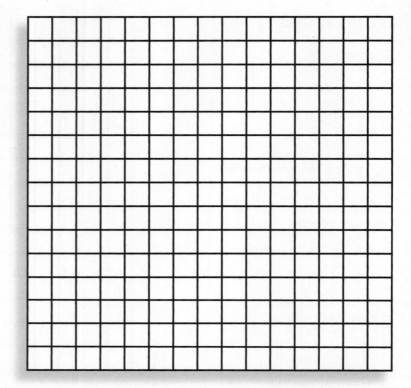

3. Suffix for differ
4. "It's a Wonderful Life" studio
5. Santa's laughs
6. Pindar poem
10. Dog-___ (well-worn)
11. Mil. award
12. Caviars
13. Bullfight bull
14. Pleads
16. Auctioneer's quest
18. Boring routine
19. Train lines: Abbr.
20. Cupid's mo.
24. Clothes
25. Oil or grease: Abbr.
27. Atlas item
28. Pier
29. Actor Gazzara
30. ___ Yutang
33. Canadian Indians

34. Emcee's amplifier
35. The "E" in QED
36. Dryly humorous
37. Educ. institution
38. More, in music
39. ABA members
40. Theology sch.
43. ___ Pinafore
47. Letters and packages
49. Freedom, briefly
50. Comic Phillips
51. Money roll
53. Hall-of-Famer Roush
54. Furthermore

1-across starts in the 4th square from the left.

Solution on page 334

Diagramless 9

Across

1. Delivery room doctors, for short
4. U.S. soldiers
7. Coffee cup
8. Lab-maze runner
9. Hushed "Hey you!"
10. Genetic material: Abbr.
11. ___-Cat (off-road vehicle)
13. Many months: Abbr.
16. Bosom buddy
17. Floor-washing implement
19. One of Alcott's "Little Women"
20. Short race
23. Porcine pads
25. Having a handle
28. Part of A&P
30. Yang partner
31. Alleged spoon-bender Geller
32. Experimentation room
34. Coastal inlet
35. "___ seeing things?"
38. Bread with a pocket
41. Stag party attendees
42. Gas pump spec.
43. Height: Abbr.
44. Silkworm

Down

1. Mantra chants
2. Commuter vehicle
3. Lt.'s subordinate
4. Doberman's warning
5. Fleming who created 007
6. "Don't move, Fido!"
9. Roly-___
11. Outpourings
12. Asian arena, for short
14. Apt. ad abbr.
15. Bread, for stew
18. 7, on a phone
21. Firenze's land
22. Diarist Anais
24. Pronounce

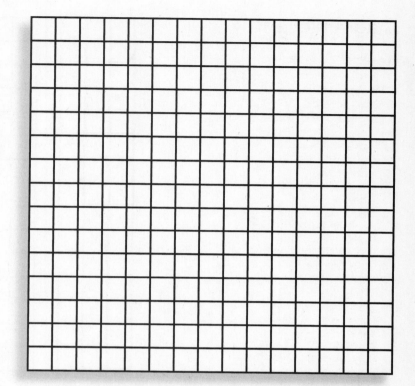

26. "Open 9 ___ 6"
27. Doe in "Bambi"
28. Surrounding glow
29. The first "T" of TNT
33. Crimson Tide, briefly
36. Gibson of film
37. Savings acct. addition
38. Before: Prefix
39. Ending with cash or bombard
40. ___ Friday's: restaurant chain

**1-across starts in the 12th square
from the left.**

Solution on page 335

Diagramless 10

Across

1. Part of m.p.h.
4. Sibling, for short
5. High-school math course: Abbr.
8. Give ___ shot
11. Have the looks of
13. Crystal ball user
15. Maple fluids
17. Former San Francisco Mayor Joseph
19. Chick of jazz
20. ___- Magnon
21. CBS forensic drama
23. Schubert's "The ___ King"
24. Oft-swiveled joint
25. Keep an ___ to the ground
27. Tin ___ Alley
28. Whodunit's essence
31. Letter holder: Abbr.
34. Three, in Torino
35. Boyfriends
36. Capuchin monkey
37. Kazakhstan, once: Abbr.
38. USN bigwigs
39. Come out even
40. Patty Hearst's kidnap grp.
42. Jan. 1, e.g.
43. "The Lord of the Rings" monster
46. Tire pressure meas.
48. April 15 addressee
49. Freeways
51. Tampa neighbor, informally
55. Long-snouted fish
56. Tot's "little piggies"
57. Swedish car
61. NYPD figure
62. The "S" in R.S.V.P.
63. Gloomy ___
64. Son-gun filler

Down

1. Charlie Rose's network
2. Before, to a sonneteer
3. 1973 Supreme Court decision name
5. "Do ___ say, . . ."
6. Virgo's predecessor
7. Wreak vengeance on
8. "Equal" word form
9. Scale deduction
10. One who mimics
12. Sailors
14. Fabled bird
16. "My gal" of song
18. Cut off, as a branch
19. Spies" org.
20. Burns the surface of
22. Hardens, as cement
26. Puts back
27. Quart parts: Abbr.
28. ___ XING: crosswalk sign
29. On the ___ (fleeing)
30. Humor finale?
32. Symbols of hardness
33. Compete (for)
35. Sheep cries
41. '60s records
42. Great success
43. Part of NATO: Abbr.
44. Hope/Crosby title word
45. Guardianship
47. Art or novel add-on
50. "Spring ahead" letters
52. How-___ (instructional books)
53. Architect I. M. ___
54. Course for new immigrants: Abbr.
58. "Fourscore and seven years ___ . . ."
59. ___ Wiedersehen
60. Jamboree grp.

1-across starts in the 1st square from the left.

Solution on page 335

Diagramless 11

Across

1. Photo ___: publicity events
4. D.D.E.'s command in WWII
7. Cambridge sch.
10. Electrified fish
11. Beach composition
13. Polynesian tuber
14. Double-helix molecule
15. Correo ___ (Spanish airmail)
16. Eagerly expecting
17. French negative
19. Curved line
20. Covert WWII org.
21. Tiny bit
22. Stetson, e.g.
25. St. Louis clock setting
26. Cry to a calf
29. Plant pockets
31. Healthful retreat
34. Modifying word: Abbr.
35. Spring holy day
38. Throw again
40. Animal that beats its chest
41. Lille lily
43. Mrs. Dithers of the comics
44. Balloon-breaking sound
45. Letters on a cornerstone
47. ___ and outs
49. Derbies and berets
50. Comedian Bernie
53. Disencumber (of)
56. Big Band or Disco period
57. NFL team
58. Loud, as the surf
60. Some ALers
63. "Do I dare to ___ peach?": Eliot
64. Author ___ Christian Andersen
65. Debt acknowledgement
66. Lacking moisture
67. "___ Beso" (1962 song)
68. Bank device: Abbr.

Down

1. Multivolume ref.
2. Animal enclosure

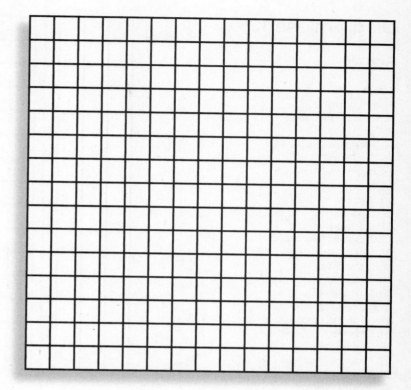

3. Leans
4. Point opposite WNW
5. Scarlett's estate
6. Unique thing
7. "Welcome" sites
8. From Donegal
9. Blouse or shirt
12. One of the Seven Dwarfs
13. Lao-tzu principle
15. In addition
18. Feed bag contents
21. Summer coolers, for short
23. Nova Scotia clock setting: Abbr.
24. Asian weight
26. Big name in China
27. Pigs out (on), briefly
28. Breakfast quaffs, for short
30. Dernier ___ (the latest thing)
32. Tennis instructor
33. Ethereal: Prefix
35. "The Raven" monogram
36. Military mail drop: Abbr.

37. Aug. follower
39. Brownish
42. Mark with a branding iron
43. Dollar parts: Abbr.
46. Sports arenas
48. Do finger painting
49. Billy Joel's "Tell ___ About It"
51. Bar association member: Abbr.
52. R. E. Lee's org.
53. Pep-rally word
54. "Dies ___"
55. Slips into
57. ___ Bartlet, president on "The West Wing"
59. Remark from Chan
61. Like stolen goods
62. Addition result

1-across starts in the 6th square from the left.

Solution on page 335

Diagramless 12

Across

1. "Yummy!"
4. Craft or skill
5. Nightclub routine
8. Caama
10. Extinct kiwi relative
11. The "I" of T.G.I.F.
14. Film director Lee
15. "It's ___ for Me to Say"
16. Thesaurus entries: Abbr.
19. Small bird
21. ___ tai (drink)
22. Typesetting mistakes
24. Feel regret over
25. Discontinues
28. Annapolis grad: Abbr.
29. TV reporter Donaldson
31. Silent film star Negri
32. ___ cit. (footnote abbr.)
34. Old what's-___-name
36. British rocker Brian
37. Three-strikes result
38. Prom-night safety grp.
42. Asner and Wynn
43. London lav
44. Japanese money

Down

1. Barnyard sound
2. "Is it Miss or ___?"
3. Rockies, e.g.
5. Amo, ___, amat
6. Not pro
7. Kids' running game
9. One, in Germany
12. Kiddie
13. Actor David Ogden ___
16. Tiny, in Troon
17. China's Sun ___-sen
18. Actress Long or Peeples
20. Makes level
23. Thrift-shop transaction
25. Corporate V.I.P.
26. Big picture?: Abbr.
27. Happy ___ lark
30. Tues. preceder
31. Attention-getters
33. Fortune 500 listings: Abbr.
34. Weed digger
35. Birth control option, briefly
39. Prince ___ Khan
40. Bambi's mother
41. Comic Rickles

1-across starts in the 2nd square from the left.

Solution on page 335

Diagramless 13

Across

1. CCL x X
4. Swiss river to the Rhine
7. German valley
8. Suffix with meth- or eth-
9. Rosary prayers
10. Putrefies
12. Bitter brews
15. Lousy grade
17. British brew
20. Mas' mates
21. Narrow waterway: Abbr.
22. Baltic or Bering
23. Airport screening org.
24. Light throw
25. Savannah summer hrs.
26. Moses' mountain
29. Letter addenda: Abbr.
31. Livy's lang.
32. Fri. follower
33. Wall St. trading group
34. First known asteroid
36. Calendar doz.
38. "Compos mentis"
40. Elbow's place
43. Sounds of doubt
44. "Boy, am ___ trouble!"
45. Narcs' agcy.
46. Opposite dir. from NNW
47. Basic version: Abbr.
48. Performed an aria
49. Spinning toys
52. Flimsy, as an excuse
55. Alliance since 1948: Abbr.
56. Smell ___ (be leery)
57. Cries of dismay
58. One of two hardy followers

Down

1. Dallas hoopster, briefly
2. Fannie ___ (federal mortgage agency)
3. Hosp. workers

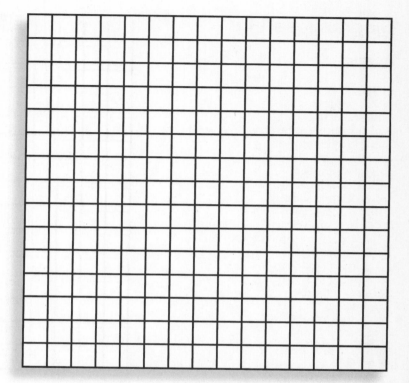

4. Alpine river
5. Year in Yucatan
6. Not active: Abbr.
7. Carrier to Sweden
11. Ms. enclosures
12. Prone (to)
13. "Leaving ___ Vegas"
14. Those, in Toledo
15. Drunk's problem
16. Ambulance destinations, for short
18. Was in charge of
19. Have breakfast
21. ". . . or ___ thought"
24. "I tawt I taw a puddy ___!"
27. They, in Calais
28. Scottish negative
29. ___ for the course
30. French holy woman: Abbr.
32. Get a look at
33. Valuable possession

34. MSNBC alternative
35. Actress Thompson of "Family"
36. Month, in Madrid
37. Surprised exclamations
38. Command to a dog
39. Pitch in for
41. Stimpy's cartoon buddy
42. Periodical, for short
47. Radiator sound
48. Harden, as cement
50. Winning tic-tac-toe row
51. Foot the bill
52. "___-di-dah!"
53. Parseghian of football
54. Cause damage to

1-across starts in the 5th square from the left.

Solution on page 336

Diagramless 14

Across

1. The "L" of L.A.
4. UFO navigators
7. Relative of -arian
10. Birmingham's state: Abbr.
11. Wide shoe designation
12. Dentists' grp.
13. Highways: Abbr.
14. Compass pt. opposite SSW
15. Present and future
19. D.D.E. opponent
20. Open ___ of worms
22. Mauna ___ (Hawaiian volcano)
23. Bread with seeds
25. Some USN officers
26. Agent: Abbr.
27. Stallone title role
31. Uncovers
32. Certifies by oath
36. Layers of paint
38. "My Heart Skips ___"
39. Latin art
42. Mikhail of chess
44. Patriotic org.
47. Mothers
48. ". . . and to ___ good night!"
50. Furry foot
52. Avoid a trial
54. 1960s radical grp.
57. Money for old age: Abbr.
58. ___ Van Winkle
59. Vowel sequence
60. Sunday address: Abbr.
61. Ooh and ___
62. "___ port in a storm"
63. All ___ up (irate)

Down

1. ___ Flynn Boyle
2. ___ but wiser
3. Smart-mouthed
4. Nighttime, to a poet
5. Coffee-break time
6. "___ pin and pick it up . . ."
7. Bother continuously
8. Paradisiacal places
9. Competed in a marathon
16. Popular camera type, for short
17. Help-wanted abbr.
18. Syrup ingredient
21. Near miss
24. Tarzan creator's monogram
28. Motor-club letters
29. "The A-Team" muscleman
30. Place a wager
33. Cry audibly
34. Menlo Park inits.
35. Railroad stop: Abbr.
37. Avenue crossers: Abbr.
39. Mornings, briefly
40. Norma ___ (Sally Field role)
41. Concorde: Abbr.
42. Shire of "Rocky"
43. First Hebrew letter
45. Prone to imitation
46. Carnival show
49. Not on shore
51. Witch's blemish
53. La-la prelude
55. Lot of noise
56. Dim sum sauce

1-across starts in the 1st square from the left.

Solution on page 336

Chapter 9
Word Ladders

Link these word pairs together with a ladder of words. Each step in the ladder must be a real word and must differ from the previous word by only one letter. For example, CAT can be linked to DOG with these steps: CAT, COT, DOT, DOG. There are many possible solutions for these puzzles, but try to use only the given number of steps.

Word Ladder 1

P	U	P
_D_	___	_G_
___	___	___
D	O	G

Word Ladder 2

P	R	O
_C_	___	_Y_
___	_O_	___
C	O	N

Word Ladder 3

O	N	E
___	___	___
___	___	___
___	___	___
___	___	___
___	___	___
T	E	N

Word Ladder 4

M	O	M
___	_A_	_D_
___	___	___
D	A	D

Word Ladder 5

B	O	Y
___	___	___
___	___	___
M	A	N

Word Ladder 6

T	E	E
___	___	___
___	___	___
___	___	___
___	___	___
O	F	F

Solution on page 337

Word Ladder 7

B	E	L	L
	A		
	A		E
		N	E
R			G
R	**I**	**N**	**G**

Word Ladder 8

W	I	L	D
W	I	L	E
T	I	L	E
T	I	M	E
T	**A**	**M**	**E**

Word Ladder 9

G	I	V	E
G	A	V	E
C	A	V	E
C	A	K	E
T	**A**	**K**	**E**

Word Ladder 10

D	R	A	G
R	**A**	**C**	**E**

Word Ladder 11

Y	E	A	R
B	E	A	R
	O		
		O	
B	**O**	**O**	**K**

Word Ladder 12

W	O	R	K
W	O	R	T
W	A	R	T
C	A	R	T
C	A	S	T
C	**A**	**S**	**H**

Solution on page 337

Word Ladder 13

S H I F T

___ ___ ___ ___ ___

___ ___ ___ ___ ___

___ ___ ___ ___ ___

___ ___ ___ ___ ___

___ ___ ___ ___ ___

G E A R S

Word Ladder 14

W O R D S

___ ___ ___ ___ ___

___ ___ ___ ___ ___

___ ___ ___ ___ ___

B O O K S

Word Ladder 15

W A L K

___ ___ ___ ___

___ ___ ___ ___

___ ___ ___ ___

P A T H

Word Ladder 16

H E A D

___ ___ ___ ___

___ ___ ___ ___

___ ___ ___ ___

T O E S

Word Ladder 17

P U S H

___ ___ ___ ___

___ ___ ___ ___

P U L L

Word Ladder 18

F A I R

___ ___ ___ ___

___ ___ ___ ___

___ ___ ___ ___

G O O D

Solution on page 337

Word Ladder 19

T R E E E

_ _ _ _ _

_ _ _ _ _

_ _ _ _ _

_ _ _ _ _

_ _ _ _ _

W O O D

Word Ladder 20

T R I C K

_ _ _ _ _

_ _ _ _ _

_ _ _ _ _

_ _ _ _ _

_ _ _ _ _

T R E A T

Word Ladder 21

R I S E

_ _ _ _

_ _ _ _

F A L L

Word Ladder 22

P I G

_ _ _

_ _ _

H A M

Word Ladder 23

R A T E

_ _ _ _

_ _ _ _

_ _ _ _

H I K E

Word Ladder 24

S W E E T

_ _ _ _ _

_ _ _ _ _

_ _ _ _ _

_ _ _ _ _

_ _ _ _ _

_ _ _ _ _

H E A R T

Solution on page 337

Word Ladder 25

D   O   C

_____   _____   _____

_____   _____   _____

_____   _____   _____

_____   _____   _____

_____   _____   _____

_____   _____   _____

F   L   U

Word Ladder 26

P   L   A   Y

_____   _____   _____   _____

_____   _____   _____   _____

_____   _____   _____   _____

_____   _____   _____   _____

_____   _____   _____   _____

_____   _____   _____   _____

G   A   M   E

Word Ladder 27

F   A   R   M

_____   _____   _____   _____

_____   _____   _____   _____

F   O   O   D

Word Ladder 28

M   I   X   E   D

_____   _____   _____   _____   _____

_____   _____   _____   _____   _____

_____   _____   _____   _____   _____

_____   _____   _____   _____   _____

_____   _____   _____   _____   _____

_____   _____   _____   _____   _____

_____   _____   _____   _____   _____

_____   _____   _____   _____   _____

_____   _____   _____   _____   _____

D   R   I   N   K

Word Ladder 29

L   O   G

_____   _____   _____

_____   _____   _____

O   A   R

Word Ladder 30

T   I   M   E

_____   _____   _____   _____

_____   _____   _____   _____

B   E   L   L

Solution on pages 337–338

Word Ladder 31

S E N D

____ ____ ____ ____

____ ____ ____ ____

____ ____ ____ ____

H O M E

Word Ladder 32

K I S S

____ ____ ____ ____

____ ____ ____ ____

____ ____ ____ ____

____ ____ ____ ____

T E L L

Word Ladder 33

B E E

____ ____ ____

____ ____ ____

W A X

Word Ladder 34

P L A Y

____ ____ ____ ____

____ ____ ____ ____

____ ____ ____ ____

G R O W

Word Ladder 35

T O W N

____ ____ ____ ____

____ ____ ____ ____

____ ____ ____ ____

____ ____ ____ ____

C I T Y

Word Ladder 36

O U T E R

____ ____ ____ ____ ____

____ ____ ____ ____ ____

____ ____ ____ ____ ____

____ ____ ____ ____ ____

B A K E D

Solution on page 338

Word Ladder 37

T   I   G   E   R

_____ _____ _____ _____ _____

_____ _____ _____ _____ _____

_____ _____ _____ _____ _____

_____ _____ _____ _____ _____

_____ _____ _____ _____ _____

_____ _____ _____ _____ _____

M   A   T   E   D

Word Ladder 38

S   I   R   E   N

_____ _____ _____ _____ _____

_____ _____ _____ _____ _____

_____ _____ _____ _____ _____

F   A   D   E   S

Word Ladder 39

P   A   P   E   R

_____ _____ _____ _____ _____

_____ _____ _____ _____ _____

_____ _____ _____ _____ _____

G   A   M   E   S

Word Ladder 40

P   O   N   D

_____ _____ _____ _____

_____ _____ _____ _____

_____ _____ _____ _____

L   A   K   E

Word Ladder 41

B   O   O   K

_____ _____ _____ _____

_____ _____ _____ _____

_____ _____ _____ _____

_____ _____ _____ _____

F   I   L   M

Word Ladder 42

Z   E   R   O

_____ _____ _____ _____

_____ _____ _____ _____

_____ _____ _____ _____

_____ _____ _____ _____

_____ _____ _____ _____

F   R   E   E

Solution on page 338

Word Ladder 43

F   O   X

___   ___   ___

___   ___   ___

___   ___   ___

D   E   N

Word Ladder 44

E   A   S   Y

___   ___   ___   ___

___   ___   ___   ___

___   ___   ___   ___

H   A   R   D

Word Ladder 45

E   A   T

___   ___   ___

___   ___   ___

___   ___   ___

___   ___   ___

A   T   E

Word Ladder 46

A   I   R

___   ___   ___

___   ___   ___

A   R   T

Word Ladder 47

C   A   R

___   ___   ___

___   ___   ___

___   ___   ___

T   O   Y

Word Ladder 48

E   G   G

___   ___   ___

___   ___   ___

___   ___   ___

___   ___   ___

___   ___   ___

___   ___   ___

H   E   N

Solution on page 338

Word Ladder 49

S I N G

____ ____ ____ ____

____ ____ ____ ____

____ ____ ____ ____

T O N E

Word Ladder 50

M O U S E

____ ____ ____ ____ ____

____ ____ ____ ____ ____

____ ____ ____ ____ ____

W O R S T

Word Ladder 51

C O A T

____ ____ ____ ____

____ ____ ____ ____

____ ____ ____ ____

S H O E

Word Ladder 52

C L U M P

____ ____ ____ ____ ____

____ ____ ____ ____ ____

____ ____ ____ ____ ____

____ ____ ____ ____ ____

T R A S H

Word Ladder 53

S T A R T

____ ____ ____ ____ ____

____ ____ ____ ____ ____

____ ____ ____ ____ ____

____ ____ ____ ____ ____

P H O N E

Word Ladder 54

M O R E

____ ____ ____ ____

____ ____ ____ ____

____ ____ ____ ____

L E S S

Solution on page 338

Word Ladder 55

S   A   D

___   ___   ___

___   ___   ___

J   O   Y

Word Ladder 56

I   C   E

___   ___   ___

___   ___   ___

___   ___   ___

___   ___   ___

H   O   T

Word Ladder 57

J   E   T

___   ___   ___

___   ___   ___

___   ___   ___

F   L   Y

Word Ladder 58

F   O   U   R

___   ___   ___   ___

___   ___   ___   ___

___   ___   ___   ___

___   ___   ___   ___

___   ___   ___   ___

F   I   V   E

Word Ladder 59

S   O   U   P

___   ___   ___   ___

___   ___   ___   ___

___   ___   ___   ___

B   O   W   L

Word Ladder 60

F   O   O   L

___   ___   ___   ___

___   ___   ___   ___

___   ___   ___   ___

___   ___   ___   ___

W   I   S   E

Solution on page 338

Word Ladder 61

W	A	R	M
—	—	—	—
—	—	—	—
—	—	—	—
C	O	L	D

Word Ladder 62

B	O	R	N
—	—	—	—
—	—	—	—
—	—	—	—
—	—	—	—
—	—	—	—
F	R	E	E

Word Ladder 63

W	H	E	A	T
—	—	—	—	—
—	—	—	—	—
—	—	—	—	—
—	—	—	—	—
B	R	E	A	D

Word Ladder 64

N	O	R	T	H
—	—	—	—	—
—	—	—	—	—
—	—	—	—	—
—	—	—	—	—
—	—	—	—	—
S	O	U	T	H

Word Ladder 65

P	A	W	N
—	—	—	—
—	—	—	—
—	—	—	—
—	—	—	—
K	I	N	G

Word Ladder 66

S	N	A	C	K
—	—	—	—	—
—	—	—	—	—
—	—	—	—	—
—	—	—	—	—
—	—	—	—	—
M	E	A	L	S

Solution on pages 338–339

Word Ladder 67

F   O   G

___   ___   ___

___   ___   ___

___   ___   ___

S   U   N

Word Ladder 68

O   W   L

___   ___   ___

___   ___   ___

___   ___   ___

___   ___   ___

F   O   X

Word Ladder 69

T   O   P

___   ___   ___

___   ___   ___

___   ___   ___

___   ___   ___

E   N   D

Word Ladder 70

D   R   Y

___   ___   ___

___   ___   ___

___   ___   ___

___   ___   ___

W   E   T

Word Ladder 71

F   L   E   S   H

___ ___ ___ ___ ___

___ ___ ___ ___ ___

___ ___ ___ ___ ___

___ ___ ___ ___ ___

___ ___ ___ ___ ___

B   L   O   O   D

Word Ladder 72

S   E   E   D

___ ___ ___ ___

___ ___ ___ ___

___ ___ ___ ___

___ ___ ___ ___

L   A   W   N

Solution on page 339

Word Ladder 73

T	E	A	R	S
___	___	___	___	___
___	___	___	___	___
___	___	___	___	___
___	___	___	___	___
___	___	___	___	___
S	M	I	L	E

Word Ladder 74

H	A	N	D
___	___	___	___
___	___	___	___
___	___	___	___
___	___	___	___
F	O	O	T

Word Ladder 75

O	L	D
___	___	___
___	___	___
___	___	___
___	___	___
___	___	___
N	E	W

Word Ladder 76

J	O	G
J	U	G
R	U	G
R	U	N

Word Ladder 77

S	M	I	L	E
___	___	___	___	___
___	___	___	___	___
___	___	___	___	___
___	___	___	___	___
___	___	___	___	___
___	___	___	___	___
___	___	___	___	___
F	R	O	W	N

Word Ladder 78

P	A	L
___	___	___
___	___	___
___	___	___
F	O	E

Solution on page 339

Word Ladder 79

S L E E P
_ _ _ _ _
_ _ _ _ _
_ _ _ _ _
_ _ _ _ _
D R E A M

Word Ladder 80

F R E S H
_ _ _ _ _
_ _ _ _ _
_ _ _ _ _
_ _ _ _ _
_ _ _ _ _
S T A L E

Word Ladder 81

W O R D
_ _ _ _
_ _ _ _
_ _ _ _
G A M E

Word Ladder 82

D A Y S
_ _ _ _
_ _ _ _
_ _ _ _
Y E A R

Word Ladder 83

S E E D
_ _ _ _
_ _ _ _
T R E E

Word Ladder 84

S H A R P
S N A R D
C N A R B
C U A R T
C U A N T
_ _ _ _ _
B L U N T

Solution on page 339

Chapter 10
Dropout Puzzles

Rearrange the letters in the vertical columns to fill the boxes directly below them. When you have filled in the grid correctly you will see a quote.

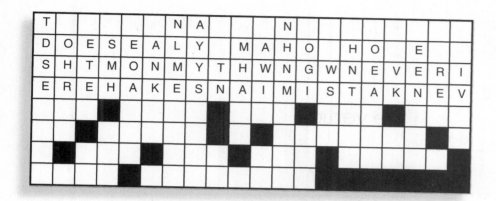

Theodore Roosevelt

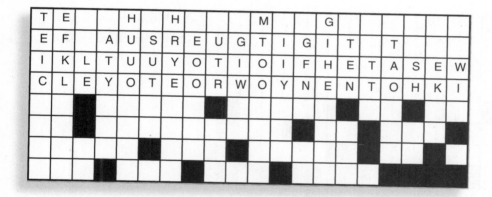

Keith Richards

	V			I		V	O	U											
E	T	E	G	H	I		T	E	E	R	E			N		T		E	
E	S	T	R	U	T	F	T	Y	A	R	K	I	Y	O	Y	L	U		J
U	R	I	N	S	N	T	O	R	H	C	R	E	F	O	U	O	L	H	G

Will Rogers

Solution on page 339

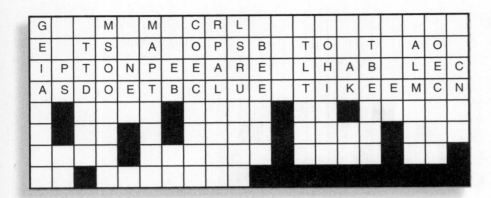

Groucho Marx

```
G     M     M     C  R  L
E     T  S     A     O  P  S  B     T  O     T     A  O
I  P  T  O  N  P  E  E  A  R  E     L  H  A  B     L  E  C
A  S  D  O  E  T  B  C  L  U  E     T  I  K  E  E  M  C  N
```

William Shakespeare

```
F  Y     E        I     T     I     R
S  Y  F  N  D     S  O  I     F  U  L  Y     S     L  D
L  I  I  A  G     A  D  D  H  T  A  F  U     T  O  G  N
B  O  U  N  N  I  N  N  A  O  T  N  G  E  L  L  I  O  F  I
```

Oscar Wilde

```
   K  H        S        T
L  H  E  T     N  L  E  N  O  G     B  G     K  E        A
B  T  U  A  N  I  B  O  I  N  T     T  E  L  W  G  R  S  A
T  O  E  D  O  A  B  Y  U  T  H  I  N  A  I  N  O  D  T  E
```

Solution on pages 339–340

John F. Kennedy

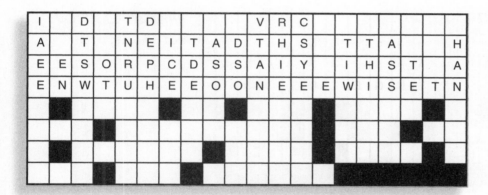

Bill Cosby

Anne Frank

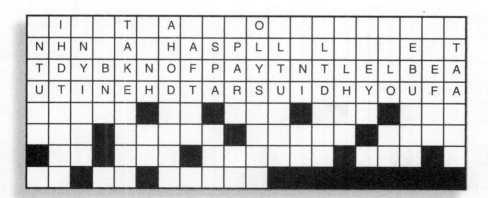

Solution on page 340

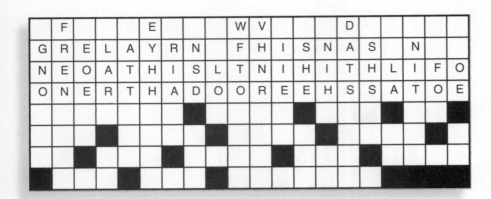

Jesus

Martin Luther King, Jr.

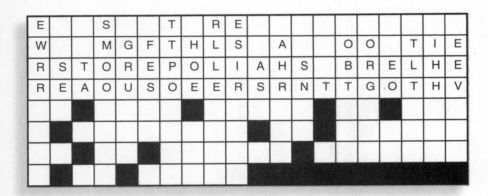

George Bernard Shaw

Solution on page 340

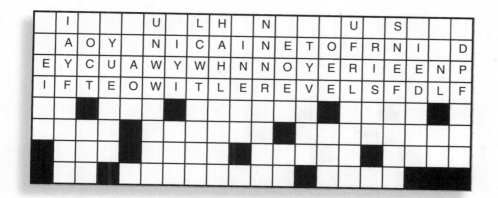

Marvin Gaye

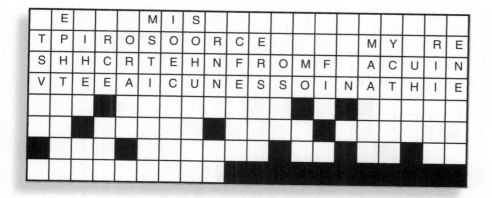

Claude Monet

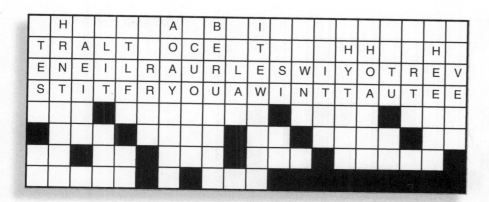

Lily Tomlin

Solution on page 340

Steve Martin

Raymond Chandler

Forrest Gump

Solution on page 340

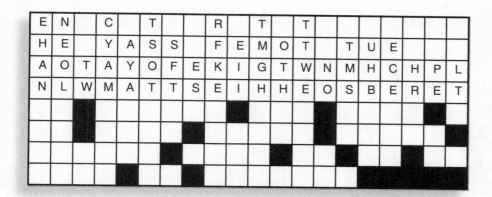

Abraham Lincoln

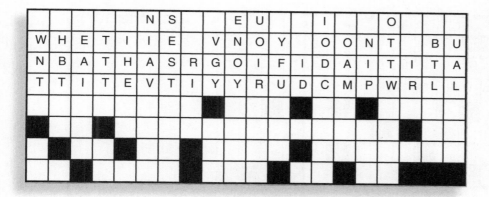

Mahatma Gandhi

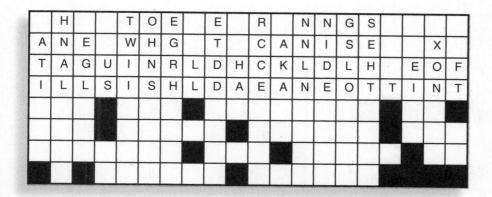

St. Francis of Assisi

Solution on page 340

Albert Einstein

1	2	3	4	5	6	7	8	9	10	11	12	13	14	15	16	17	18	19	20
A		I		P				E		H			T	E					
A	S	E	N	F	I	T	O		W	N	T	U	T		R	O			S
U	T	H	S	O	N	Y	D	M	D	W	E	I	L	T	H	E	O		R
E	C	H	A	T	P	E	T	H	A	I	F	L	S	U	T	O	O	P	M

Jimi Hendrix

1	2	3	4	5	6	7	8	9	10	11	12	13	14	15	16	17	18	19	20
		L			H	E		W		T		A		O					
V	H	E	N		E	R	W	O	R		P	E	E		E			L	O
E	E	I	F	L	P	O	C	E	M	E	W	E	T	C	E	O	L	O	D
W	W	O	O	V	T	K	N	O	P	O	S	H	R	H	W	F	R	L	V

Harry S. Truman

1	2	3	4	5	6	7	8	9	10	11	12	13	14	15	16	17	18	19	20
	U		C				N		O		P		R	E					
	G		I	S		T	A	C	C	T	M	G	A	W	S				O
O	T	O	U	S	N	O	H	E	Z	C	N	E	D	I	T	A	W	I	Y
I	Y	E	T	A	D	A	M	A	O	I	R	C	L	I	H	H	T	H	F

Solution on page 340

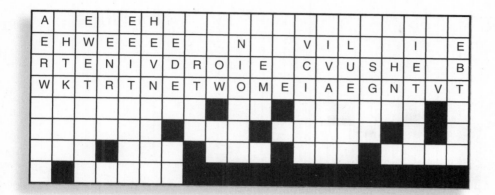

Mae West

Basho

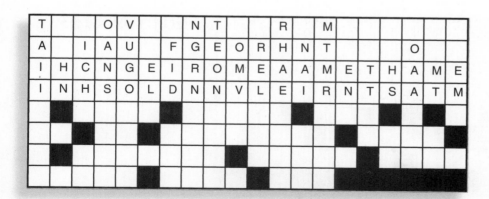

Galileo Galilei

Solution on page 340

Victor Hugo

T			O			B	N			O	O			I					
A		N	E	N		A	S		C	D	M	A				H	O		I
T	I	M	I	T	V	A	S		I	N	S	O	S	W	E	D	M	B	U
S	N	C	A	N	H	A	E	I	R	E	E	E	F	T	A	R	S	E	E

Ann Landers

E			H	I			N		A		L				L	L	
T	E	L	H	A	A		A	E	Y	C	H	A	O	T	I	R	O	H
O	R	K	T	A	T	N	P	O	O	T	H	E	N	G	H	R	A	V	E
D	O	T	E	V	T	S	I	E	N	P	H	I	S	W	P	E	R	T	L

Edith Wharton

I	N			O										
O	F	G		N	H	M	B	W		H		S	P	O			Y		C
I	O	D	D	T	L	Y	E	E		A		P	R	Y	T	W	T		Y
O	U	L	O	T	I	A	V	E	E	D	A	P	T	E	P	T	E	R	G

Solution on page 340

T		O	A	L			T			A	T			I	N			
O	P	E	L	Y	I	S		E	H	A	W	T		H	T		R	B
I	L	I	T	R	S	T	Y	H	S	T	O	B	I	L	I	E	E	N	O
V	I	T	N	Y	I	T	O	T	S	B	U	R	S	T	O	V	Y	A	T

F. Scott Fitzgerald

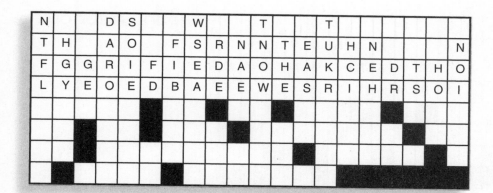

John Rushkin

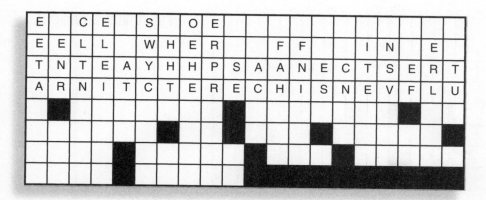

Henry Adams

Solution on pages 340–341

Eleanor Roosevelt

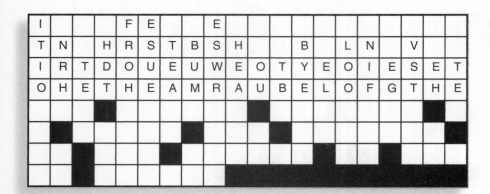

Jean Giraudoux

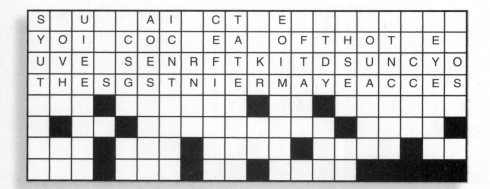

Thomas Edison

Solution on page 341

Kurt Vonnegut

W	R			R			W		B					W						
N	E		B	E				E	H	A	T	E	W	R			U	L		W
E	D		T	W	E	V	P	R	E	T	C	A	E	E	F	R	E	T	T	
H	A	T	A	O	E	B	E	R	Y	U	T	N	D	E	P	B	E	T	E	

George Burns

	E			E	N											
R	A	N	I	R	F		I	M		W		I		G		N	E		O
N	E	T	T	I	L		S	M		T	O	E	N	O	I	L	O		S
T	U	Y	L	I	E	T	I	H	O	G	H	B	U	S	N	T	Y	S	S

Douglas Adams

U		E		V												
I		F			T	H	E	Y		A	A	O	S		E	N			E
I	N	L	L	T	H	B	Y	E	M	D	K	I	N	I	S		I	S	L
Y	K	D	O	Y	E	E	D	W	H	O	L	E	H	A	S	G	T	H	O

Solution on page 341

Henry Miller

St. Thomas
Aquinas

Robert Frost

Solution on page 341

Chapter 11
Brain Teasers

Many people enjoy solving brainteasers—they keep your mind in tiptop shape while boosting creativity and mental flexibility. For some, the satisfaction comes from figuring out the solution to a difficult puzzle. For others, it's just the entertainment derived from the amusing stories and clever answers that accompany a good brainteaser. Whatever the reason, it is clear that brainteasers are highly popular for puzzlers of all ages. The language, logic, math, and trivia teasers in this chapter are sure to please!

Language Teaser #1

▲ *Difficulty: Easy*

Below are four epitaphs that appear on some fictional gravestones. From the writings, can you figure out the occupation of each person?

1. Here lies Mortimer Bibbs. He took part of ours and gave it to big brother, but he always had good form.
2. Here lies Dirk McDuff, who toppled giants with weapons of steel. If only he'd heard his partner's shout before the giants found their revenge. *LUMBER JACK*
3. Here lies Suzy Smelt. She constructed many a bomb but mostly brought smiles to our faces. *Fireworks*
4. Here lies Ethel Grant. She spent her whole life fighting with what she will now become.

Language Teaser #2

▲ *Difficulty: Easy*

Fill in the blanks in the following sentences with rhyming words.

1. The _____ of a stoplight is to make a road _____ safer.
2. Like the saying goes, you can't _force_ a _____ to drink. He'll do it in due _____.
3. The _____ was terrible at _____ because he was much too short and kept slipping on the ice.

Language Teaser #3

▲ *Difficulty: Easy*

The blanks in these sentences will be filled in with three different homonyms (words that sound alike but are spelled differently) to make valid sentences. The dashes indicate the number of letters in the words. Can you fill in the blanks?

1. The cut on his _heel_ won't _heal_ in time for the race, so _he'll_ have to drop out.
2. The man was so upset about being _bald_ that he regularly _____ himself up on the bed and _____ his eyes out.
3. I couldn't _sense_ any of the _____ in the flower shop, because for some strange reason I had 50 _____ crammed up my nose.
4. A pirate will wander the _seas_ and essentially _____ everything he _____.

Language Teaser #4

▲ *Difficulty: Easy*

In the following sentence, fill in the blanks with words that are the same except for their first letters.

My _father_ , the _b_____ , would _r_____ _____ with soap than with body wash.

Solution on page 341

Language Teaser #5

▲ *Difficulty: Easy*

Below are clues to words that start with the prefix "man." Can you figure out the words?

1. Cuffs: _____
2. Sea cow: _____
3. Command: _____
4. Dummy: _____
5. Guide: _____

Language Teaser #6

▲ *Difficulty: Medium*

To find the answers to the following questions, you start with words that start with the prefix "in." But the words will only answer the questions when a space is added after the "in." For example, the answer to the question "Where is the horse?" would be INSTALL (in stall). Obviously it's not proper grammar, but you get the point. Can you figure out the "in" words that answer the following questions?

1. Where is my sleeping bag?
2. Where is my wife's stomach?
3. Where does the air go after the fan sucks it up?
4. I put some food down in the seabird's cage. Where did it go?
5. Where is the church bell?

Language Teaser #7

▲ *Difficulty: Medium*

Use the clue to figure out what two smaller words will combine to make one compound word. For example: Elevated + Easy to carry = Highlight (high + light)

1. Not over + Not sit = ?
2. Not tall + Slice or divide = ?
3. Large four-legged animal + Foot protection = ?
4. Hot beverage + Eating utensil = ?
5. Natural sweet substance + Planetary satellite = ?

Language Teaser #8

▲ *Difficulty: Medium*

Here are some more compound word puzzles. Use the clues to figure out which two smaller words will fit together to make one compound word.

1. Clear liquid + Plummet = ?
2. Something to read + Type of container = ?
3. Celestial body + Swimming animal = ?
4. Head topping + Piece of furniture = ?
5. Sandwich spread + Whiskey = ?

Solution on page 341

Language Teaser #9

▲ Difficulty: Medium

You'll need to mix things up twice to solve this puzzle. Each word on the left can be scrambled and used to fill in the blanks in one of the words on the right to make a new word. For example, you would scramble "Lot" to fill in "S _ _ _ E N" and make the word "STOLEN." Can you figure out which word goes where?

a. Access   1. D I _ A _ V _ N _ A _ _

b. Strain   2. _ O M _ R _ _ U _ _

c. Staged   3. _ _ N I _ E N _ I A _ _

d. Pretty   4. _ E _ _ _ _ E R _

e. Slates   5. _ _ _ R _ I T I _ _

Language Teaser #10

▲ Difficulty: Medium

In each of the following clues, a definition is given. Fill in the blanks with two rhyming words that fit the definition.

1. A T-bone for a pickpocket: _____ for a _____

2. A fool with an open sore: A _____ with a _____

3. Don't stop the horse: Don't _____ the _____

4. Smart mousy creature: A _____ with a _____

Language Teaser #11

▲ Difficulty: Hard

Each clue below describes two words that differ by only one letter. The extra letter has been either added to the beginning or the end of the second word—all the rest are in the same order. For example "Writing on the wall of Noah's boat" would result in "Ark mark." Can you get the rest?

1. Complaint about a golf club part
2. Insect being angry and vocal
3. Angry buccaneer
4. The second of the two dishes
5. Scrawny unidentified object

Language Teaser #12

▲ Difficulty: Hard

The words in the following list are out of order. Can you figure out the pattern (which is NOT alphabetical) and put them in the proper order?

1. Leaf
2. Part
3. Mitt
4. Corn
5. Saw

Solution on page 342

Language Teaser #13

⚠ *Difficulty: Hard*

The following words, when modified according to the same general rule, will each fit one of the definitions listed below. Can you figure out how to properly modify each word and then match it with the proper definition?

PICKLE, KNIGHT, CHOIR, PAN, TIRE, TREE, FIN, TENT

1. Peace-talks goal
2. Man's title
3. Fairylike
4. Join
5. High-pitched flute
6. Garden flower
7. Whole

Language Teaser #14

⚠ *Difficulty: Hard*

The clues will lead you to two words that are anagrams of each other. (That is, both words contain the same letters, just in a different order.) For example, the clue "Attach father" would lead you to the anagram "Add Dad."

1. Not above the arm joint
2. Tutors a mutant creature
3. Swindler of a large area of land
4. Mountainous friends
5. Directional soup

Solution on page 342

Logic Teaser #1

⚠ *Difficulty: Easy*

One evening, Bobby Braingle sits at home waiting for his favorite television show to come on. As he glances at the clock face (analog, with numerals 1 to 12 correctly positioned), Bobby makes an observation. If he were to draw a straight line in the right place, the clock face would be divided in such a way that the sum of the numbers on one side of the line would equal the sum of the numbers on the other side of the line.

Where could Bobby draw the line, and what is the total of the numbers on either side?

Logic Teaser #2

⚠ *Difficulty: Easy*

Bobby either always lies or always tells the truth. Regardless of which it is, there is one statement that Bobby can never make. What is it?

Logic Teaser #3

▲ *Difficulty: Easy*

You have four pieces of chain. Each piece is made of three links. What is the smallest number of cuts and mends you need to make to produce a circular chain with all 12 links? 3/3

Logic Teaser #4

▲ *Difficulty: Easy*

At the annual Puzzleonia Tennis Tournament, 128 players compete in a system where the winner of each round goes on to play another winner until there is a champion. How many games are played in the entire tournament? 127

Logic Teaser #5

▲ *Difficulty: Easy*

Twice a year, the time in Florida is the same as the time in Oregon. How is this possible?

Logic Teaser #6

▲ *Difficulty: Medium*

Potato Pete is getting ready to ship a bunch of barrels of potatoes to the local French fry factory. He knows that the French fry factory only buys potatoes that weigh exactly one pound, so he has sorted all the 1-pound potatoes into barrels. He also sorts the potatoes that weight exactly 1.1 pounds into other barrels that he sends to the potato chip factory. Any potatoes that do not weigh 1 or 1.1 pounds are sent to the mashed potato plant.

The problem is that Pete has accidentally swapped one barrel from the potato-chip order with a barrel from the French fry order—and he doesn't know which barrel it is. Luckily, Pete has a scale that will read the weight to three decimal places. What is the smallest number of weighings Pete can make to correct his mistake? You should know that each order has exactly ten barrels and that no two barrels have the same number of potatoes inside.

Solution on page 342

Logic Teaser #7

▲ *Difficulty: Medium*

The king of Puzzleonia is at a fundraiser, and he must personally shake hands with all 99 guests— a lot of handshaking. How many handshakes would be made if all 100 people at the fundraiser shook hands with every other person once?

Logic Teaser #8

▲ *Difficulty: Medium*

Three aliens are on the alien basketball team. Each alien has a different number of limbs (either two, three, or four). Each alien is wearing a jersey with a number printed on it. Coincidentally, the numbers are 2, 3, and 4. The alien wearing the #4 jersey says, "Isn't it odd that our jersey numbers match the number of our limbs, but none of us is actually wearing the jersey number that matches our own number of limbs?" The three-limbed alien turns around and says, "Yeah, that is strange."

Which alien is wearing which jersey number?

Logic Teaser #9

▲ *Difficulty: Medium*

Five customers (Candy, Derek, John, Rose, and Steve), order lunch at a fast-food restaurant. They order the following things, not in order: cheeseburger, salad, chicken strips, hamburger, and fried fish. Each customer asks for his or her meal with extra sauce (ketchup, mustard, barbeque sauce, mayo, and ranch dressing). Can you figure out who got what and in which order they were standing in line?

Clues:

1. The first customer (who wasn't a girl) isn't the one who ordered a salad.
2. The salad did not have barbeque sauce on it.
3. Candy ate chicken for lunch and wasn't last in line.
4. The person who asked for extra ketchup had a cheeseburger.
5. John did not eat the mustard-drenched fish.
6. Derek was in the exact middle of the line.
7. Steve was in line after the salad eater but before the mayo lover.

Logic Teaser #10

▲ *Difficulty: Medium*

A chessboard has eight rows and eight columns. In chess, a rook can move any number of squares at a time, either sideways or forward, but

Solution on page 343

it cannot move diagonally. What is the smallest possible number of moves the rook would have to make to pass over every single square on the board and finish in the same position where it began? The rook can start anywhere.

Logic Teaser #11

▲ *Difficulty: Hard*

Some very clever aliens have captured you. As a test of your intelligence, they have poisoned you and placed the antidote in one of two vials, with the second vial containing more of the same poison. They won't tell you which is which. Instead, Vial A has a label that reads, "The label on the other vial is true, and this is the antidote." Vial B has a label that reads, "The label on the other vial is false, but it contains the antidote." Which vial should you drink?

Logic Teaser #12

▲ *Difficulty: Hard*

Since the turn of the last century, the canal has provided one of the quickest ways to travel from one end of the legendary land of Puzzleonia to the other. Every day, the Sinc or Schwim cruise company provides cruises for passengers to travel the length of the canal.

On one particular cruise, six passengers all required specific conditions during the three-day cruise. The six cabins available are numbered 1 through 6 successively, and all are on the same floor. The walls of the cabins are extremely thin. These six cabins must be allotted to the passengers according to the following set of instructions.

1. Miss Fortune's work as a traveling salesperson requires that she must use the phone regularly during the journey.
2. Miss D. Werk's lucky number is 5, and she insists on having Cabin 5.
3. Mr. Buss and Mr. Allot often talk to each other during their work as secondhand clock repairmen, and they have a preference for adjacent cabins.
4. Mr. Lastrain, Mr. Buss, and Mr. Meaner are all smokers. Miss D. Werk is affected by smoke and insists upon nonsmokers adjacent to her cabin.
5. Mr. Meaner requires silence to work during his travels.

Can you determine how the cabins were allotted?

Logic Teaser #13

▲ *Difficulty: Hard*

What is the fewest number of colors you can use to color in a map of the United States without using the same color on any adjoining states?

Solution on page 343

Logic Teaser #14

⚠ *Difficulty: Hard*

Five friends (Bobby, Isaac, Isabel, Mimi, and Shane) are playing a baseball game against some other people. Each friend plays a different position (first base, pitcher, shortstop, catcher, right field) and makes a different number of hits (one, two, three, four, or five). From the clues can you figure out who did what?

Clues:

1. Bobby, the furthest from home plate, had exactly twice as many hits as the pitcher.
2. The shortstop was tired after getting her fifth hit.
3. Shane had more hits than all the other infielders except for Isabel.
4. Isaac wears a mask.

Math Teaser #1

⚠ *Difficulty: Easy*

Wally Rus and Rod Lightning decide to race each other to the Puzzle Shop, exactly one mile away, and then back again. Wally, being on the chubby side, runs at 10 mph to the shop, but he manages a whopping 30 mph on the way back (downhill with a tailwind). Rod Lightning, on the other hand, being less weight-challenged than Wally, runs at a constant rate of 20 mph each way.

Who wins the race?

Math Teaser #2

⚠ *Difficulty: Easy*

In Puzzleonia, every horse is required to be licensed. A horse license number is made up of one letter and one digit. What is the maximum number of horses that can be licensed in Puzzleonia under this system?

Math Teaser #3

⚠ *Difficulty: Easy*

Bobby Braingle and Hyde Enceek are on a backpacking trip. Bobby carried the heavy backpack for the first 4 miles, and Hyde carried it the rest of the way into the campsite. The next morning they fished a bit and packed up to return home along the same trail they had used yesterday. This time Bobby started again with the heavy backpack, and Hyde finished off by carrying it out the last 5 miles. Who carried the backpack the most and by how much?

Solution on pages 343–344

Math Teaser #4

▲ *Difficulty: Easy*

Bobby Braingle works at the Freshest Donut Store. The donut machine normally produces one fresh donut every 18 seconds, but it broke some time ago. The last nine donuts produced are still sitting on the tray. The oldest donut is five times older than the freshest donut. Bobby is trying to figure out how long ago the machine broke. What is the shortest amount of time it could have been broken?

Math Teaser #5

▲ *Difficulty: Easy*

A monk has a very specific ritual for climbing up the steps to the temple, which for religious reasons are odd in number. First he climbs up to the middle step and meditates for one minute. Then he climbs up eight steps and faces east until he hears a bird singing. Then he walks down 12 steps and picks up a pebble. He takes one step up and tosses the pebble over his left shoulder. Now, he walks up the remaining steps two at a time, which only takes him 14 paces. How many steps are there at the temple?

Math Teaser #6

▲ *Difficulty: Medium*

If you take all the prime numbers under 1,000,000 and multiply them together, what digit will be in the ones place?

Math Teaser #7

▲ *Difficulty: Medium*

You have a bag of pennies, and you are arranging them on the table. You notice that you can make a solid triangle with six pennies and a solid square with nine pennies. What is the smallest number of pennies that you can use, with none left over, that can be used to make either a triangle or a square?

Solution on page 344

Math Teaser #8

⚠ Difficulty: Medium

Bobby Braingle just got one of those new hybrid automobiles that get great gas mileage. He tests out the car on his drive to work. To get to work, Bobby must drive 10 miles uphill and 5 miles on flat land; to get home, it's 5 miles flat, and 10 miles downhill. After several weeks of testing, he determines that his new car gets 35 miles per gallon (mpg) going uphill, 80 mpg downhill, and 50 mpg on level terrain. What is the average mileage Bobby gets on his complete round trip?

Math Teaser #9

⚠ Difficulty: Medium

In a five-day workweek, Bobby Braingle manufactures 1,000 pogo sticks at the factory. Each day he builds 30 more sticks than the day before. How many pogo sticks did Bobby build on Monday?

Math Teaser #10

⚠ Difficulty: Medium

A 10-foot rope is tied from a hook on the ceiling to a hook on the floor. There is no slack in the rope. Bobby Braingle wants to tie up his dog so he can go do a little shopping. He detaches the rope from the hook on the floor and attaches the free end to the dog's collar, which happens to be 2 feet off the floor. (It's a big dog.) The dog can now run around in a circle, and because the rope goes to the ceiling the dog won't trip or get tangled up in the rope. What a good idea! What is the radius of the circle in which the dog can wander?

Math Teaser #11

⚠ Difficulty: Hard

Santa Claus sometimes helps the elves make toys. He's not as fast as they are, but he can still make 30 toys each hour. In order to keep from getting bored he starts each day by building 50 trains and then switches to building 50 airplanes. Then he switches back to trains and keeps switching back and forth doing 50 of each until the day is finished. If Santa starts work at 8:00 a.m., when will he finish his 108th train?

Solution on pages 344–345

Math Teaser #12

▲ *Difficulty: Hard*

Predictably, Bobby Braingle is once again waiting for the Puzzle Shop to open (he always gets there early). This time, he has arrived over an hour early, and as a consequence stands looking at his watch and counting the seconds and minutes until the shop opens. He noticed something strange about his watch: The minute and the hour hands of his watch meet exactly every 65 minutes. How much time would Bobby's watch gain or lose in an hour, if any?

Math Teaser #13

▲ *Difficulty: Hard*

Bobby Braingle is at his local newsstand, looking at the various magazines on display. He picked up a copy of Pretzels and Me, a copy of Wooden Puzzles Digest, and a copy of Indoor Hang Gliding. He passes the magazines to the shopkeeper, who enters the amounts of each magazine into the cash register.

"Hang on a minute!" says Bobby. "You just pressed the multiplication button each time between amounts instead of the addition button." The shopkeeper smiles with new false teeth and replies, "It doesn't matter. Either way, it comes to $5.70."

What were the prices of the magazines?

Math Teaser #14

▲ *Difficulty: Hard*

Several contestants were in a chocolate bunny–eating contest. After the contestants stuffed their faces for 20 minutes, all of the bunnies were eaten. One of the contestants remarked, "Isn't it interesting that there were seven times as many bunnies as contestants, but that each of us ate a different number of bunnies?" Another contestant replies, "That certainly is interesting. I always eat the ears first, and I noticed that when we had eaten a third of the bunnies, there were four fewer than 10 times as many bunny ears as human noses in the contest."

How many bunnies and contestants were in the contest?

Trivia Teaser #1

▲ *Difficulty: Easy*

Bobby is at a coin-collecting convention, walking down the rare and valuable coin aisle. He stops at a stand claiming that it has one of the oldest and most valuable nickels in existence. Bobby sees that they do indeed have a nickel from 1812. Bobby instantly knows that it is a fake. How?

Solution on page 345

Trivia Teaser #2

▲ *Difficulty: Easy*

Sometimes state borders are designated by a river or mountain range, but many times they are simply straight lines drawn across the land. Which state has no straight lines in its borders?

Trivia Teaser #3

▲ *Difficulty: Easy*

There is a funny race called the Four States Race. In it, the contestants must run inside of four different U.S. states. The interesting thing about the race is that the contestants can pick whichever four states they want, and they can start and end wherever they want. Assume that a runner can run at a constant 5 miles per hour without getting tired. What states should the runner pick, and how long will it take to complete the race?

Trivia Teaser #4

▲ *Difficulty: Easy*

A professor is giving a lecture to his students. He says, "Albert Einstein and Stephen Hawking are two of the smartest physicists of our time. In a historic meeting, they argued about Einstein's theory of relativity. Hawking said that it was too complicated and that it could be simplified. In spite of this, they remained friends." A student raised his hand, "Professor, I'm sorry, but you are clearly making this up." How did the student know?

Trivia Teaser #5

▲ *Difficulty: Easy*

Crocodile Pete is famous for his tall tales of hunting expeditions. One day in a local Sydney bar, he is recalling his last adventure during his Christmas trip to Argentina. He had been building a snowman, when all of a sudden a wild dog jumped out and attacked him. After wrestling for 15 minutes, he was able to subdue the dog. Everyone in the bar instantly knew that he was lying. How did they know?

Solution on page 345

Trivia Teaser #6

▲ *Difficulty: Medium*

Vera Dangerous was one of the worst female criminals of all time. When she was arrested in California in 1954, she was accused and convicted of 17 murders. For the last 30 years, incorrigible murderers had been sent to Alcatraz Island, but Vera was not sent there. Why not? (Alcatraz didn't close until 1963.)

Trivia Teaser #7

▲ *Difficulty: Medium*

Bobby Braingle is playing a game of golf with his boss. Bobby is not a very good golfer, and on the second hole, he hits his ball into a sand trap. His boss, who is very skilled, hits his ball onto the green. When Bobby arrives at the sand trap, he notices that there are two golf balls in the sand trap. Both are face down so he cannot identify which one is his. What should he do so as not to incur a penalty?

Trivia Teaser #8

▲ *Difficulty: Medium*

What is the answer to this strange math problem?

Lincoln + Jefferson + Roosevelt +Washington + Kennedy = ?   91¢

Trivia Teaser #9

▲ *Difficulty: Medium*

If you write out the names of all the states in the United States, you will have written every letter except for one. Which letter would be left out?

Trivia Teaser #10

▲ *Difficulty: Medium*

Bobby Braingle recounts the details of a hunting trip to entertain a bunch of his buddies. "We were deep in the Amazon, when all of a sudden a 10-foot alligator jumped into our boat. After about 15 minutes of wrestling, I strangled the gator, and now I have this trophy on my wall."

After hearing this, an acquaintance spoke up, "That story is completely made up, you liar!"

How did the acquaintance know?

Solution on pages 345–346

Trivia Teaser #11

⚠ *Difficulty: Hard*

Inspector Bobby Braingle is a collector of rare and unusual coins. On a visit to a nearby market, he comes upon a stall selling collectible coins. The stall is run by the well-known female villain Maude Upname. Inspector Bobby browses the contents of her stall, looking at several interesting commemorative coins celebrating 100 Years of Puzzles. Maude Upname sees Inspector Bobby's interest and decides to offer him a special coin she has been saving.

"It's a special one-of-a-kind coin," she tells Bobby. "It was minted to celebrate the birth of Queen Elizabeth the Second." Inspector Bobby views the coin and reads the inscription on its reverse side. It says, "In celebration of the birth of Princess Elizabeth, daughter to the Duke and Duchess of York, heir to the throne of the United Kingdom and the colonies of the Empire."

"Where did you get this?" asks Inspector Bobby.

"It was given to my grandmother in 1926, the year of the Queen's birth. It's 100 percent genuine, honest, I swear on it."

"Well, in that case, you are under arrest for forgery!" the inspector cries.

How did Bobby know the coin was a fake?

Trivia Teaser #12

⚠ *Difficulty: Hard*

What is the missing word in this group? (The following words are in no particular order.)

SCAPHOID, LUNATE, TRIQUETRUM, PISIFORM, TRAPEZIUM, TRAPEZOID, CAPITATE

NAVICULAR   HAMATE

Trivia Teaser #13

⚠ *Difficulty: Hard*

The following math equation is true under a very special circumstance. What is it?

$$11 + 8 + 8 = 17$$

19

Trivia Teaser #14

⚠ *Difficulty: Hard*

A bunch of dogs is called a pack, and a bunch of cows is called a herd. Do you know what a bunch of the following animals are called?

1. Buzzards
2. Cobras
3. Turtles
4. Sharks

Solution on page 346

Chapter 12
Groupies

Groupies have lots of blanks and no clues. Actually, there is one clue, the one word supplied for you in each puzzle. This word is a member of the category from which all of the other words are taken. For example, if the word is POKER, then the other words to be fit in the blanks could be card games.

Groupie 1

Groupie 2

Solution on page 347

Groupie 3

Groupie 4

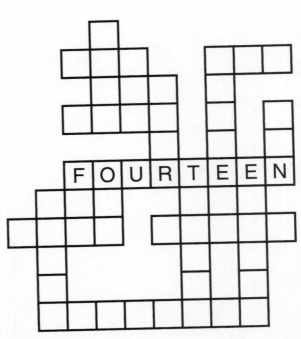

Solution on page 347

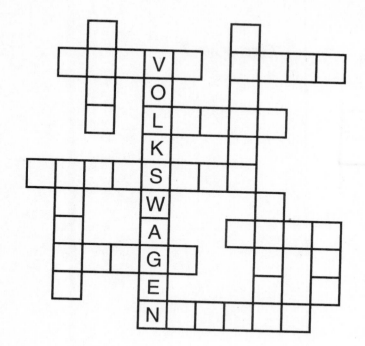

Groupie 5

Groupie 6

Solution on page 347

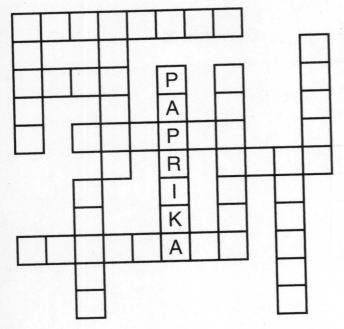

Groupie 7

Groupie 8

Solution on page 348

Groupie 9

Groupie 10

Solution on page 348

Groupie 11

N O V E M B E R

Groupie 12

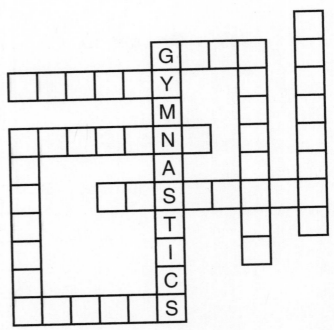

G
Y
M
N
A
S
T
I
C
S

Solution on page 348

Groupie 13

Groupie 14

Solution on page 349

Groupie 15

Groupie 16

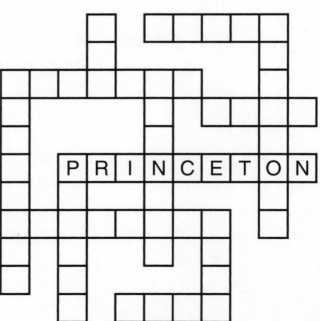

Solution on page 349

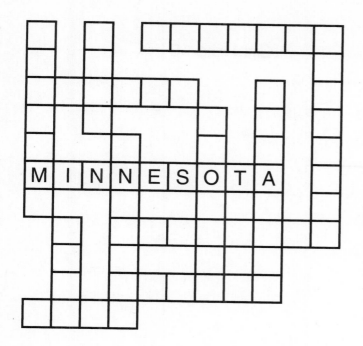

Groupie 17

M I N N E S O T A

Groupie 18

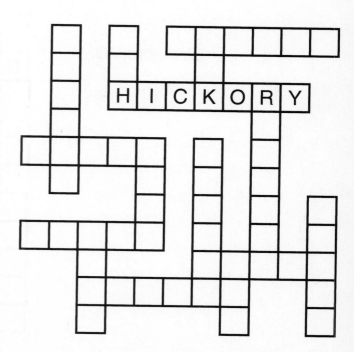

H I C K O R Y

Solution on page 349

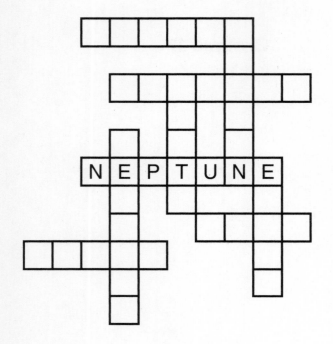

Groupie 19

Groupie 20

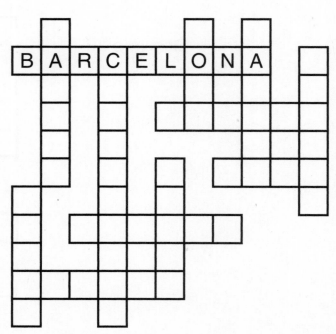

Solution on page 350

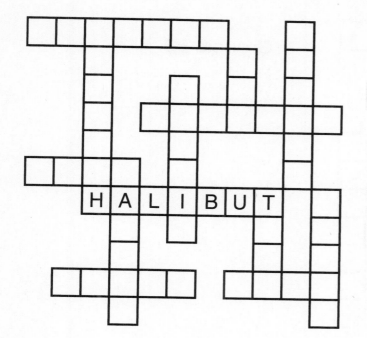

Groupie 21

Groupie 22

Solution on page 350

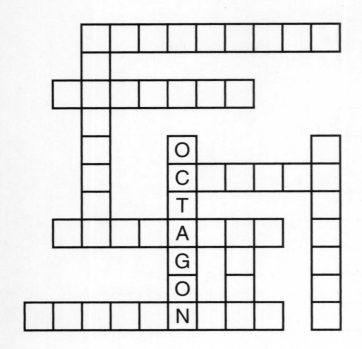

Groupie 23

Groupie 24

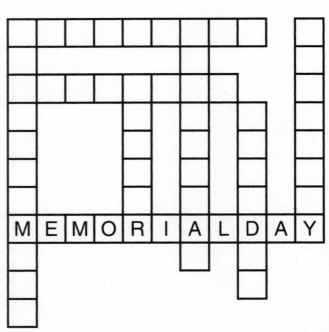

Solution on page 350

Groupie 25

Groupie 26

Solution on page 351

Groupie 27

E I S E N H O W E R

Groupie 28

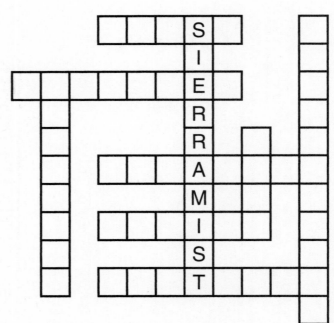

SIERRAMIST

Solution on page 351

Chapter 13

Cryptograms

Cryptograms are fun word puzzles that involve phrases and text that have been converted into code. Most letters of the alphabet (A–Z) have been substituted with another letter. Your challenge is to break the code for each puzzle and decipher the quote and author. If you get stumped, there are hints for the puzzles at the end of this chapter (page 222).

Example:

U   KLNV   Q   HLX.   MV   HLVA

ZLCMUZX   OLJ   RLKUCUIQK   JVQALZA.

—GUKK JLXVJA

The answer is:

I love a dog. He does nothing for political reasons.

—Will Rogers

Cryptogram 1

(handwritten above: YOU HEAR A VOICE WITHIN YOU SAY)
SL NJV KGTH T WJSMG PSXKSY NJV ZTN

(handwritten above: YOU CANNOT PAINT THEN BY ALL MEANS)
"NJV MTYYJX QTSYX," XKGY ON TUU EGTYZ

(handwritten above: PAINT AND THAT VOICE WILL BE SILENCED)
QTSYX, TYD XKTX WJSMG PSUU OG ZSUGYMGD.

(handwritten: √ Vincent Van Gogh)
—WSYMGYX WTY BJBK

Cryptogram 2

(handwritten above: POWER WITHOUT PRINCIPLE IS BARREN)
OUBJS BAWZUCW OSAEXAOKJ AH MVSSJE,

(handwritten above: BUT PRINCIPLE WITHOUT POWER IS FUTILE)
MCW OSAEXAOKJ BAWZUCW OUBJS AH RCWAKJ.

(handwritten above: THIS IS A PARTY OF GOVERNMENT AND)
WZAH AH V OVSWN UR YUGJSEPJEW, VEL A

(handwritten above: WILL LEAD IT AS A PARTY OF GOVERNMENT)
BAKK KJVL AW VH V OVSWN UR YUGJSEPJEW.

(handwritten: Tony Blair)
—WUEN MKVAS

Cryptogram 3

(handwritten above: USE WHAT TALENT YOU POSSESS)
OTH XFLD DLKHGD RWO NWIIHII:

(handwritten above: THE WOODS WOULD BE VERY SILENT)
DFH XWWYT XWOKY QH MHSR IEKHGD

(handwritten above: IF NO BIRDS SANG EXCEPT THOSE THAT)
EP GW QESYI ILGJ HATHND DFWIH DFLD

(handwritten above: SANG BEST)
ILGJ QHID.

(handwritten: Henry Van Dyke)
—FHGSR MLG YRBH

Solution on page 352

Cryptogram 4

WE'RE ALL CAPABLE OF MISTAKES BUT I
US'AS KMM PKVKCMS FO GBZEKHSZ, CJE B

IF NOT CARE TO ENLIGHTEN YOU ON THE
IF NFE PKAS EF SNMBYWESN QFJ FN EWS

MISTAKES WE MAY OR MAY NOT HAVE MADE
GBZEKHSZ US GKQ FA GKQ NFE WKXS GKIS.

GEORGE W BUSH
—YSFAYS U. CJZW

Cryptogram 5

NO MORE TEARS NOW I WILL THINK UPON
EX JXBS DSRBW EXV; L VLFF DZLEQ HPXE

REVENGE
BSOSENS.

MARY QUEEN OF SCOTS
—JRBM IHSSE XT WCXDW

Cryptogram 6

GYND   GN   QHS   IDSH   HFFIPN,   SYN   SYIDQ

SYWS   UEAMAIUNZ   CN   SYN   CHUS   GWU   SYWS

SYIDQU   GNAN   WU   VWZ   WU   GN'Z   VNND

UWRIDQ   SYNR   GNAN.

—KHYD F. ONDDNZR

Solution on page 352

Cryptogram 7

GVHE   KXGTA   SXG   SBHH   MBTY   PGBVP   KGG

ODM   UDV   QGTTBJHE   OBVI   GFK   XGS   ODM

GVA   UDV   PG.

—K. T. AHBGK

Cryptogram 8

THE JOURNEY   OF A THOUSAND MILES MUST
BQI   VRTEGIM   RZ   W   BQRTXWGS   UALIX   UTXB

BEGIN WITH A SINGLE STEP
KIOAG   PABQ   W   XAGOLI   XBIY.

LAO TZU
—LWR BJT

BCKQVWXJ

Cryptogtam 9

SRMR   GZ   U   YRZY   YJ   PGTA   JDY   BSRYSRM

FJDM   QGZZGJT   GT   IGPR   GZ   HJQNIRYR.   GP

FJD'MR   UIGVR,   GY   GZT'Y.

—MGHSUMA LUHS

Solution on page 352

Cryptogram 10

DZ   DI   ACNCIIJWL   ZS   ZWL   ZS   IFWHJII

SACICGP   JGUJLI;   ZTDI   SNNFHJZDSA   SFBTZ

ZS   GJIZ   JI   GSAB   JI   GDPC.

—QFCCA NTWDIZDAJ

Cryptogram 11

IWDS,   CBSDS   XDS   KEIBVJSIC   NSJ   EJ   TVYXT

LVHSDJNSJC.   PWC   CBSDS   XDS   KEIBVJSIC   NSJ

EJ   JXCEVJXT   LVHSDJNSJC,   CVV.

—DEYBXDK JERVJ

Cryptogram 12

UNKCT   RBPCOMC,   KFUK   GFBMF   MZICR   OCUTCRK

KZ   CYHTCRRBOQ   KFC   BOCYHTCRRBXPC   BR

IDRBM.

—UPWZDR FDYPCJ

Solution on page 352

Cryptogram 13

VRECMADCAL SY ARL MCJYRA; SL SY ARL CKRHPCAL; SL SY NRMGC. KSBC NSMC, SL SY J QJAVCMRPY YCMEJAL JAQ J NCJMNPK DJYLCM.

—VCRMVC ZJYOSAVLRA

Cryptogram 14

RA REJV. ZL SEN'FA DEZKD IE WXPA XK AFFEF, WXPA X VEEHS, XKV VEK'I RA XLFXZV IE UZI IUA RXJJ.

—RZJJZA QAXK PZKD

Cryptogram 15

SMI XIKS NZF LWKS XINPSVEPJ SMVZHK VZ SMI YWOJF BNZZWS XI KIIZ WO IRIZ SWPBMIF. SMIU LPKS XI EIJS YVSMVZ SMI MINOS.

—MIJIZ DIJJIO

Solution on page 352

Cryptogram 16

W   RYKI   NBIVVIE   MOB   OVMZ   BRWN   VXYBFMCH
BRYB   W   HYP   NII   PMO   YZE   BRYB   PMO
HYP   NII   HI,   YZE   WZ   BRI   YCCYZJIHIZB   W
RYKI   BRI   SINB   MF   BRI   SYCJYWZ.

—YSCYRYH   XWZLMXZ

Cryptogram 17

ATASV   JSEFKE   HFZK   LFK   PSMKL   FB   LFK
YNB   KYMG,   JBH   ZJFBEK   LFK   YNB   BJEMSA
FBEY   LFK   ZFIEMSAK.

—LABSV   NJSH   PAAILAS

Cryptogram 18

XIUDNDZC   DC   AIN   R   ORW   XQIHKCCDIA.   DH
BIG   CGZZKKW   NYKQK   RQK   TRAB   QKFRQWC,
DH   BIG   WDCLQRZK   BIGQCKUH   BIG   ZRA
RUFRBC   FQDNK   R   OIIS.

—QIARUW   QKRLRA

Solution on page 352

Cryptogram 19

ZNSPYFY   YDMYKKYXMY   MGXZAZQZ   AX   VPYTRAXU
QIY   YXYFC'Z   PYZAZQTXMY   EAQIGNQ   LAUIQAXU.

—ZNX - QJN

Cryptogram 20

UIJOJ   WA   OJLD   GLEWP   WY   JYUIHAWLAG.   WU
ATJDDA   UIJ   FWSSJOJYPJ   CJUZJJY   GJFWBPOWUN
LYF   LPPBGTDWAIGJYU.

—YBOGLY   XWYPJYU   TJLDJ

Cryptogram 21

JOG   BIDHVX   IS   JOG   AEGMHVAU   RIYGMUEGUJ   HN
JI   DGAYG   JOGHM   VHJHZGUN   SMGG,   UGHJOGM
MGNJMAHUHUR   UIM   AHFHUR   JOGE   HU   JOGHM
BWMNWHJN.

—JOIEAN   CGSSGMNIU

Solution on pages 352–353

Cryptogram 22

GV'H FSFXGCI VMFV VMA FSJWCV JY CAQH
VMFV MFTTACH GC VMA QJPOZ AUAPK ZFK
FOQFKH BWHV ADFNVOK YGVH VMA CAQHTFTAP.

—BAPPK HAGCYAOZ

Cryptogram 23

GYHALJG LO XKT GXNTZLXP LI LT JKXOLOTO
KI HGJZ KI BO. LT LO OKYHTZLXP KXDN
LI LT JKXOLOTO KI GDD KI BO.

—UKKVAKU ULDOKX

Cryptogram 24

JZQGRBD HF WZHOB KERY IZQ RGD RAGRHW
YZ WZ. YEDGD JRO TD OZ JZQGRBD
QOSDFF IZQ'GD FJRGDW.

—DWWHD GHJNDOTRJEDG

Solution on page 353

Cryptogram 25

TRWG   FPXV   SXRPKH   MV   WKH   TRWG   FPXV
SXIUCX   MV   WCX   GPKZ   WGGXCV   DUAOWCXH   GU
TRWG   FPXV   TPGRPK   MV.

—CWFOR TWFHU XAXCVUK

Cryptogram 26

MBO   ENAYM   BDPUX   IBJ   BDAWOF   UX   NXYDWM
NXYMOUF   JE   U   YMJXO   IUY   MBO   EJDXFOA   JE
KNSNWNVUMNJX.

—YNHPDXF EAODF

Cryptogram 27

T   VTN   GHZII   Z   FTOYUTQ   TB   SZOYV   NUII
VTIK   PG   NVSQ   NS   ZOS   KSZK,   NVT
ZHMUYUTPGID   GSSW   ZBYSO   YVS   NVTIS   NTOIK
NVUIS   NS   ZOS   IUXUQJ.

—FVUIUF UU

Solution on page 353

Cryptogram 28

HFF ECXHDZS HDR CSXXJKFS SUSDCE HXS
BSFQOPS, KVC QOPWOXCE BS RSEAJES.

—QFSOAHCXH

Cryptogram 29

LBY GBSCY GSWCX IR IK WYVSCL. RSSK
LBYWY GICC ZY SKCA EIVY DIKMR CYEL—LBY
DIKM SE YKMCPKX, LBY DIKM SE RQPXYR,
LBY DIKM SE NCFZR, LBY DIKM SE BYPWLR,
PKX LBY DIKM SE XIPUSKXR.

—DIKM EPWSFD

Cryptogram 30

TQL RD, VP CUWWDH TVUMGNTQR: TRS QDX
HFTX PDZM NDZQXMP NTQ LD CDM PDZ–TRS
HFTX PDZ NTQ LD CDM PDZM NDZQXMP.

—EDFQ C. SUQQULP

Solution on page 353

Cryptogram 31

R HEJK OSQWX RC RZNSYYRBLK CS AEDDT
(I HAVE FOUND IF IMPOSSIBLE TO ARRY)

CHK HKEJT BQDXKW SO DKYNSWYRBRLRCT...
(THE HEAVY BURDEN OF RESPONSIBILITY)

—GRWP KXUEDX JRRR
(KING EDWARD VIII)

Cryptogram 32

YMGWAEIZLA   JIZLWJN   GKNZ   ZED   ZW   ULJY   QIDN

ZW   NZIESM   ZCM   ZMEEWELNZ   IJY   ZCM   CLPIABME

WU   ZCM   WXDVMJ   WU   FKOHLALZD   WJ   QCLAC

ZCMD   YMFMJY.

—GIEVIEMZ   ZCIZACME

Cryptogram 33

FSD   ERU'A   GUTKDVUEV   VDLSBV'O   TDADLV   TLSX

AHV   AVLLREVO.   FSD   HRIV   AS   CV   SU   AHV

BGAEH   RUQ   BKRFGUJ   HRLQ.

—NSHU   XRNSL

Solution on page 353

Cryptogram 34

XPY   WBCO   YAAYOXCBRA   KU   B   AGSSYAAUGR

MHCWY   WCOCAXYH   [BHY]   ARYYM   BOI   B

AYOAY   KU   PCAXKHN.

—PBHKRI   DCRAKO

Cryptogram 35

ESRZTAHZAB   HDUB   XZZY   YVFZ   PJBC   BCZ

FCVAEJAE   AZZQU   SW   SDT   UBVBZ   VAQ   JBU

YZSYOZ   BS   KZ   UDTZ   BCVB   ESRZTAHZAB   FVA

WDOWJOO   JBU   OZEJBJHVBZ   SKOJEVBJSAU.

—TSAVOQ   TZVEVA

Cryptogram 36

GDXBRSG   MRM   IAK   RIFXIK   QCDGI   BRTQKJ.   RI

G   FXBY   BXGV   JXIJX   QCDGI   BRTQKJ   RIFXIKXM

GDXBRSG.

—URDDY   SGBKXB

Solution on page 353

Cryptogram 37

N   UPEUQT   ZMDY   ZB   ZJV   TFBDZT   FURVT   SNDTZ
EJNGJ   DVGBDHT   FVBFPV'T   UGGBIFPNTJIVYZT.   ZJV
SDBYZ   FURV   JUT   YBZJNYR   LMZ   IUY'T   SUNPMDVT.

—GJNVS   OMTZNGV   VUDP   EUDDVY

Cryptogram 38

RUAQIXDNB   AJFD   TX   DJBTDN   XU   CU   J   MUX
UW   XGTZLB,   HIX   AUBX   UW   XGD   XGTZLB   XGDO
AJFD   TX   DJBTDN   XU   CU   CUZ'X   ZDDC   XU
HD   CUZD.

—JZCO   NUUZDO

Cryptogram 39

HSM   GEM   YMFK   US   NEOOK   XNSM   BNSK   TY
MYB   EWWVHS   BNEB   BNS   YUCSGB   YD   FJDS
JW   NEOOJMSWW.

—ISYPIS   YPXSFF

Solution on page 353

Hints

Cryptogram 1: The word "voice" is found in this puzzle.

Cryptogram 2: The word "power" is found in this puzzle.

Cryptogram 3: The word "possess" is found in this puzzle.

Cryptogram 4: The word "capable" is found in this puzzle.

Cryptogram 5: The word "tears" is found in this puzzle.

Cryptogram 6: The word "things" is found in this puzzle.

Cryptogram 7: The word "only" is found in this puzzle.

Cryptogram 8: The word "miles" is found in this puzzle.

Cryptogram 9: The word "alive" is found in this puzzle.

Cryptogram 10: The word "ought" is found in this puzzle.

Cryptogram 11: The word "local" is found in this puzzle.

Cryptogram 12: The word "nearest" is found in this puzzle.

Cryptogram 13: The word "force" is found in this puzzle.

Cryptogram 14: The word "ball" is found in this puzzle.

Cryptogram 15: The word "things" is found in this puzzle.

Cryptogram 16: The word "bargain" is found in this puzzle.

Cryptogram 17: The word "nature" is found in this puzzle.

Cryptogram 18: The word "always" is found in this puzzle.

Cryptogram 19: The word "breaking" is found in this puzzle.

Cryptogram 20: The word "magic" is found in this puzzle.

Cryptogram 21: The word "pursuits" is found in this puzzle.

Cryptogram 22: The word "news" is found in this puzzle.

Cryptogram 23: The word "only" is found in this puzzle.

Cryptogram 24: The word "scared" is found in this puzzle.

Cryptogram 25: The word "tiny" is found in this puzzle.

Cryptogram 26: The word "insult" is found in this puzzle.

Cryptogram 27: The word "earth" is found in this puzzle.

Cryptogram 28: The word "strange" is found in this puzzle.

Cryptogram 29: The word "revolt" is found in this puzzle.

Cryptogram 30: The word "fellow" is found in this puzzle.

Cryptogram 31: The word "found" is found in this puzzle.

Cryptogram 32: The word "oxygen" is found in this puzzle.

Cryptogram 33: The word "pitch" is found in this puzzle.

Cryptogram 34: The word "sleep" is found in this puzzle.

Cryptogram 35: The word "people" is found in this puzzle.

Cryptogram 36: The word "sense" is found in this puzzle.

Cryptogram 37: The word "front" is found in this puzzle.

Cryptogram 38: The word "done" is found in this puzzle.

Cryptogram 39: The word "object" is found in this puzzle.

Chapter 14
Providers

Fit all of the words into the grids. To get you started, one of the words is already entered. If you have trouble, approach the problem from another angle—search the puzzle for words that fit the blanks.

Provider 1

Solution on page 354

3 Letters

ACE
ANI
APT
AWL
BAA
CUM
DOE
FAS
GOT
INN
KOI
LOP
OHM
ONE
ORS
OSE
PAX
REP
RHO
RUN
SAE
SOS
TAP

4 Letters

ACRE
ADDS
AGON
ANEW
ANNA
APEX
ARCO
AWOL
BAKE
BANE
BORE
DADA
DEAN
ELMS
FOIL
FRAT
HARE
HAST
LOCA
LOUT
MASS
MORE
OBOE
OUTS
PASS
PLAT
PROS
RETE
ROPE
SALT
SENT
SHUN
SLAP
SLIM
SNIP
SOME
STEW
TUNA

5 Letters

ALONE
BASED
LATHE
LEFTS
SCOLD
SHAMS
SLASH
TESTA
TREES

Provider 2

3 Letters

ADO
AVA
BAD
BOS
DAP
EVE
FAR
FOB
HAH
HEP
NET
ODE
PIS
TAB

4 Letters

ALFA
ALMS
AMEN
ANTA
BEAR
CITE
CLAM
CLOD
DRAY
DROP

DRYS
ERRS
ERST
EYRE
FEAT
ISMS
LAMA
LAWS
LEAN
LEAS
LILT
LIMA
MARS
MELD
OMER
OYER
PEAL
PEAS
PERT
RIEL
ROTA
SCAB
SOLI
STAY
TATE
VANE

5 Letters

ARCED
AVERS
MODES
SASSY
SETTS
SLAMS
SLAPS
SOLAR
TEENS
TORSI

6 Letters

AMERCE
ENSILE
REDONE
WISEST

8 Letters

RESTATED
TOOLSHED

Solution on page 354

Provider 3

3 Letters

ALB
ALT
AXE
BID
BRR
CAD
EAU
EFT
EKE
EMU
HEH
HIT
HMM
HUE
LAC
LAD
MON
NAN
OKA
ROE
SAL
SOT
SOU
SOW
TEA
WIG

4 Letters

ABED
ALBA
ALEF
AMAS
ARMS
ASHY
AWES
AXON
BASE
BATE
BEST
BIKE
BLOB
BRAT
DELE
EGER
EWES
MAID
MAMA
MARE
MOUE
MUTE
NAME
ORAD
ORCA
PEND
PESO
REBS
REES
ROLE
SAKI
SAND
STAT
SULK
TSKS
TUBS

5 Letters

ANTES
BASER
BASTE
OREAD
REMAP
SERAC
SLEEP
STYES

Solution on page 354

Provider 4

3 Letters

ADD
ASK
DAY
ELM
ETA
ICH
LIN
ORC
OUR
OXO
OXY
PEN
PER
PHI
PIA
POP
POW
PRO
RID
RUE
RYE
TWO
URN
WOE

4 Letters

ACTA
ACTS
ALGA
ANAS
ANIL
ARIL
BEER
CARE
CODE
COPE
DEAR
HIRE
IDLE
INNS
LEST
NOES
ODDS
ORCS
PALE
PIED
PLUS
PORK
PORN
RIDS
SCAM
SHAY

SPUD
TELS
TOGA
TRAM
URGE
WIDE

5 Letters

ASSET
ATRIA
EGEST
LOSES
MESAS

MOLDS
ORCAS
ORLES
PASSE
SCABS

6 Letters

CASTLE
SEAMEN

Solution on page 354

Provider 5

3 Letters

BRO
CHI
CUE
EAR
EGO
ELL
GHI
GNU
HEW
IVY
LED
MOM
NIP
RUT
SEX
SKI
SOL
TWA
USE
UTA
WRY
YAR
YOU

4 Letters

AGHA
ALEC
ALTO
AUTO
AVER
AWRY
BALL
BEAM
BEGS
BOIL
CYST
DOOR
DRUM
DYNE
HAKE
HEAR
IDOL
IRIS
LENT
LIMB
LOIN
MILT
MYNA
OGLE
ORAL
ORTS
PHEW
RUSE
SALS
SCUM
SLAY
SUPS
TEAR
TEXT
TOYS
TREE
USES
YAWP

5 Letters

ALPHA
ESTER
IONIC
LAMBS
MADRE
RASPY
SABRA
SANTO
TATES

R	U	S	E

Solution on page 355

Provider 6

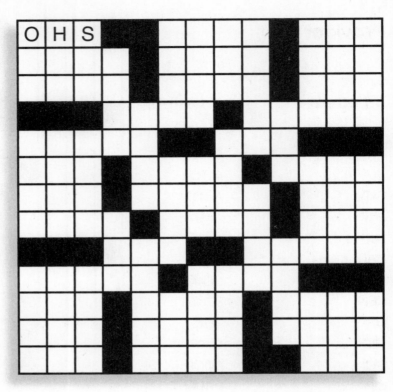

3 Letters

ABS
ANY
BYE
CAN
DEE
DIP
DUG
DUI
DYE
ERG
GOA
HOW
LIB
NEE
NUB
OHS
OPE
PRY
REB
RUG
SUE
TUG
URB
YAY
ZOO

4 Letters

ABBE
ADOS
ADZE
ALLY
ASKS
BADE
BIOS
BOSS
DEED
EELS
EGGS
EGGY
EWER
GUNK
LEAP
LIDO
OGRE
OWES
PLAN
POPS
POUT
PURR
SAGS
SECS
SEED
SINE
SLUE
SOAR
SOUR
SPOT
STEP
SUNS
TARO
TONG
TROT
TRUE
ULNA
WEBS

5 Letters

ADAGE
APERS
CREST
SLUES
SPACE
SPEED
STATE

Solution on page 355

Provider 7

3 Letters

ALA
ANT
ARS
AVE
AYE
BOY
DAD
ERA
ERN
GAT
GEN
MAY
MOA
NAE
ORT
PAP
PUT
RAP
SAT
SET
TEN
TOM
TSK

4 Letters

AGEE
ALEE
AMPS
APED
APES
ASPS
BARE
BRAD
EYES
LAVA
NENE
ONES
PATS
PELE
PLEA
POLL
PSST
RARE
ROUT
SALE
SASS
SATE
SCAT
SEAS
SERE
SLOE

SLOG
SOLO
SPAT
STAB
TEED
TENS
TOIL
TORE

5 Letters

ALTAR
BLAST
ESSES

KAPPA
MINCE
ROAST
SEEDS
STABS
STEED

6 Letters

ARMADA
ASTERS

Solution on page 355

Provider 8

3 Letters

AGA
ANA
BRA
DOS
GAS
HES
MAD
MOB
MOP
NOR
OAT
ODS
ORE
PAS
POI
RIG
SAG
TAT
TOE
YEA

4 Letters

AEON
AERO
AGIO
AMAH
ARID
CARD
DEAL
DRAT
ELSE
EPEE
ERGS
EVES
HERO
HITS
MAGS
OARS
OSES
OTTO
OWED
SEGO
SETA
SNAG
SODS
TARS
TEEN
THAT
TOMS
TOPE
TRIM
TSAR
TYNE
WOES

5 Letters

DENSE
RAGES
RAVEN
STATS
STOAT
TRESS

6 Letters

ARENAS
ARREST
PESETA
ROASTS
STREET
THRONE

7 Letters

CAMERAS
NEATENS

Solution on page 355

Provider 9

3 Letters

ACT
AGE
AGO
AHA
ALS
ASP
ATE
BAM
COO
EON
HOP
LAB
LAS
LAT
LIE
MAT
MIL
NUN
OBI
RAS
RES
ROD
SEN
SHY
SPY
TAS

4 Letters

ABLE
ACHE
AGAR
AGUE
ALBS
ANTE
APER
ARBS
BRAE
BRAG
BRAS
BROS
CORE
GLEE
KEEL
LEER
LOCI
LOOT
MANE
METE
MOPE
OAST
ODES
RACE
RATE
ROTE

SANS
SASH
SEAL
SEMI
SOAK
SOMA
SOTS
TEND
THEE
VISE

5 Letters

GATOR
GESTE
MATES
PSALM
SATES
SAVER
SLATS
TREED

Solution on page 356

Provider 10

3 Letters

ALL
ANE
BAY
BOO
ELD
ERS
HAY
HON
HUH
ICE
LAG
LET
MED
MEN
OCA
OHO
OLE
PAL
SON
SPA
TAE
TAN
WIN

4 Letters

ABET
AGED
ALAS
ALIT
ANSA
AURA
BOWS
CORN
DICE
ELLS
EPOS
ERAS
GOBS
LAIN
LANE
MADE
OLDS
PREP
ROAN
ROSE
SAIL
SCAD
SEAT
SHAD
SHES
SHMO
SHOO
SLAM
SLED
SONS
SYNE
TAEL
TAPA
THEM
TOLE
TOON
TRIO
YENS

5 Letters

ANGST
ASSES
BESTS
PANED
PICOT
RESTS
SLATE
SNARE
TASSE

Solution on page 356

Provider 11

3 Letters

AAH
AMP
ARM
ASS
BEE
BOA
EEL
ELS
EMS
ERE
HAE
ION
LEA
OPS
OPT
PAR
PEE
ROB
ROT
SEE
TAO
TEE
THE
TIS
WET

4 Letters

ABRI
ALMA
ANTS
AREA
ASEA
BARN
CELL
ETHS
HEAT
IOTA
LAMP
LAPS
LASE
LASS
LOAM
OATS
OLES
OPES
OPTS
PEEP
PHAT
PROA
PSIS
RENT
SABE
SARI

SEAM
SEAR
SEER
SEPT
SETS
SIRE
SOON
TENT
TONE
TOOL
TORA
TWAS

5 Letters

ALINE
CASAS
MATTE
SPARS
STARS
START
TESTS

Solution on page 356

Provider 12

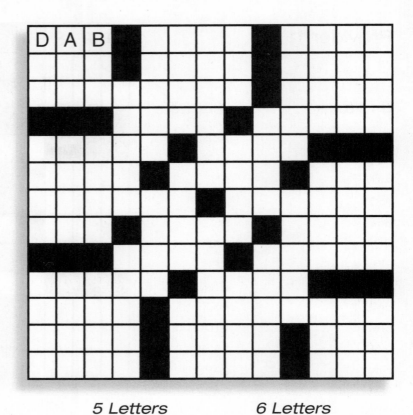

3 Letters

AMA
AMI
AWE
BEG
DAB
DOR
MAN
OWE
RED
REF
SIT
TAM
TED
TIN

4 Letters

AGER
AKIN
ALAN
ALAR
AMID
CAKE
CLAY
CREW
EARN
ELAN

FLEE
GAME
HERE
IDES
LOOS
LOPE
LUNA
MANO
NAVE
ORES
ORLE
PANE
PENS
SAVE
SCUP
SLOT
SONE
SURE
TAPS
TERN
THRU
TOWS
TROP
TUBE
UNIT
WANE

5 Letters

ACRES
AWARE
CRESS
CRONE
ECRUS
MASON
SPATS
STETS
STILE
TONES

6 Letters

ENISLE
LETHAL
OBEYER
PSEUDO

8 Letters

REGAINED
RHEOSTAT

Solution on page 356

Provider 13

3 Letters

APE
ARC
BEN
BUY
COS
DOM
EYE
FIB
FLU
FRO
LAW
LUV
OOH
RAH
SAW
SRI
THO
TOY
WAD
WAG
WEB
WOO
YES

4 Letters

ACES
AMIE
ARES
ARFS
AWED
AWLS
AYES
COVE
GENE
HOES
HOOT
LACE
MILS
MORT
OHMS
OMIT
OOPS
PAPA
PARA
PFFT
REST
RILE
ROUE
SETT
SHOW
SILO
SLAT
SLAW
SORE
STAR
STET
TARE
TEST
TODS

5 Letters

BROOD
IMAMS
MOCHA
POSTS
REAPS
RESEE
SEEPY
SPATE
TESTY

6 Letters

EMBRYO
TRADER

Solution on page 357

Provider 14

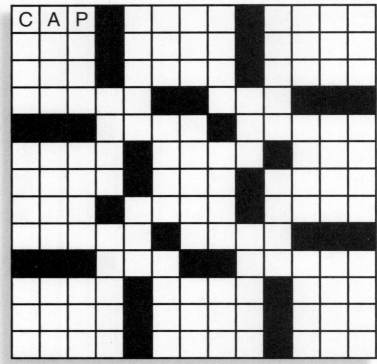

3 Letters

AAS
ABA
ALP
AND
CAP
ELK
EWE
FOE
GOD
HAS
HIE
HOE
IDS
ILL
LAM
LEI
NOT
OAR
OVA
PSI
SHA
SHE
VIA

4 Letters

AFAR
AIDE
ALES
ALLS
ALSO
AVOW
BRIT
BYTE
CHIS
CONE
DIME
EAVE
GREW
HOBO
ILIA
IRES
LOSS
MALE
MITE
NEAT
PATE
PEPS
PEST
POLE
READ
RUES

SAKE
SEIS
SHAG
SKIP
SOPS
SPAS
STOA
SWAT
TEES
TELE
TOGS
YULE

5 Letters

ADAPT
AREAS
PASEO
RECAP
SETAE
SHRED
SOAKS
TASTE
TEETH

Solution on page 357

Chapter 15
What's in a Name?

Find words using only the letters in a given name. Each letter in a name can be used only once in your word. For example, if the name is George Washington, then you could make the words soar, grow, note, and many others. Words that are always capitalized or require a hyphen or an apostrophe are not included in the answer lists. Words with variant or British spellings are also not included.

Conan O'Brien

Find 10 four-letter words:

1. CONE MANE BANE
2. CORNA IRON BOON
3. CORE IRON BOOR
4. CORN NOON BIER
5. CRANE OBOE BARE
6. CRAB ONCE BRIE
7. CARE ONER BRAN
8. CANE ANON BARN
9. CAIRN RICE BORN
10. CARBON BANE BONE

Jimmy Carter

Find 10 four-letter words:

1. CART ARMY TEAR
2. CARE AIRY TARE
3. ARTY FAME
4. TRAY
5. MARE TRAM
6. MITE TIRE
7. RICE REAR
8. RIME REAM
9. MART RIME
10. MATE TIER RICE

Henry Fonda

Find 7 five-letter words:

1. HEARD — AFORE
2. HARDY
3. HENNA FOYER
4. HONEY FORAY
5. HEADY FREON
6. HORNY
7. HANDY DRONE

Lauren Bacall

Find 10 four-letter words:

1. CALL CURL NEAR
2. CLAN CLUE NULL
3. CELL CULL CURE
4. CUBE AREA LACE
5. CLUB UREA LUNE
6. CURE REAL LANE
7. BLUE RACE ABLE
8. BULL RALE ALEE
9. BALE RUNE ANAL
10. BALL RULE ULNA

Solution on page 358

Stephen King

Find 7 five-letter words:

1. _____
2. _____
3. _____
4. _____
5. _____
6. _____
7. _____

Ross Perot

Find 7 five-letter words:

1. _____
2. _____
3. _____
4. _____
5. _____
6. _____
7. _____

Gene Wilder

Find 10 four-letter words:

1. _____
2. _____
3. _____
4. _____
5. _____
6. _____
7. _____
8. _____
9. _____
10. _____

Farrah Fawcett

Find 10 four-letter words:

1. _____
2. _____
3. _____
4. _____
5. _____
6. _____
7. _____
8. _____
9. _____
10. _____

Solution on page 358

John Malkovich

Find 7 five-letter words:

1. _____
2. _____
3. _____
4. _____
5. _____
6. _____
7. _____

Johnny Carson

Find 10 four-letter words:

1. _____
2. _____
3. _____
4. _____
5. _____
6. _____
7. _____
8. _____
9. _____
10. _____

Fred MacMurray

Find 10 four-letter words:

1. _____
2. _____
3. _____
4. _____
5. _____
6. _____
7. _____
8. _____
9. _____
10. _____

Vincent Price

Find 7 five-letter words:

1. PIECE   CIVET
2. PRICE   TRINE
3. VIPER   TRIPE
4. INEPT   RIPEN
5. INERT   NICER
6. INTER   NIECE
7. PRINT   NERVE
                  NEVER

Solution on pages 358–359

James Baker

Find 10 four-letter words:

1. _____
2. _____
3. _____
4. _____
5. _____
6. _____
7. _____
8. _____
9. _____
10. _____

Meryl Streep

Find 10 four-letter words:

1. _____
2. _____
3. _____
4. _____
5. _____
6. _____
7. _____
8. _____
9. _____
10. _____

Pablo Picasso

Find 7 five-letter words:

1. POOLS   SALSA
2. SLOBS   SILOS
3. SLAPS   SOAPS
4. CLASS   SPOIL
5. CLASP   BASIC
6. ASPIC   BASIL
7. LASSO   BOLAS
                  BASSO

Petula Clark

Find 7 five-letter words:

1. _____
2. _____
3. _____
4. _____
5. _____
6. _____
7. _____

Solution on page 359

Kurt Cobain

Find 7 five-letter words:

1. _____
2. _____
3. _____
4. _____
5. _____
6. _____
7. _____

Dudley Moore

Find 7 five-letter words:

1. _____
2. _____
3. _____
4. _____
5. _____
6. _____
7. _____

Van Morrison

Find 10 four-letter words:

1. _____
2. _____
3. _____
4. _____
5. _____
6. _____
7. _____
8. _____
9. _____
10. _____

Milton Berle

Find 7 five-letter words:

1. TIMER   TRIWE
2. BERET   TILER
3. INTER   REMIT
4. MELON   TONER
5. MILER   LEMON
6. MINER   INERT
7. MITER

Solution on pages 359–360

George C. Scott

Find 10 four-letter words:

1. _____
2. _____
3. _____
4. _____
5. _____
6. _____
7. _____
8. _____
9. _____
10. _____

Willem Dafoe

Find 7 five-letter words:

1. _____
2. _____
3. _____
4. _____
5. _____
6. _____
7. _____

Margaret Thatcher

Find 7 five-letter words:

1. _____
2. _____
3. _____
4. _____
5. _____
6. _____
7. _____

Bing Crosby

Find 7 five-letter words:

1. _____
2. _____
3. _____
4. _____
5. _____
6. _____
7. _____

Solution on page 360

J. Edgar Hoover

Find 10 four-letter words:

1. _____
2. _____
3. _____
4. _____
5. _____
6. _____
7. _____
8. _____
9. _____
10. _____

Quincy Jones

Find 10 four-letter words:

1. _____
2. _____
3. _____
4. _____
5. _____
6. _____
7. _____
8. _____
9. _____
10. _____

Arthur Ashe

Find 7 five-letter words:

1. SNARE   HARSH
2. ASTER   HEATH
3. HEART   TRASH
4. HATER   SHEAR
5. EARTH   HARES
6. TRUER   HEATS
7. WASTE   TRUES

Ansel Adams

Find 10 four-letter words:

1. AMEN   SANE
2. MSS   SAND
3. MESS   LAND
4. MESA   LENS
5. LASS   SEND
6. LAME   MADE
7. MEAL   MEAD
8. MILE   EDAM
9. LAMA   DAME
10. SAME   LEAS

Solution on pages 360–361

Chris Evert

Find 10 four-letter words:

1. _____
2. _____
3. _____
4. _____
5. _____
6. _____
7. _____
8. _____
9. _____
10. _____

Jack Nicklaus

Find 10 four-letter words:

1. _____
2. _____
3. _____
4. _____
5. _____
6. _____
7. _____
8. _____
9. _____
10. _____

Ginger Rogers

Find 10 four-letter words:

1. _____
2. _____
3. _____
4. _____
5. _____
6. _____
7. _____
8. _____
9. _____
10. _____

Federico Fellini

Find 7 five-letter words:

1. _____
2. _____
3. _____
4. _____
5. _____
6. _____
7. _____

Solution on page 361

Goldie Hawn

Find 7 five-letter words:

1. _____
2. _____
3. _____
4. _____
5. _____
6. _____
7. _____

Amelia Earhart

Find 7 five-letter words:

1. _____
2. _____
3. _____
4. _____
5. _____
6. _____
7. _____

Lionel Richie

Find 10 four-letter words:

1. _____
2. _____
3. _____
4. _____
5. _____
6. _____
7. _____
8. _____
9. _____
10. _____

Will Rogers

Find 10 four-letter words:

1. _____
2. _____
3. _____
4. _____
5. _____
6. _____
7. _____
8. _____
9. _____
10. _____

Solution on pages 361–362

Regis Philbin

Find 7 five-letter words:

1. _____
2. _____
3. _____
4. _____
5. _____
6. _____
7. _____

Glen Campbell

Find 7 five-letter words:

1. _____
2. _____
3. _____
4. _____
5. _____
6. _____
7. _____

Greg LeMond

Find 10 four-letter words:

1. _____
2. _____
3. _____
4. _____
5. _____
6. _____
7. _____
8. _____
9. _____
10. _____

Gerard Depardieu

Find 7 five-letter words:

1. _____
2. _____
3. _____
4. _____
5. _____
6. _____
7. _____

Solution on page 362

Dianne Feinstein

Find 7 five-letter words:

1. _____
2. _____
3. _____
4. _____
5. _____
6. _____
7. _____

Keanu Reeves

Find 10 four-letter words:

1. _____
2. _____
3. _____
4. _____
5. _____
6. _____
7. _____
8. _____
9. _____
10. _____

Jason Robards

Find 10 four-letter words:

1. _____
2. _____
3. _____
4. _____
5. _____
6. _____
7. _____
8. _____
9. _____
10. _____

Cat Stevens

Find 10 four-letter words:

1. _____
2. _____
3. _____
4. _____
5. _____
6. _____
7. _____
8. _____
9. _____
10. _____

Solution on pages 362–363

Sam Donaldson

Find 10 four-letter words:

1. _____
2. _____
3. _____
4. _____
5. _____
6. _____
7. _____
8. _____
9. _____
10. _____

Richard Gere

Find 10 four-letter words:

1. _____
2. _____
3. _____
4. _____
5. _____
6. _____
7. _____
8. _____
9. _____
10. _____

Art Linkletter

Find 7 five-letter words:

1. _____
2. _____
3. _____
4. _____
5. _____
6. _____
7. _____

Barry Manilow

Find 7 five-letter words:

1. _____
2. _____
3. _____
4. _____
5. _____
6. _____
7. _____

Solution on page 363

Carrie Fisher

Find 7 five-letter words:

1. _____
2. _____
3. _____
4. _____
5. _____
6. _____
7. _____

Dean Martin

Find 7 five-letter words:

1. _____
2. _____
3. _____
4. _____
5. _____
6. _____
7. _____

Golda Meir

Find 7 five-letter words:

1. _____
2. _____
3. _____
4. _____
5. _____
6. _____
7. _____

Anton Chekhov

Find 7 five-letter words:

1. CHORE   HAVOC
2. CHEAT   MATCH
3. CANON   CHANT
4. COVET
5. TEACH
6. NEATH
7. KNACK   HOOCH

Solution on pages 363–364

Jacques Cousteau

Find 10 four-letter words:

1. COST — JEST
2. CASE — JUST
3. COAT — JUTE
4. COTE
5. COST — SECT — EASE
6. CUTE — SCAT — AUTO
7. OAST — SUET — OUST
8. CESS — STOA — EAST
9. SOTE — AQUA
10. SEAT — OAST

Alfred Nobel

Find 7 five-letter words:

1. ABLER — ELDER — OLDEN
2. ADORN — LADEN — RADON
3. BREED — LADEN — BLEAR
4. BRAND — DROLL — BLAND
5. FABLE — DOLER
6. FARED — NOBLE
7. ENDER — BREAD

Liam Neeson

Find 7 five-letter words:

1. INANE — ALINE — LEMON
2. INION — ALIEN — AISLE
3. EASEL — ANISE
4. ANILE — SLAIN
5. ANION — SNAIL
6. MASON — SLIME
7. MESON — SMILE

Frankie Valli

Find 7 five-letter words:

1. AVAIL — RIVEN
2. ANKLE — RAVEN
3. APIRE — FINAL
4. ANVIL — FLAIN
5. FINER — FLANK
6. FAKER — INKER
7. FREAK — VILL — KNIFE

Solution on page 364

Chapter 16
Kakuro Puzzles

Kakuro is played on a grid that looks much like a crossword puzzle. In kakuro, the clues are sums located above or to the left of each entry. The object is to fill in the blank squares using the numbers 1 to 9 so that they add up to the sums. No number can be used more than once in a sum. There will always be just one solution for each puzzle. Some of the answer numbers have been included in the initial puzzles. As the chapter progresses, fewer and fewer answer numbers are given until you are sailing completely on your own.

Kakuro Puzzle 1

Solution on page 365

Kakuro Puzzle 2

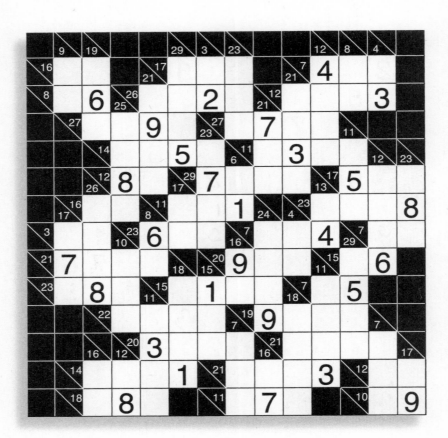

Solution on page 365

Kakuro Puzzle 3

Solution on page 365

Kakuro Puzzle 4

Solution on page 365

Kakuro Puzzle 5

Solution on page 366

Kakuro Puzzle 6

Solution on page 366

Kakuro Puzzle 7

Solution on page 366

Kakuro Puzzle 8

Solution on page 366

Kakuro Puzzle 9

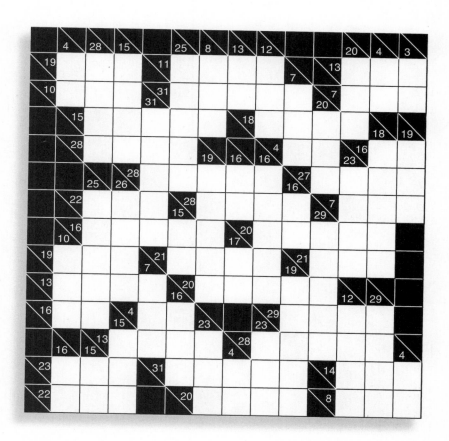

Solution on page 367

Kakuro Puzzle 10

Solution on page 367

Kakuro Puzzle 11

Solution on page 367

Kakuro Puzzle 12

Solution on page 367

Kakuro Puzzle 13

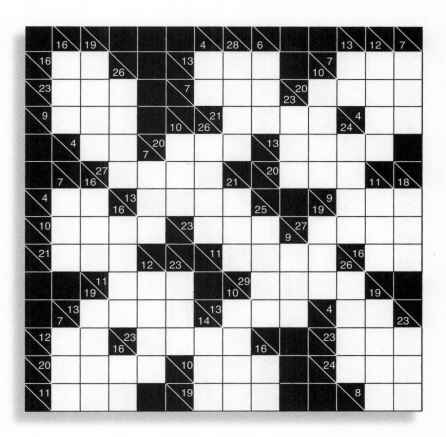

Solution on page 368

Kakuro Puzzle 14

Solution on page 368

Chapter 17
Quotagrams

Answer the clues and then put the letters into the corresponding parts of the grid. Some clues might have multiple word answers. Work back and forth between the clues and the grid until you figure out the quote in the grid.

Stanley Kubrick

A. Bait shop crawler

_84_ _82_ _68_ _91_ _73_ _53_ _87_ _102_ _88_

B. Give it a shot

T̲ _86_ _30_
62

C. "___ me?"

W̲ _32_ _65_
92

D. A to Z

A̲ _101_ _18_ _93_ _100_ _107_ _16_ _15_
22

E. Particular bit of info

_50_ _69_ _77_ _104_ _46_ _109_

F. Soup cracker

_61_ _94_ _5_ _21_ _42_ _47_ _98_

G. Cruise quarters

S̲ _81_ _66_ _96_ _51_ _90_ _74_ _45_ _24_
36

H. California national park

_72_ _25_ _52_ _59_ _10_ _49_ _27_ _103_

I. Fourscore

E̲ _33_ _35_ _56_ _95_ _99_
64

J. Pleasure boat

Y̲ _28_ _48_ _97_ _55_
80

K. Paradise

_78_ _79_ _70_ _112_ _108_ _34_

L. Testimony giver

W̲ _110_ _31_ _29_ _111_ _26_ _12_
60

M. Rural wagon outing

_63_ _89_ _106_ _19_ _13_ _105_ _113_

N. Netflix mailing

D̲ _57_ _71_
76

O. Oryx, bushbuck, or addax

_40_ _14_ _38_ _20_ _23_ _37_ _4_ _6_

P. Salad heart ingredient

A̲ _17_ _41_ _54_ _44_ _39_ _3_ _83_ _2_
8

Q. Paper holder

_7_ _75_ _58_ _1_

R. Fire igniter

M̲ _67_ _11_ _9_ _43_
85

1Q	2P	3P	4O	5F	6O		7Q	8P	9R		10H
11R	12L	13M	14O	15D	16D	17P	18D	19M	20O	21F	
22D	23O	24G	25H	26L	27H		28J	29L	30B	31L	32C
33I	34K	35I		36G	37O		38O	39P	40O	41P	
42F	43R		44P	45G	46E	47F	48J	49H	50E	51G	52H
	53A	54P	55J	56I		57N	58Q	59H	60L	61F	
62B	63M	64I	65C		66G	67R	68A	69E	70K	71N	72H
	73A	74G	75Q	76N			77E	78K	79K	80J	
81G	82A	83P	84A		85R	86B	87A	88A		89M	90G
91A		92C	93D	94F	95I		96G	97J	98F	99I	
100D	101D	102A	103H	104E	105M	106M		107D	108K	109E	110L
111L	112K	113M									

Solution on page 369

Albert Einstein

A. Carved Polynesian pendant

$\overline{97}$ $\overline{70}$ $\overline{89}$ $\overline{88}$

B. Mental quickness

$\overline{50}$ $\overline{109}$ $\overline{59}$

C. Glass growing structure

$\overline{24}$ $\overline{63}$ $\overline{45}$ $\overline{23}$ $\overline{92}$ $\overline{51}$ $\overline{94}$ $\overline{13}$ $\overline{44}$ $\overline{103}$

D. The L of XXL

$\overline{87}$ $\overline{28}$ $\overline{74}$ $\overline{18}$ $\overline{64}$

E. Dashboard counter

$\overline{79}$ $\overline{81}$ $\overline{12}$ $\overline{37}$ $\overline{73}$ $\overline{100}$ $\overline{52}$ $\overline{96}$

F. Connecting flight, up or down

$\overline{57}$ $\overline{106}$ $\overline{91}$ $\overline{16}$ $\overline{102}$ $\overline{69}$ $\overline{75}$ $\overline{101}$ $\overline{83}$

G. Yo!

$\overline{98}$ $\overline{35}$ $\overline{111}$

H. Sidewalk material

$\overline{46}$ $\overline{67}$ $\overline{71}$ $\overline{78}$ $\overline{33}$ $\overline{36}$ $\overline{68}$ $\overline{42}$

I. Park or Fifth

$\overline{43}$ $\overline{108}$ $\overline{77}$ $\overline{80}$ $\overline{56}$ $\overline{84}$

J. Take a load off

$\overline{82}$ $\overline{21}$ $\overline{15}$

K. The Ocean State

$\overline{26}$ $\overline{66}$ $\overline{60}$ $\overline{49}$ $\overline{90}$ $\overline{107}$ $\overline{76}$ $\overline{104}$ $\overline{99}$ $\overline{5}$ $\overline{3}$ $\overline{65}$

L. Place to get steamed

$\overline{34}$ $\overline{62}$ $\overline{95}$ $\overline{17}$ $\overline{105}$

M. Bankrupt energy giant

$\overline{10}$ $\overline{61}$ $\overline{14}$ $\overline{55}$ $\overline{48}$

N. One's early years

$\overline{54}$ $\overline{47}$ $\overline{32}$ $\overline{110}$ $\overline{93}$

O. Device with a snooze button

$\overline{19}$ $\overline{39}$ $\overline{89}$ $\overline{85}$ $\overline{11}$ $\overline{27}$ $\overline{31}$ $\overline{22}$ $\overline{41}$

P. Polished, as shoes

$\overline{86}$ $\overline{30}$ $\overline{58}$ $\overline{29}$ $\overline{5}$

Q. Magician Harry

$\overline{2}$ $\overline{6}$ $\overline{7}$ $\overline{72}$ $\overline{25}$ $\overline{20}$ $\overline{40}$

R. Current events

$\overline{4}$ $\overline{3}$ $\overline{138}$

1R	2Q	3R	4R		5P	6Q	7Q		8O	9O	10M
	11O	12E	13C	14M	15J	16F	17L	18D		19O	
20Q	21J	22O	23C		24C	25Q	26K	27O		28D	29P
	30P	31O	32N	33H		34L	35G	36H	37E	38R	
39O	40Q	41O	42H		43I		44C	45C	46H	47N	48M
49K			50B	51C	52E	53K		54N	55M	56I	
57F	58P	59B		60K	61M		62L		63C	64D	65K
	66K	67H	68H		69F	70A	71H	72Q	73E	74D	
75F		76K	77I	78H	79E	80I	81E		82J	83F	84I
85O	86P		87D	88A	89A	90K		91F	92C		93N
94C	95L	96E			97A	98G	99K	100E		101F	
102F	103C	104K	105L	106F	107K	108I	109B	110N	111G		

Solution on page 369

Clint Eastwood

A. Skyscraper ride

<u>106</u> <u>98</u> <u>68</u> <u>75</u> <u>102</u> <u>79</u> <u>110</u> <u>11</u>

B. Velodrome vehicle

<u>77</u> <u>82</u> <u>59</u> <u>26</u> <u>43</u> <u>32</u> <u>39</u>

C. Have a go at

<u>99</u> <u>29</u> <u>70</u>

D. Tune from "Annie"

<u>100</u> <u>93</u> <u>84</u> <u>27</u> <u>19</u> <u>16</u> <u>51</u> <u>66</u>

E. Haystack hider

<u>64</u> <u>76</u> <u>12</u> <u>48</u> <u>36</u> <u>65</u>

F. Volkswagen bug

<u>96</u> <u>53</u> <u>97</u> <u>103</u> <u>45</u> <u>31</u>

G. Restaurant final course

<u>89</u> <u>42</u> <u>104</u> <u>58</u> <u>46</u> <u>83</u> <u>50</u>

H. _____ Madness

<u>38</u> <u>90</u> <u>112</u> <u>81</u> <u>35</u> <u>113</u>

I. Dental care item

<u>55</u> <u>54</u> <u>71</u> <u>3</u> <u>34</u>

J. Poisonous brown snake

<u>24</u> <u>15</u> <u>41</u> <u>61</u> <u>20</u> <u>91</u> <u>101</u> <u>23</u> <u>74</u> <u>56</u>

K. Tot's constant question

<u>111</u> <u>67</u> <u>86</u>

L. Helper

<u>107</u> <u>52</u> <u>21</u> <u>63</u> <u>49</u> <u>44</u> <u>47</u> <u>88</u> <u>25</u>

M. Waffle topper

<u>40</u> <u>92</u> <u>95</u> <u>72</u> <u>22</u>

N. Einstein's "_____ of relativity"

<u>17</u> <u>73</u> <u>5</u> <u>78</u> <u>105</u> <u>8</u>

O. To mix cards

<u>30</u> <u>80</u> <u>87</u> <u>37</u> <u>33</u> <u>85</u> <u>2</u>

P. 1994 John Travolta film

<u>109</u> <u>94</u> <u>62</u> <u>4</u> <u>14</u> <u>60</u> <u>6</u> <u>7</u> <u>57</u> <u>9</u> <u>69</u>

Q. Gunpowder element

<u>18</u> <u>28</u> <u>108</u> <u>13</u> <u>10</u> <u>1</u>

1Q	2O	3I	4P	5N	6P	7P		8N	9P	10Q	11A
	12E	13Q	14P	15J	16D	17N	18Q ,			19D	20J
21L	22M	23J	24J	25L		26B	27D	28Q	29C	30O	31F
32B	33O			34I	35H	36E	37O		38H	39B	40M
41J	42G	43B	44L		45F	46G	47L	48E -	49L		50G
51D		52L	53F	54I	55I		56J	57P	58G	59B	60P
61J	62P	63L	64E	65E		66D	67K	68A	69P		
70C	71I	72M		73N	74J	75A	76E		77B	78N	79A
80O		81H	82B	83G	84D	85O	86K		87O	88L	89G
90H	91J		92M	93D	94P	95M		96F	97F	98A	99C
		100D	101J	102A	103F	'	104G		105N	106A	107L
, 108Q		109P	110A	111K	112H	113H					

Solution on page 369

Mark Twain

A. Language of China

$\overline{100}$ $\overline{96}$ $\overline{64}$ $\overline{107}$ $\overline{99}$ $\overline{85}$ $\overline{94}$ $\overline{110}$

B. Bronze medalist's place

$\overline{113}$ $\overline{90}$ $\overline{86}$ $\overline{88}$ $\overline{111}$

C. Largest city in Iowa

$\overline{67}$ $\overline{68}$ $\overline{79}$ $\overline{51}$ $\overline{69}$ $\overline{43}$ $\overline{49}$ $\overline{106}$ $\overline{95}$

D. Corridor

$\overline{72}$ $\overline{40}$ $\overline{77}$ $\overline{76}$

E. Use a loom

$\overline{6}$ $\overline{24}$ $\overline{101}$ $\overline{11}$ $\overline{81}$

F. Take to court

$\overline{47}$ $\overline{75}$ $\overline{91}$

G. Mr. Fixit

$\overline{92}$ $\overline{78}$ $\overline{52}$ $\overline{102}$ $\overline{46}$ $\overline{114}$ $\overline{105}$ $\overline{109}$ $\overline{44}$

H. Metropolis

$\overline{103}$ $\overline{50}$ $\overline{16}$ $\overline{108}$

I. Large

$\overline{57}$ $\overline{66}$ $\overline{116}$

J. Nitrous ___ (laughing gas)

$\overline{104}$ $\overline{82}$ $\overline{56}$ $\overline{74}$ $\overline{10}$

K. Doohickey

$\overline{45}$ $\overline{112}$ $\overline{97}$ $\overline{31}$ $\overline{26}$ $\overline{23}$

L. Yell

$\overline{65}$ $\overline{39}$ $\overline{53}$ $\overline{37}$ $\overline{61}$

M. Pester

$\overline{48}$ $\overline{30}$ $\overline{22}$ $\overline{87}$ $\overline{119}$

N. Nun

$\overline{55}$ $\overline{21}$ $\overline{36}$ $\overline{28}$ $\overline{35}$ $\overline{98}$

O. Fill with air

$\overline{63}$ $\overline{20}$ $\overline{70}$ $\overline{32}$ $\overline{115}$ $\overline{41}$ $\overline{73}$

P. They hit the ground running

$\overline{34}$ $\overline{84}$ $\overline{117}$ $\overline{89}$

Q. "___ the season . . ."

$\overline{71}$ $\overline{29}$ $\overline{54}$

R. Traveler's outline

$\overline{33}$ $\overline{83}$ $\overline{60}$ $\overline{18}$ $\overline{93}$ $\overline{13}$ $\overline{17}$ $\overline{25}$ $\overline{62}$

S. Bloody Mary stalk

$\overline{38}$ $\overline{15}$ $\overline{59}$ $\overline{12}$ $\overline{4}$ $\overline{14}$

T. Inhabited by a ghost

$\overline{42}$ $\overline{7}$ $\overline{19}$ $\overline{9}$ $\overline{80}$ $\overline{5}$ $\overline{118}$

U. Grad student's dissertation

$\overline{1}$ $\overline{2}$ $\overline{3}$ $\overline{27}$ $\overline{58}$ $\overline{8}$

1U	2U	3U	4S	5T		6E	7T	8U		9T	10J
11E	12S	13R		14S	15S	16H		17R	18R		19T
20O	21N	22M	23K	24E	25R	26K	27U	28N	29Q	30M	31K
	32O	33R	34P	35N			36N	37L	38S	39L	
40D		41O	42T	43C	44G	45K		46G	47F		48M
49C		50H	51C	52G	53L	54Q	55N	56J	57I	58U	59S
60R	61L	62R			63O	64A	65L	66I	67C	68C	
69C	70O		71Q	72D	73O		74J	75F	76D	77D	78G
79C	80T	81E	82J	83R	84P	85A	86B	87M	88B		
89P	90B	91F	92G	93R		94A	95C		96A		97K
98N	99A	100A	101E			102G		103H	104J	105G	106C
107A	108H		109G	110A	111B		112K		113B	114G	115O

Solution on page 369

Van Gogh

A. Sign after Taurus

$\overline{23}$ $\overline{18}$ $\overline{98}$ $\overline{43}$ $\overline{17}$ $\overline{104}$

B. Twister

$\overline{33}$ $\overline{50}$ $\overline{13}$ $\overline{22}$ $\overline{90}$ $\overline{82}$ $\overline{14}$

C. Pre-cable need

$\overline{34}$ $\overline{70}$ $\overline{89}$ $\overline{47}$ $\overline{81}$ $\overline{77}$ $\overline{62}$

D. Underground passage

$\overline{57}$ $\overline{83}$ $\overline{25}$ $\overline{28}$ $\overline{52}$ $\overline{48}$

E. Court sport

$\overline{41}$ $\overline{86}$ $\overline{35}$ $\overline{39}$ $\overline{21}$ $\overline{55}$

F. Sheet costume

$\overline{73}$ $\overline{103}$ $\overline{38}$ $\overline{32}$ $\overline{58}$

G. Big Band music

$\overline{61}$ $\overline{46}$ $\overline{93}$ $\overline{44}$ $\overline{95}$

H. Heartless one in Oz

$\overline{65}$ $\overline{66}$ $\overline{84}$ $\overline{63}$ $\overline{99}$ $\overline{51}$

I. Pizza topping

$\overline{107}$ $\overline{80}$ $\overline{27}$ $\overline{71}$ $\overline{54}$ $\overline{106}$ $\overline{30}$

J. Pants material

$\overline{85}$ $\overline{68}$ $\overline{105}$ $\overline{6}$ $\overline{8}$

K. Parents and children group

$\overline{15}$ $\overline{56}$ $\overline{67}$ $\overline{76}$ $\overline{49}$ $\overline{101}$

L. Cowboy contest

$\overline{87}$ $\overline{79}$ $\overline{92}$ $\overline{64}$ $\overline{16}$

M. Insult

$\overline{96}$ $\overline{97}$ $\overline{2}$ $\overline{40}$ $\overline{94}$ $\overline{36}$

N. Wall Street

$\overline{88}$ $\overline{102}$ $\overline{3}$ $\overline{91}$ $\overline{60}$

O. Dusk to dawn

$\overline{100}$ $\overline{72}$ $\overline{45}$ $\overline{74}$ $\overline{78}$

P. Things to do in the sink after dinner

$\overline{29}$ $\overline{69}$ $\overline{37}$ $\overline{59}$ $\overline{12}$ $\overline{10}$

Q. Something to shake with

$\overline{53}$ $\overline{24}$ $\overline{4}$ $\overline{26}$

R. Top 40 songs

$\overline{42}$ $\overline{1}$ $\overline{75}$ $\overline{7}$

S. Indication of impending danger

$\overline{19}$ $\overline{20}$ $\overline{31}$ $\overline{5}$ $\overline{9}$ $\overline{11}$

1R	2M		3N	4Q	5S		6J	7R		8J	9S
10P	11S	12P	13B		14B	15K		16L	17A	18A	
19S	20S	21E	22B	23A		24Q	25D	26Q		27I	28D
29P	30I	31S	32F	33B	34C	35E	36M	37P		38F	39E
40M		41E	42R	43A	44G	45O		46G	47C	48D	49K
		50B	51H	52D		53Q	54I	55E		56K	57D
,	58F	59P	60N		61G	62C	63H	64L		65H	66H
67K	68J		69P	70C	71I	72O	73F	74O	75R	
76K	77C	78O	79L		80I	81C	82B		83D	84H	85J
86E	87L	88N	89C	90B	91N	92L	93G	94M	95G		96M
97M		98A	99H	100O	101K		102N	103F	104A	105J	106I
107I	.										

Solution on page 369

Abraham Lincoln

A. Lousy car

96 91 57 101 76

B. Place for a plug

29 69 79 42 48 17

C. Disciple of Jesus

26 92 22 55 89 43 93

D. Poppy product

56 95 35 73 108

E. Where the heart is

62 59 66 97

F. Hot breakfast food

44 75 103 36 105 98 27

G. Switch position

51 30 60

H. Helium symbol

90 63

I. Mama Cass ____

109 24 83 107 72 31

J. Put on the payroll

67 13 52 85 78 71

K. Run off to get hitched

58 99 94 49 54

L. Carnival confection

74 81 34 46 82 77 4 84 39
40 1

M. North American bison

68 3 88 7 38 86 87

N. Chewy candy

64 15 102 45 33 50

O. H of HMO

47 37 41 100 61 104

P. Skin

16 53 25 11 32

Q. Home on the Range

5 6 106 21 28 12 23 19

R. Well-mannered

20 9 10 65 70 14

S. Horse's foot

18 8 2 80

1L	2S	3M		4L	5Q	6Q		7M	8S	9R	10R
	11P	12Q	13J	14R		15N	16P		17B	18S	19Q
	20R	21Q	22C	23Q	24I	25P		26C	27F	28Q	
29B	30G		31I	32P	33N		34L	35D	36F	37O	
	38M	39L	40L		41O	42B	43C		44F	45N	
46L	47O	48B		49K	50N	51G	52J	53P	54K		55C
56D	57A	58K		59E	60G		61O	62E	63H		64N
65R	66E	67J		68M	69B	70R		71J	72I	73D
83I	74L	75F	76A		77L	78J	79B		80S	81L	82L
		84L	85J	86M		87M	88M		89C	90H	91A
	92C	93C	94K	95D	96A	97E		98F	99K	100O	
101A	102N		103F	104O	105F		106Q	107I	108D	109I	

Solution on page 370

Amy Bloom

A. Business person's motive

48 76 24 77 63 23

B. Joke reaction

49 52 25 65 90

C. Acting technique

87 68 6 39 61 27

D. Once more

66 14 69 104 64

E. Pick

107 74 44 47 101 109

F. Look without purchasing

55 79 60 43 37 88

G. Semiformal evening wear

95 81 91 97 62 67 86 19

H. Place for books

30 15 100 108 83

I. Lift between floors

75 59 84 53 80 31 72 105

J. Simple

28 5 21 22

K. Fool

82 34 93 98 89

L. San Francisco transport

18 73 29 4 96 16 70 102 9

M. Hand warmer

99 35 85 36 57 58

N. Flick

103 78 3 17 40

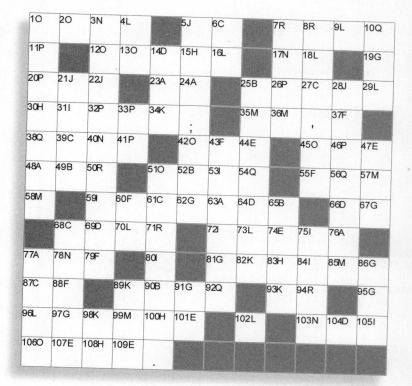

O. Medical site

51 2 12 45 13 42 106 1

P. Reception aid

32 26 11 46 41 33 20

Q. Sugary

10 38 56 54 92

R. Pickpocket

94 71 8 50 7

Solution on page 370

Dale Carnegie

A. Hard yellow candy

$\overline{110}$ $\overline{71}$ $\overline{47}$ $\overline{98}$ $\overline{75}$ $\overline{54}$ $\overline{89}$ $\overline{102}$ $\overline{72}$

B. 1995 Mel Gibson movie

$\overline{99}$ $\overline{77}$ $\overline{36}$ $\overline{68}$ $\overline{29}$ $\overline{52}$ $\overline{84}$ $\overline{43}$ $\overline{32}$ $\overline{73}$

C. First daughter of the '90s

$\overline{45}$ $\overline{28}$ $\overline{9}$ $\overline{111}$ $\overline{91}$ $\overline{38}$ $\overline{67}$

D. Kitchen fixture

$\overline{44}$ $\overline{107}$ $\overline{39}$ $\overline{50}$ $\overline{42}$ $\overline{69}$ $\overline{76}$

E. National park in California

$\overline{56}$ $\overline{74}$ $\overline{51}$ $\overline{100}$ $\overline{11}$ $\overline{79}$ $\overline{86}$ $\overline{92}$

F. Detroit record label

$\overline{94}$ $\overline{104}$ $\overline{97}$ $\overline{31}$ $\overline{30}$ $\overline{80}$

G. Actress Goldberg

$\overline{82}$ $\overline{83}$ $\overline{65}$ $\overline{59}$ $\overline{57}$ $\overline{25}$

H. Camp shelter

$\overline{108}$ $\overline{40}$ $\overline{85}$ $\overline{27}$

I. Inner-city area

$\overline{81}$ $\overline{64}$ $\overline{53}$ $\overline{19}$ $\overline{18}$ $\overline{13}$

J. Young cat

$\overline{70}$ $\overline{21}$ $\overline{15}$ $\overline{7}$ $\overline{41}$ $\overline{101}$

K. First-year students

$\overline{6}$ $\overline{14}$ $\overline{58}$ $\overline{24}$ $\overline{66}$ $\overline{1}$ $\overline{62}$ $\overline{26}$

L. Wool source

$\overline{3}$ $\overline{103}$ $\overline{88}$ $\overline{90}$ $\overline{60}$

M. Parka feature

$\overline{87}$ $\overline{46}$ $\overline{5}$ $\overline{96}$

N. Invoice

$\overline{55}$ $\overline{10}$ $\overline{33}$ $\overline{49}$

O. Smiling Dwarf

$\overline{35}$ $\overline{109}$ $\overline{12}$ $\overline{105}$ $\overline{78}$

P. Called up

$\overline{48}$ $\overline{20}$ $\overline{2}$ $\overline{22}$ $\overline{106}$ $\overline{34}$

Q. Surfer's ride

$\overline{63}$ $\overline{16}$ $\overline{37}$ $\overline{93}$

R. Pants measure

$\overline{61}$ $\overline{95}$ $\overline{17}$ $\overline{23}$ $\overline{4}$ $\overline{8}$

1K	2P	3L	4R		5M	6K		7J	8R	9C	
10N	11E	12O	13I	14K	15J	16Q	17R	18I		19I	20P
21J	22P	23R	24K		25G	26K		27H	28C	29B	
30F	31F	32B	33N	34P		35O	36B	37Q	38C		39D
40H	41J	42D		43B	44D	45C	46M	47A	48P	49N	50D
51E	52B	53I	54A		55N	56E		57G	58K	59G	60L
61R	62K		63Q	64I	65G		66K	67C	68B	69D	
70J	71A	72A	73B		74E	75A		76D	77B	78O	79E
80F	81I		82G	83G	84B	85H		86E	87M	88L	89A
90L		91C	92E	93Q	94F	95R	96M		97F	98A	
99B	100E		101J	102A		103L	104F	105O	106P		107D
108H		109O	110A	111C							

Solution on page 370

Nathaniel Hawthorne

A. America's Cup racer

$\overline{23}\ \overline{12}\ \overline{68}\ \overline{25}\ \overline{17}$

B. Breadmaker's material

$\overline{39}\ \overline{51}\ \overline{74}\ \overline{57}\ \overline{66}$

C. Pain reliever

$\overline{94}\ \overline{79}\ \overline{33}\ \overline{67}\ \overline{58}\ \overline{5}\ \overline{85}$

D. Beat to a froth

$\overline{24}\ \overline{100}\ \overline{98}\ \overline{61}$

E. Like a wallflower

$\overline{60}\ \overline{69}\ \overline{92}$

F. Hamper filler

$\overline{97}\ \overline{96}\ \overline{55}\ \overline{105}\ \overline{53}\ \overline{56}\ \overline{46}$

G. Knit pullover

$\overline{36}\ \overline{44}\ \overline{89}\ \overline{59}\ \overline{10}\ \overline{31}\ \overline{35}$

H. Student

$\overline{103}\ \overline{87}\ \overline{4}\ \overline{70}\ \overline{91}$

I. Commuter's home

$\overline{47}\ \overline{102}\ \overline{62}\ \overline{34}\ \overline{20}\ \overline{48}$

J. Hive ruler

$\overline{86}\ \overline{63}\ \overline{38}\ \overline{7}\ \overline{32}$

K. Minimum or maximum

$\overline{77}\ \overline{76}\ \overline{93}\ \overline{88}\ \overline{64}$

L. 50th state

$\overline{30}\ \overline{42}\ \overline{75}\ \overline{45}\ \overline{80}\ \overline{40}$

M. Peanuts

$\overline{41}\ \overline{52}\ \overline{54}\ \overline{104}\ \overline{3}\ \overline{50}$

N. Third place at the track

$\overline{13}\ \overline{28}\ \overline{107}\ \overline{65}$

O. Opinion piece

$\overline{49}\ \overline{11}\ \overline{9}\ \overline{14}\ \overline{72}$

P. Road Runner's foe

$\overline{27}\ \overline{73}\ \overline{95}\ \overline{83}\ \overline{81}\ \overline{19}$

Q. Made before blowing out the candles

$\overline{29}\ \overline{10}\ \overline{8}\ \overline{1}$

R. Merriment

$\overline{21}\ \overline{108}\ \overline{6}$

S. Executor's concern

$\overline{84}\ \overline{26}\ \overline{78}\ \overline{43}$

T. Spotted beetle

$\overline{22}\ \overline{2}\ \overline{82}\ \overline{106}\ \overline{15}\ \overline{37}\ \overline{99}$

U. Clump of hair

$\overline{90}\ \overline{16}\ \overline{71}\ \overline{101}$

1Q	2T	3M	4H	5C	6R	7J	8Q	9O		10Q	11O
	12A	13N		14O		15T	16U	17A	18G	19P	20I
21R	22T	23A		24D	25A	26S	27P	28N		29Q	30L
31G	32J		33C	34I	35G	36G	37T	38J	39B		40L
41M		42L	43S	44G	45L	46F	47I		48I	49O	50M
51B	52M	53F		54M	55F	56F		57B	58C	59G	60E
61D			62I	63J	64K		65N	66B	67C	68A	69E
	70H	71U		72O	73P	74B		75L	76K	77K	78S
	79C	80L	81P		82T	83P	84S	85C		86J	87H
88K	89G	90U	91H	92E		93K	94C	95P		96F	97F
98D	99T	100D	101U		102I	103H	104M	105F		106T	107N
108R	.										

Solution on page 370

Carl Jung

A. Field

75 45 16 67 55 23

B. Spring or summer

34 32 104 103 91 49

C. Brewing whistler

73 107 30 60 19 85

D. Manifest ___

100 99 70 25 24 17 62

E. Ten to the third

92 52 69 28 46 33 78 105

F. Evening disappearing act

108 35 44 47 71 51

G. Parade component

83 95 38 94 20

H. Nephew's sister

80 72 14 98 37

I. Response

96 90 74 54 76 36

J. Louisiana's state bird

9 22 66 79 15 41 97

K. Hawk's opposite

40 27 2 53

L. Cookout staple

26 59 31 21 65 88 81 87 42

M. Dumbo or Babar

89 68 3 61 58 77 106 29

N. Fish in a tin

109 48 56 57 84 18 1

O. Door opener

43 4 64 93

P. Slight odor

86 6 82 39 13

Q. Side road

101 102 63 7 10

R. Tartan pattern

8 11 5 12 50

1N	2K	3M	4O	■	5R	■	6P	7Q	8R	9J	10Q
■	11R	12R	13P	14H	■	15J	16A	17D	18N	19C	20G
■	21L	22J	■	23A	24D	25D	26L	27K	28E	29M	■
30C	■	31L	32B	33E	34B	35F	36I	37H	■	38G	39P
■	40K	41J	42L	43O	44F	45A	46E	47F	■	■	48N
49B	50R	■	51F	52E	53K	■	54I	55A	56N	57N	■
58M	59L	60C	61M	62D	■	63Q	64O	65L	66J	67A	■
68M	69E	70D	71F	■	72H	73C	74I	■	75A	76I	77M
78E	79J	80H	81L	■	82P	83G	■	84N	85C	■	86P
87L	88L	89M	■	90I	91B	92E	■	93O	94G	95G	96I
97J	98H	99D	100D	■	101Q	102Q	■	103B	104B	105E	106M
107C	108F	109N	■	■	■	■	■	■	■	■	■

Solution on page 370

Alfred Hitchcock

A. Guacamole ingredient

94 103 77 92 75 57 106

B. Winter forecast

80 41 40 33

C. Sardine or salmon

59 21 82 84

D. Highest point

43 107 53 110 23 68

E. Miss Saigon's homeland

65 51 30 74 56 72 81

F. Conestoga wagon rider

32 58 61 73 85 2 91

G. Old Faithful, for one

101 17 60 52 90 13

H. Iowa city

11 111 54 88 14 79 78 104 96

I. Tropical lizard

76 42 26 36 109

J. Big house

89 27 67 108 93 87 70

K. Bee product

63 49 45 66 71

L. Performer with a painted face

86 31 37 97 50

M. Quiz show info

83 35 102 20 98 69

N. _____ of Liberty

22 46 64 16 9 19

O. Pay

1 44 95 55 10 105

P. Groundbreaking tool

29 34 12

Q. Pink wading bird

38 100 47 8 4 28 48 24

R. Pajama material

39 99 7 25 15 3 18

S. Firearm

6 62 5

1O	2F	3R	4Q	5S	6S		7R		8Q	9N	10O
11H	12P	13G		14H	15R		16N	17G	18R	19N	20M
21C	22N	23D	24Q	25R		26I	27J	28Q		29P	30E
31L	32F		33B	34P	35M	36I		37L	38Q	39R	
40B	41B	42I		43D		44O	45K	46N	47Q	48Q	49K
50L	51E	52G	53D	54H			55O	56E	57A		58F
59C		60G	61F	62S		63K	64N	65E	66K	67J	
68D		69M	70J	71K		72E	73F	74E	75A	76I	77A
78H	79H	80B	81E	82C			83M	84C	85F		86L
87J	88H	89J	90G	91F	92A	93J	94A	95O	96H		97L
98M	99R	100Q		101G	102M	103A	104H			105O	106A	107D
	108J	109I	110D	111H							

Solution on pages 370–371

Ray Bradbury

A. Duke it out

61 94 57 93 84

B. Letters after F

96 114 26

C. Mork's mate

103 102 64 49 98

D. Toy on a string

106 19 52 39

E. Place to fill up

117 47 58 118 85 82 88 115 99 40

F. Jurassic Park

90 71 4 112 33 50 69 86

G. Fork or knife

100 110 13 116 70 67 36

H. Without sound

97 28 105 59 48 92

I. Nocturnal marsupial

44 104 63 101 109 108 107

J. Business mogul

53 77 81 89 91 83

K. Any of the original 13

66 79 73 68 51 30

L. Shiny photo

8 60 74 34 41 87

M. ____ on the Bounty

17 75 32 55 56 78

N. Thin's opposite

113 54 43 38 5

O. Dawn follower

65 80 95 22 31 46 35

P. Pupil

76 11 45 111 14 15 29

Q. Uncertain

6 37 20 18

R. Peace Train

21 24 25 72 1 23 27 16 7 10

S. Golfer Rodriguez

62 12 9 42 2 3

Solution on page 371

Calvin Coolidge

A. Nutty ice cream flavor

`92` `81` `49` `89` `63` `112` `90` `39` `60`

B. Neverending afternoon story

`58` `26` `108` `55` `100` `40` `48` `110` `53`

C. Five-sided shape

`1` `8` `72` `42` `33` `52` `66` `54`

D. Tentacled sea creature with a flower name

`77` `13` `69` `98` `85` `109` `104`

E. Abba's home country

`65` `80` `11` `70` `57` `44`

F. Dog command

`105` `32` `88` `96`

G. Actor Keanu

`56` `35` `16` `87` `113` `99`

H. Beach memento

`59` `91` `28` `64` `47` `97` `29` `50`

I. Michael of "Little House on the Prairie"

`67` `23` `31` `14` `94` `61`

J. Wedding assistant

`95` `43` `79` `102` `107` `71` `38`

K. Christmas tree decoration

`30` `34` `27` `111` `37` `18` `22` `45`

L. Toddler's wheels

`84` `46` `93` `51` `75` `82` `2` `19`

M. Dilbert

`6` `10` `41` `24` `17` `74` `73` `12` `20` `4`

N. Piano key material

`5` `68` `36` `3` `78`

O. Ship's bottom

`62` `106` `83` `86`

P. Gone ____ the Wind

`76` `25` `7` `103`

Q. Discover

`101` `21` `9` `15`

1C	2L	3N	4M	5N	6M	7P	8C	9Q	10M	11E	
12M	13D	14I		15Q	16G	17M	18K	19L	20M	21Q	22K
23I	24M	25P	26B	27K		28H	29H	30K	31I	32F	
33C	34K	35G		36N	37K	38J	39A	40B	41M	42C	43J
44E	45K			46L	47H	48B		49A	50H	51L	52C
53B	54C			55B	56G	57E	58B	59H		60A	61I
		62O	63A	64H		65E	66C	67I	68N	69D	70E
	71J	72C	73M		74M	75L	76P	77D	78N	79J	
80E	81A	82L	83O		84L	85D	86O	87G	88F		89A
90A	91H		92A	93L	94I	95J	96F	97H	98D	99G	
100B	101Q		102J	103P	104D		105F	106O	107J	108B	109D
	110B	111K	112A	113G							

Solution on page 371

Douglas Adams

A. Larry, Moe, or Curly

 10 112 104 21 97 91

B. Apollo destination

 49 67 40 32

C. San Francisco transport

 85 51 83 42 82 102 106 89 71

D. San Francisco bread

 118 48 100 34 81 57 79 55 93

E. Newton fruit

 66 44 38

F. Movie

 105 101 23 88

G. Golfer's last hole

 14 36 45 52 92 24 84 99

H. Eighth prime number

 96 87 80 20 39 50 61 46

I. A fairy may leave money for it

 62 68 72 11 30

J. The Who's rock opera

 86 115 4 25 103

K. Nonstick coating

 33 63 74 60 107 54

L. Office note

 58 94 108 73

M. Roadside stopover

 8 78 90 98 64

N. Birds do it

 114 69 35

O. Picnic side dish

 59 116 77 26 15 6 43 17 110 12 41

P. Rookie piano tune

 56 16 3 19 47 18 75 2 27 76

Q. Hawaiian fruit

 22 95 37 113 1 109 70 117 31

R. Fuzzy fruit

 13 53 29 9

S. Foe

 28 7 111 5 65

1Q		2P	3P	4J	5S	6O	7S		8M	9R	10A
11I	12O	13R	14G		15O	16P	17O	18P		19P	20H
21A	22Q	23F	24G		25J	26O	27P	28S		29R	30I
31Q	32B		33K	34D	35N	36G	37Q	38E		39H	40B
	41O	42C	43O	44E	45G	46H		47P	48D	49B	50H
51C	52G	53R	54K	55D		56P	57D	58L	59O	60K	61H
62I	63K	64M	65S		66E	67B	68I	69N	70Q	71C	72I
73L	74K		75P	76P		77O	78M		79D	80H	81D
82C	83C	84G	85C	86J	87H	88F	89C	90M	91A		92G
93D	94L		95Q	96H	97A	98M	99G	100D	101F	102C	103J
	104A	105F		106C	107K	108L	109Q	110O	111S	112A	113Q
	114N	115J	116O	117Q	118D						

Solution on page 371

Chapter 18
Transadditions

Add a letter to a word, scramble all of the letters, and form another word. The clues suggest what word is to be formed. The words formed can be any part of speech.

Example

Transadd This Word: Teach

1.   Add an L, scramble, and get a Swiss dwelling.
2.   Add an S, scramble, and a perfume packet.
3.   Add a C, scramble, and get a mark of distinction.

The answers are:

1.   chalet
2.   sachet
3.   cachet

Transsadd This Word: Rides

1. Add an E, scramble, and get a longing for something. _D_____

2. Add an N, scramble, and get washed off. _R_____

3. Add a B, scramble, and get some trash. _D_____

Transsadd This Word: Scout

1. Add an L, scramble, and get an insect. _L_____

2. Add a C, scramble, and get a house exterior. _S_____

3. Add an R, scramble, and get a place for tennis games. _C_____

Transsadd This Word: Model

1. Add a U, scramble, and get a component. _M_____

2. Add a Y, scramble, and get a tune. _M_____

3. Add an S, scramble, and get something rarely. _S_____

Transsadd This Word: Loser

1. Add an M, scramble, and get a tidbit. _M_____

2. Add a V, scramble, and get a couple. _L_____

3. Add a V, scramble, and get someone with answers. _S_____

Solution on page 372

Transadd This Word: Medal

1. Add an S, scramble, and get a maiden.   _____

2. Add an F, scramble, and get burned.   _____

3. Add a B, scramble, and get crazy.   _____

Transadd This Word: Purse

1. Add a B, scramble, and get really high quality.   _____

2. Add a P, scramble, and get some dinner.   _____

3. Add a C, scramble, and get an evergreen.   _____

Transadd This Word: Actor

1. Add an S, scramble, and get an acting sidekick.   _____

2. Add an N, scramble, and get a Jewish musical leader.   _____

3. Add an R, scramble, and get a vegetable.   _____

Transadd This Word: Heart

1. Add a T, scramble, and get some animosity.   _____

2. Add a B, scramble, and get someone getting clean.   _____

3. Add a W, scramble, and get a ring of flowers.   _____

Solution on page 372

Transadd This Word: Miner

1. Add a V, scramble, and get some rats. _____

2. Add an A, scramble, and get some air force guys. _____

3. Add an A, scramble, and get a soldier. _____

Transadd This Word: Press

1. Add an A, scramble, and get some long weapons. _____

2. Add an A, scramble, and get what a quarterback could be called. _____

3. Add a U, scramble, and get what some ladies carry. _____

Transadd This Word: Skate

1. Add a C, scramble, and get the last resting spot. _____

2. Add a B, scramble, and get something woven. _____

3. Add an S, scramble, and get some meat. _____

Transadd This Word: Ridge

1. Add an L, scramble, and get something that soars. _____

2. Add a G, scramble, and get a hole maker. _____

3. Add an N, scramble, and get surrounded. _____

Solution on page 372

Transadd This Word: Snail

1. Add an E, scramble, and get some creatures from outer space.   _____

2. Add a D, scramble, and get some surrounded land.   _____

3. Add an F, scramble, and get the last tests.   _____

Transadd This Word: Nurse

1. Add a P, scramble, and get dried fruit.   _____

2. Add an R, scramble, and get something already seen.   _____

3. Add a T, scramble, and get some trouble.   _____

Transadd This Word: Range

1. Add an H, scramble, and get something in your closet.   _____

2. Add an L, scramble, and get one who fishes.   _____

3. Add a D, scramble, and get a male goose.   _____

Transadd This Word: Canoe

1. Add a B, scramble, and get a guiding light.   _____

2. Add a T, scramble, and get a gasoline rating.   _____

3. Add an R, scramble, and get an eye piece.   _____

Solution on page 372

Transadd This Word: Score

1. Add a C, scramble, and get football in Europe.

2. Add a T, scramble, and get one to accompany you.

3. Add a U, scramble, and get a point of origin.

_____

_____

_____

Transadd This Word: Noise

1. Add a C, scramble, and get a trigonometry function.

2. Add an L, scramble, and get part of a shoe.

3. Add a P, scramble, and get some small horses.

_____

_____

_____

Transadd This Word: North

1. Add an E, scramble, and get a king's chair.

2. Add an E, scramble, and get a stinger.

3. Add an S, scramble, and get part of a rosebush.

_____

_____

_____

Transadd This Word: Organ

1. Add an S, scramble, and get some sounds of displeasure.

2. Add an E, scramble, and get a fruit.

3. Add a J, scramble, and get some special language.

_____

_____

_____

Solution on page 372

Transadd This Word: Grand

1. Add an E, scramble, and get in a risky situation. _____

2. Add an O, scramble, and get a monster. _____

3. Add an E, scramble, and get a flower plot. _____

Transadd This Word: Pride

1. Add an S, scramble, and get eight legs. _____

2. Add an A, scramble, and get baby's underwear. _____

3. Add an O, scramble, and get what is at the end of this sentence. _____

Transadd This Word: Panel

1. Add an S, scramble, and get some jets. _____

2. Add a T, scramble, and get Saturn. _____

3. Add an I, scramble, and get high in the mountains. _____

Transadd This Word: Raise

1. Add a T, scramble, and get something funny. _____

2. Add a B, scramble, and get a dog disease. _____

3. Add an R, scramble, and get a rugged mountain range. _____

Solution on pages 372–373

Transadd This Word: Sharp

1. Add a G, scramble, and get some diagrams. _____

2. Add an E, scramble, and get a short sequence of words. _____

3. Add an E, scramble, and get a Tibetan mountaineer. _____

Transadd This Word: Sight

1. Add an L, scramble, and get some illuminating things. _____

2. Add an E, scramble, and get some numbers just above seven. _____

3. Add an F, scramble, and get some brawls. _____

Transadd This Word: Horse

1. Add a C, scramble, and get some work. _____

2. Add a W, scramble, and get some rain. _____

3. Add an E, scramble, and get some courageous people. _____

Transadd This Word: Moral

1. Add an S, scramble, and get some teeth. _____

2. Add an N, scramble, and get something that conforms. _____

3. Add a C, scramble, and get some hubbub. _____

Solution on page 373

Transadd This Word: Naked

1. Add an S, scramble, and get what a baker does. _____

2. Add an R, scramble, and get ordered. _____

3. Add an R, scramble, and get blacker. _____

Transadd This Word: Earth

1. Add an L, scramble, and get a bareback top. _____

2. Add a B, scramble, and get some exhalation. _____

3. Add an F, scramble, and get the old man. _____

Transadd This Word: React

1. Add an S, scramble, and get wooden containers. _____

2. Add an N, scramble, and get a sweet liquid. _____

3. Add a P, scramble, and get something to walk on. _____

Transadd This Word: Relay

1. Add a W, scramble, and get an attorney. _____

2. Add a G, scramble, and get a diamond pattern on socks. _____

3. Add a Y, scramble, and get something annual. _____

Solution on page 373

Transadd This Word: Easel

1. Add a P, scramble, and get a polite word.   _____

2. Add a P, scramble, and get a naptime condition.   _____

3. Add a V, scramble, and get some foliage.   _____

Transadd This Word: Elder

1. Add an A, scramble, and get one who is followed.   _____

2. Add an N, scramble, and get a loaner.   _____

3. Add an A, scramble, and get one who sells.   _____

Transadd This Word: Feast

1. Add an R, scramble, and get quicker.   _____

2. Add an I, scramble, and get a festival.   _____

3. Add a C, scramble, and get the surfaces of a gemstone.   _____

Transadd This Word: Ideal

1. Add an S, scramble, and get some women.   _____

2. Add an R, scramble, and get put off the track.   _____

3. Add a J, scramble, and get locked up.   _____

Solution on page 373

Transadd This Word: Later

1. Add an N, scramble, and get a moose horn.   _____

2. Add a T, scramble, and get a baby's noisy toy.   _____

3. Add a K, scramble, and get one who gabs.   _____

Transadd This Word: Noted

1. Add a C, scramble, and get a guide.   _____

2. Add an A, scramble, and get asked for a contribution. _____

3. Add an R, scramble, and get a mouse.   _____

Transadd This Word: Field

1. Add an M, scramble, and get put into a camera.   _____

2. Add a D, scramble, and get a violin.   _____

3. Add an L, scramble, and get full.   _____

Transadd This Word: Point

1. Add an S, scramble, and get some beans.   _____

2. Add an O, scramble, and get a choice.   _____

3. Add an S, scramble, and get a car part.   _____

Solution on page 373

Transadd This Word: Slide

1. Add an O, scramble, and get songs that were once popular. _____

2. Add an E, scramble, and get some fuel. _____

3. Add an H, scramble, and get some armor. _____

Transadd This Word: Prime

1. Add an E, scramble, and get a kingdom. _____

2. Add a U, scramble, and get a judge. _____

3. Add a T, scramble, and get an OK. _____

Transadd This Word: Crisp

1. Add an H, scramble, and get bird noises. _____

2. Add an E, scramble, and get what is on tags in stores. _____

3. Add a T, scramble, and get what an actor reads. _____

Transadd This Word: Rates

1. Add a V, scramble, and get very hungry. _____

2. Add an H, scramble, and get a game suit. _____

3. Add an M, scramble, and get a small river. _____

Solution on pages 373–374

Transsadd This Word: Reach

1. Add an R, scramble, and get an arrow shooter. _____

2. Add a K, scramble, and get a computer buff. _____

3. Add a G, scramble, and get what is done with a credit card. _____

Transsadd This Word: Least

1. Add a C, scramble, and get a queen's abode. _____

2. Add a P, scramble, and get some dinnerware. _____

3. Add a B, scramble, and get a horse's abode. _____

Transsadd This Word: Bread

1. Add a V, scramble, and get a part of speech. _____

2. Add an L, scramble, and get less hair. _____

3. Add a G, scramble, and get a mammal. _____

Transsadd This Word: Eager

1. Add a G, scramble, and get a type of music. _____

2. Add an S, scramble, and get deep-fryer juice. _____

3. Add an M, scramble, and get very little. _____

Solution on page 374

Transadd This Word: Great

1. Add a T, scramble, and get a bull's eye.   _____

2. Add an R, scramble, and get a room in the attic.   _____

3. Add an R, scramble, and get a leg band.   _____

Transadd This Word: Price

1. Add an O, scramble, and get a duplicator.   _____

2. Add an E, scramble, and get some kitchen directions.   _____

3. Add an H, scramble, and get a secret code.   _____

Transadd This Word: Scale

1. Add an M, scramble, and get some humps.   _____

2. Add a B, scramble, and get some wires.   _____

3. Add a V, scramble, and get some young cows.   _____

Transadd This Word: Class

1. Add a P, scramble, and get fasteners.   _____

2. Add an E, scramble, and get something on a snake.   _____

3. Add a K, scramble, and get some pants.   _____

Solution on page 374

Transadd This Word: Radio

1. Add an H, scramble, and get a style for your head.   H_____

2. Add an E, scramble, and get a rock helper.   R_____

3. Add an N, scramble, and get priestly authority.   O_____

Transadd This Word: Scare

1. Add a D, scramble, and get something holy.   B_____

2. Add an M, scramble, and get a loud noise.   S_____

3. Add an R, scramble, and get some fast drivers.   R_____

Transadd This Word: Pearl

1. Add an O, scramble, and get released from jail.   PA_____

2. Add a C, scramble, and get a package.   PA_____

3. Add a Y, scramble, and get someone in the game.   PL_____

Transadd This Word: Loves

1. Add an I, scramble, and get some fruit.   O_____

2. Add an H, scramble, and get a scoop.   S_____

3. Add an N, scramble, and get stories.   N_____

Solution on page 374

Answers

Chapter 1: Word Search Puzzles

Holidays

```
E D C Y S H A N A H S A H H S O R K Z U
E A C R Y A A Y A D E L L I T S A B L Y S
F O A R E A L D N F A T H E R S D A Y Y A D
O U R S A D S A S T E A R T H D A Y Y A D S
U T H A A I L A C V T A F L A G D A Y A D S N
R H Y A E I N Y U I T I U W B D J H G E N I K
T O F A Y R O P S A D A E E S I O K S I I W A
H O D S A G E M A A R D S R S F L A W U X T A
O F J U E T O R M A S U N E N L D K O N N E R
F J U L K O M T R G K A M R B E N R A A B E E A
U L E W H Y I I T N Y A E M W E E N Y L I A P
L Y A A D A C D Z E G D D H U Y W T Z A D P D
Y A A F N U D K R Z U T P A A T L E Y N V A D
A Z Y U O O D S A G J K Q X Y N O O A E A S N
N A G R B A Y M Y A D R O B R A M C R A L A
A W K G G A Y R Y A D S L O O F L I R P A R R
K L I L N A O Y A M E D O C N I C B D A
```

Classical Music

```
R L I P H L K I J T H E F T R B F P O X
E X N A U A O P N O E B D O H F L R A A
R I N R K Q G F S S O T T U K E T Z C P
B O A H C S M U R D T C N C L S M W R E
O N R Y I O P I U I U R H I E R J E P M
L C R E N R V V A D W A U A U P E E F N
A C P A Q O D V E N R R T M M V Q R T E P
Q O K Q N U A M Q O O R M T W N R E C G Y N K
V K E R A M H N Y Y U B E S M M T Q P O
G E M T H E Y O U M M R S H E E V A G T
O J E E L Q B R R A P I E L C R V K L R
V R N T I O S D H A O H F L Z R O O L E
G X T L H W R C A N L D O M Q T O C M C
P L F F P R E S O P M O C N T R D T S N O
P A S S A G E M E L O D Y F Y E N N P O
H D B W J S T R I N G D M I H C W H A C
Z C I U W P E N S E M B L E A N C S R B
Q N Y Q K Z V S O N A T A O V O P A Q G
D T G B H P X S Z I N K L S V C P N W R
```

Actors

```
D D A L N A L A E Y E N R A C T R A Z H
C H I C O M A R X S E H C E M A N O D Y
B J A M E S D E A N E Y E S U B Y R A G
J Y D N A C N H O J Y E A L P A C I N O
E N Y A W N H O J G K M L S E S O G Q A
T Q P E T E R F O N D A G C N R K V A R
Y O E E L B A G K R A L C O N Y K C V R
N U M R Z A A R F G Q R T I B H H Q O W
E X L M R K D C X F E T I S V E O C I A D
L E T B I O M L T R U N O P V E K J D N
L A C G R X L Y A B A R E Y T H C L A N O
A A R E N Y U F D N C M C K U O I X N O F Y
Y D N A R G A A W N E L G A H O D E Y R C A Y R
O O R R A U S A C K V I E S N O A A R X L H K R
O W K I N T E S N B R E R N N Q P H A V V Y R N
N B U T Y A L K C A S U C N H O J Q U E D I
U O Q F J V J O H N N Y D E P P X D O V
```

Careers

```
P R P B E N Z C B Q I H D T H M R R Q R
H O O P C A P X I M T W L D S O E P E N
X T G N P M J N W A I T E R T K O Y U R
P C G A M K C I W M T S D C A S W R F O
N O I W R R G A N E H Q A B T A S E K H
A D P S I O D T G C A L B M L E H R R T U
I T O H W F U H P R A U N C E V E U A
C O S E L O Q A K A R N E O T T M Z E N X
I U I M G I E C P N P E D G N L V E N I F
S M C W A D C M Z I T F H I A F E N I I R
U P A N A I U E A C Z N A C J N I R G I E
M E M M O I D J M K A P E D T H A J N R E M
A N R K F E T L N A E T Y Y E U Q M E A M
A D A N R R G R G I N R E P F N B S R A
J Z H Q W E M R E R E I H S A C T P H A
T I P C E K L Q U S R E G N I S I I H
B Q V O N L P C V S T E A C H E R S B
C H E M I S T R N U R O L I A T D N J T
F U J R T M N U Q U X B G V A D I T O E
Y W W J M L V G X L V F M O B X Q C K R
```

On the Baseball Field

Transportation

Novels

Candy

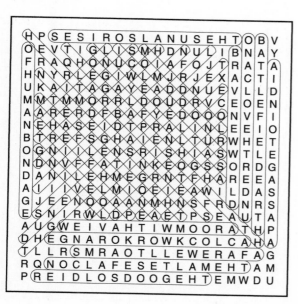

Lawyers

```
F F G Q W J Y R D I R S M L I V I C E Z
N P V R E N I A T E R E L A A D V I C E
P O G W E I W C T T F V V I C E T I C U
W M B R N G L K I I I B Z I T C V I B F
W K G E I D U C W U Z W T D I U R Z E
A L I V E E S U C R Q Q E W N E G S A E
W C K N J G V L J L Q H C J H W N A E S
T B T J H H A A F Q D L I A J L C C T X
G D W I P W G T N E T U C E S O R P E E
P D B Y B J Z A Q C H R A E W S S R C E
E V Q K B K I J F B E C Z S O M E A A I
X X L A N I M I R C W G N C T G E E F
A M A Z M L Q J L P A Y E T M R E E J
U W O B B D R T Y T M Z U B C A D E U
A B R X I P Y E N R O T T A O L H I U U
T W A D S N B T E Z T V L U D E C S S R
Y Z I P Y R X S K N K A N N O I T C A Y
V W G K I L A G E L I S N O M M U S B A
P K N E O S Q F D R E L O U M W D Y F Z
N F F P D Y I C T L V V T G B I P I O S
```

Greek Gods

```
G E V J S O E H O Y L C P Q N I K E S B
W T S N P T Q W B N J D Q B N Q Y P T U
G I S E Y S S N M D W N A H I G E R K X
P M C Q R S B I V U C P S U S Y N O I D
T V P R U A C S C M H M T A R E H P B A
B S G L E V Q S N R S E D A H Q O Y R K
A E Y U T T E A O S U E Z R Y S E N A P
R H N T H M E D P S U V G S E A T I S W
K E C Q R E I M U T Z C I I K A H U V
A I R E S T S E E S H M D J N Q C W L H
Z I H I E U H T J D E O X Y N E T O E S
Z U E S N P T S I T N S U R E U H E E P
X E O G R Y I S R A S E L U C R E H A A
A R P O Y S E A E E N O H P E S R E P E
E Z M H E H H S R A O L L O P A A T S R
L Y T M Y Y R E H S S I R E V T B U A
T C E L P R H E Z O I P F E Q A H R T O
Q N R N M T B L C K K R E H G V E W O N
A S O O E E M F E K K U I H Q A N Q O M
W S P A X D G S S A E R O B X V A G I M
```

Dinosaurs

```
E A N U R O G N A T H U S Z X R S S C Q
W U N O D O R U E L P O I L N U U S A V
S M S S U R U A S O E T A L P A L R L A
A U U T O O A I S Y L I N I D S T U S U
N L H T R R R T N O D O N Y C O A A U U
A O L C T E N N W D H S O G I L L O S D
S R D O U A P I I P F T C A U L S O I R
I X A O S S B T T T C X M V R A A N L U
N W O J N A O U O H H K K C Y F Z N C A
R C I L E A U N R S O O V P U R T A O S
O W L C R K L A G U E A O E H G W U Y H
S A H C K L A G U E A O E H G W U Y H
E Z D T J R A T I S D S N S E D Q T Y L
M C O E L O P H Y S I S A D T I R C R A
O S U R U A S O L Y K N A U Y E R B C H
R S U R U A S O N I E T E P R I S U E T
E A R U A S A N Y L L E A E L U U X S H
B U J B R A C H I O S A U R U S S S L P
I C S M E T R I O R H Y N C H U S M F O
R H A M P H O R H Y N C H U S E S A B G
```

Electronics

```
A L T E R N A T O R N B F T R G O D O D
G U L P K R A P S O R U E R I S M E S N
T Q A G G H R R T U S H D G C M D N C U
T Q N U E E F T O E R O E I R O E R I O
B E L A P N U G R T R E L O H A E R L R
R P N M E B E O A G I L S T S G H Q L G
R E U G H L T R N L A C A I R T E C O R
E J K S A C E I A T V C A A S P A C S O
M R U A U M N C O T E A H P O T O T O T
R P E D E T R R T L O C N C A M O R O U
O L N I H R T O E R B S O P C E R P B I
F I A G F E B C T L O O A E S S E B E R
S D I N L I T T K A R L N R N C A R T T
N L Y T I R T C I T L S Y E M T O E M S
A A U N O M I C C U A U D T T A K P E I
R O E D A R R E E T C N S E I C T D E D
T H E N T M L E O R O R P R N O C O U R D
Y A L E R E O R T C E Y I S I N V X R L
C I T A T S O R T C E L E C A C O I L E
D R R O T A L U G E R E G A T L O V I G
```

Sea

```
A A E W A Y I P N I Y L M S V Z V B R L
M Q I F H T O P I A B F N C V C X Y E Y
L W T V U K I E N V F N Z O Y P C V P Z
L U U Q W S O D E C B E X A A J Q O P A V
E T K D W I U V E Q E U D S C H J S I V
S B T C D S X G L S J R S T H N L K L W
S P M U T O Z D A C A T Y J T A W E C I
E O S T I Z C I L O J Z N D C T A T U N
V R L T W N L K B F W A U I A O V C I Y J
X T O E N X Z R R D R V T O H J E H Y J
Y M O R C K A W N A J U B M H K S B G A
A A P Z T T D Y M A A R E N O O H C S M
S W W S S X R A H N Y E L L A G H F N M
B M I L D K T A M G S E T E T L K E N E
J Y Y M D A M S D E N R K S G N B R C R
A H J U C P A H E D F I A A A A N R V B
C J B L R R N I R M O M D E L R Y Y X R
B G Z E J N Q P P G R S C B E Q X O S I
N B W V O W Q N I D E O E T O K X K V G
C K A X Q Y C E A N N M S M G W L V V S
```

Green Words

```
Q B N A V N U I D S Q B Y I P C F Y L F
T F V N U G P C A R D P E A K J E S S C
F C Z V M Y J E H J E O T L K Q B B T L
O R R M J J Y N A B R K A K G E P M R P
W I N T E R Y H P C C L E D R O L U O V
R X K C S P T W N A E L E E M N S H P B
E P D W C U R B B F L Y T A Y I S T A J
V D Z I T B A K L Y E F I Y I O X Y Y Y
E X M F L A P F E H C L X F E N M O O R
P D B E V J D K G T F N J B L N W Q P W
T A X S R F Z W A P E P P E R E S U O H
M A P G D W T O L T S V N C N E W W W G
X M Z V N B L M L P J A O A V T L E B E
V O R G Q I O K I W S L L I E G D A E S
G T A P L S T W V C D H L A R B X N S F
R W G U F V W T L Y D O Y O D H T C A P
K V C B M D V B U I H W C P O G L H X L
S S B J X B M Y U P N E C R F A E T B U
O D Q V G C T P E S R G N C T Y A N S A
A L V B W N G E R M J R E P M P G G C A
```

Chapter 3: Triplet Puzzles

Triplet 1

OUT: checkout, outsmart, outstretch

Triplet 2

KICK: kickstand, kick boxer, sidekick

Triplet 3

SHORT: sell short, shortfall, shortcake

Triplet 4

WASH: whitewash, brainwash, washcloth

Triplet 5

WORD: word processor, crossword, password

Triplet 6

HEART: sweetheart, heart attack, heartbreak

Triplet 7

SWEET: bittersweet, sweetheart, sweet tooth

Triplet 8

FIELD: minefield, force field, field trip

Triplet 9

SOUND: soundproof, sound effect, sound bite

Triplet 10

BOARD: boardwalk, baseboard, bulletin board

Triplet 11

SHOW: showdown, game show, showcase

Triplet 12

STOP: pit stop, stopgap, stopwatch

Triplet 13

OUT: blackout, outcast, breakout

Triplet 14

PEN: fountain pen, pen pal, bullpen

Triplet 15

CELL: stem cell, cell phone, cancer cell

Triplet 16

BREAD: white bread, breadwinner, breadstick

Triplet 17

TIME: bedtime, Christmastime, timekeeper

Triplet 18

HAND: backhand, firsthand, handheld

Triplet 19

BELL: bell-bottom, bluebell, dumbbell

Triplet 20

CHAIR: easy chair, chairman, highchair

Triplet 21

WHEEL: wheelchair, big wheel, cartwheel

Triplet 22

FOUR: fourscore, four-wheeler, four-eyes

Triplet 23

FLOOR: dance floor, floor plan, ground floor

Triplet 24

BALL: basketball, ballpoint, cornball

Triplet 25

UP: blowup, uproar, cleanup

Triplet 26

CHECK: checkbook, paycheck, checkmate

Triplet 27

BOARD: blackboard, boardroom, surfboard

Triplet 28

WASH: brainwash, washcloth, whitewash

Triplet 29

MOUTH: badmouth, mouthwash, loudmouth

Triplet 30

HONEY: honeymoon, honeydew, honeybee

Triplet 31

TAIL: coattail, tailgate, cottontail

Triplet 32

BREAK: breakneck, spring break, heartbreak

Triplet 33

DROP: raindrop, dropkick, gumdrop

Triplet 34

EYE: bull's-eye, eyewitness, eyeball

Triplet 35

TOOTH: toothpaste, sweet tooth, toothpick

Triplet 36

DOG: hotdog, dogwood, bulldog

Triplet 37

FIRE: ceasefire, firecracker, wildfire

Triplet 38

COFFEE: coffee bean, coffee table, coffee break

Triplet 39

LAND: landmark, landlocked, Iceland

Triplet 40

POLE: pole vault, fishing pole, north pole

Triplet 41

SHIP: flagship, shipshape, spaceship

Triplet 42

POWER: power trip, horsepower, power grid

Triplet 43

FREE: freeloader, carefree, freehand

Triplet 44

HOLD: stranglehold, holdup, household

Triplet 45

BODY: bodyguard, busybody, somebody

Triplet 46

WORK: homework, workbench, patchwork

Triplet 47

POINT: needlepoint, viewpoint, pinpoint

Triplet 48

CARD: flashcard, cardboard, postcard

Triplet 49

FRY: stir-fry, small fry, French fry

Triplet 50

HOUR: happy hour, hourglass, rush hour

Triplet 51

LITTLE: little dipper, chicken little, little league

Triplet 52

STREAM: bloodstream, mainstream, streamline

Triplet 53

COLD: common cold, cold cuts, cold shoulder

Triplet 54

RING: brass ring, ringworm, wedding ring

Triplet 55

PLATE: boilerplate, plate glass, paper plate

Triplet 56

LINE: linebacker, clothesline, borderline

Triplet 57

BASE: base station, home base, database

Triplet 58

PAGE: home page, page-turner, pageboy

Triplet 59

BACK: background, backpack, horseback

Triplet 60

STEP: stepladder, footstep, stepmother

Triplet 61

BOX: box office, soapbox, mailbox

Triplet 62

ZONE: combat zone, end zone, comfort zone

Triplet 63

PLAY: playground, playmate, wordplay

Triplet 64

PACK: six-pack, backpack, pack rat

Triplet 65

MAIL: mailbox, junk mail, blackmail

Triplet 66

BOOK: bookmarker, bookkeeper, yearbook

Triplet 67

STAR: starfish, superstar, stardust

Triplet 68

LETTER: scarlet letter, letterhead, love letter

Triplet 69

STOCK: laughingstock, Woodstock, stockbroker

Triplet 70

HOME: homecoming, motor home, homemaker

Triplet 71

ROOM: bathroom, roommate, classroom

Triplet 72

DUST: dust cover, sawdust, dust storm

Triplet 73

LIFE: lifesaver, wildlife, lifestyle

Triplet 74

CRY: cry wolf, battle cry, crybaby

Triplet 75

DOWN: countdown, meltdown, downstairs

Triplet 76

FLASH: flashbulb, newsflash, flashback

Triplet 77

PHOTO: photocopy, photo finish, photojournalism

Triplet 78

WATER: watermelon, dishwater, waterproof

Triplet 79

DUCK: lame duck, duck soup, sitting duck

Triplet 80

GIRL: flower girl, girl scout, girl Friday

Triplet 81

SHOP: shoplifter, barbershop, window-shop

Triplet 82

PARK: parallel park, parkway, trailer park

Triplet 83

END: end table, end zone, bitter end

Triplet 84

BRUSH: toothbrush, brush up, paintbrush

Triplet 85

CUP: buttercup, cupcake, suction cup

Triplet 86

PAPER: paper clip, paperback, newspaper

Triplet 87

HEART: heartache, artichoke heart, heartworm

Triplet 88

WILL: goodwill, willpower, living will

Triplet 89

BELLY: belly dance, belly button, pork belly

Triplet 90

WOOD: driftwood, woodchuck, redwood

Triplet 91

SHORT: shortcake, shortstop, shortwave

Triplet 92

NOTE: notebook, keynote, noteworthy

Triplet 93

LIGHT: light bulb, flashlight, moonlight

Triplet 94

UP: roundup, checkup, upstage

Triplet 95

SCORE: scorekeeper, underscore, fourscore

Triplet 96

YARD: courtyard, yardstick, yard sale

Triplet 97

FOOT: tenderfoot, footwear, foothill

Triplet 98

PRIME: prime minister, prime time, prime rate

Triplet 99

REPORT: underreport, report card, annual report

Triplet 100

BALL: blackball, cornball, ballroom

Triplet 101

AFTER: aftershock, afternoon, aftertaste

Triplet 102

CROSS: double cross, crosswind, cross-examine

Triplet 103

GAME: fair game, big game, game plan

Triplet 104

ORGAN: internal organ, organ grinder, organ donor

Triplet 105

OFF: buzz off, polish off, off-road

Triplet 106

CELL: cell phone, cellblock, blood cell

Triplet 107

LINE: battle line, party line, line drive

Triplet 108

ABOUT: runabout, about-face, turnabout

Triplet 109

DAY: day trade, rainy day, daylight

Triplet 110

SPRING: spring chicken, offspring, springboard

Triplet 111

HOME: homemade, nursing home, homespun

Triplet 112

SLIP: pink slip, slipknot, slipstream

Triplet 113

TANK: gas tank, tank top, think tank

Triplet 114

TREE: Christmas tree, treetop, tree-hugger

Triplet 115

EGG: goose egg, egg white, egghead

Triplet 116

FLY: fly ball, butterfly, dragonfly

Triplet 117

LINE: deadline, lineman, hairline

Triplet 118

WIRE: haywire, wire service, hotwire

Triplet 119

BLUE: bluegrass, baby blue, bluebird

Triplet 120

LAND: heartland, landlord, mainland

Triplet 121

ROAD: railroad, road rage, roadkill

Triplet 122

FACE: boldface, poker face, face card

Triplet 123

SHOT: big shot, gunshot, long shot

Triplet 124

BALL: mothball, ballpoint, ballroom

Triplet 125

KNOCK: knockdown, knock-knee, knockoff

Triplet 126

STOP: stopgap, stopwatch, shortstop

Triplet 127

BACK: drawback, backspace, horseback

Triplet 128

TALK: talk show, sweet talk, talk shop

Triplet 129

MASTER: mastermind, grand master, masterpiece

Triplet 130

GAME: word game, fair game, game plan

Triplet 131

PAPER: paperback, sandpaper, paper-thin

Triplet 132

WEATHER: weathervane, fair-weather, weatherproof

Triplet 133

MARK: hallmark, postmark, bookmark

Triplet 134

NOTE: footnote, notebook, keynote

Triplet 135

SHAKE: milkshake, shakedown, shakeup

Triplet 136

PITCH: sales pitch, pitch dark, fever pitch

Triplet 137

CHAIR: chairlift, highchair, armchair

Triplet 138

POINT: checkpoint, needlepoint, point blank

Triplet 139

DOG: top dog, doghouse, dog tag

Triplet 140

MOON: blue moon, honeymoon, moonstruck

Triplet 141

PACK: packhorse, backpack, fanny pack

Triplet 142

OVER: overcast, once-over, overdrive

Triplet 143

LIFE: still life, lifestyle, wildlife

Triplet 144

MONKEY: monkey bars, monkey business, monkey wrench

Triplet 145

SERVICE: answering service, Secret Service, service charge

Triplet 146

SCREEN: smokescreen, sunscreen, silkscreen

Triplet 147

CAR: carpet, carpool, car seat

Triplet 148

BROW: eyebrow, lowbrow, brow band

Triplet 149

PEN: penname, fountain pen, pen point

Triplet 150

PASS: pass away, overpass, passage

Triplet 151

BANK: piggy bank, bank account, bank note

Triplet 152

EYE: hawk eye, eyesore, eye socket

Triplet 153

STOCK: stock market, chicken stock, livestock

Triplet 154

LOVE: puppy love, loveless, lovebird

Triplet 155

RING: ringworm, ring finger, ring bearer

Triplet 156

ENGINE: engine block, engine room, engine driver

Triplet 157

TIRE: tire iron, tireless, tiresome

Triplet 158

LIGHT: taillight, light pollution, light show

Triplet 159

SLAP: slap shot, slapstick, slaphappy

Triplet 160

CLUB: club card, club sandwich, club soda

Triplet 161

STROKE: backstroke, stroke symptoms, pen stroke

Triplet 162

WORD: word game, crossword, word count

Triplet 163

BUTTON: button-down, button hole, button mushroom

Triplet 164

DOG: hot dog, dog catcher, dog-eared

Triplet 165

RELAY: relay race, relay switch, relay call

Triplet 166

HAIR: hairpin, body hair, hair dryer

Triplet 167

DIG: dig in, dig out, dig up

Triplet 168

ROOM: mushroom, roommate, room service

Chapter 4: Sudoku Puzzles

Sudoku Puzzle 1

1	5	2	9	4	7	3	6	8
3	4	6	2	8	1	9	7	5
8	9	7	5	3	6	2	1	4
4	2	8	1	7	5	6	9	3
9	3	1	4	6	8	5	2	7
6	7	5	3	9	2	4	8	1
5	1	4	7	2	9	8	3	6
7	6	9	8	5	3	1	4	2
2	8	3	6	1	4	7	5	9

Sudoku Puzzle 2

9	5	6	8	2	1	4	7	3
4	3	8	5	7	6	1	9	2
1	7	2	9	3	4	5	8	6
2	8	3	1	6	9	7	5	4
6	1	7	2	4	5	8	3	9
5	4	9	7	8	3	6	2	1
7	6	4	3	9	8	2	1	5
8	9	5	6	1	2	3	4	7
3	2	1	4	5	7	9	6	8

Sudoku Puzzle 3

2	7	6	5	9	8	3	4	1
8	4	1	2	7	3	6	9	5
5	9	3	4	1	6	8	7	2
7	3	8	6	2	4	5	1	9
6	1	4	9	8	5	7	2	3
9	5	2	7	3	1	4	8	6
1	6	5	8	4	9	2	3	7
3	8	7	1	5	2	9	6	4
4	2	9	3	6	7	1	5	8

Sudoku Puzzle 4

3	4	2	8	6	9	7	1	5
8	1	7	5	3	2	9	6	4
5	6	9	1	4	7	8	3	2
9	2	1	4	8	6	3	5	7
6	8	5	7	1	3	4	2	9
4	7	3	2	9	5	6	8	1
7	5	4	6	2	8	1	9	3
2	9	6	3	7	1	5	4	8
1	3	8	9	5	4	2	7	6

Sudoku Puzzle 5

6	2	8	7	9	1	3	5	4
1	3	4	8	6	5	7	2	9
7	9	5	4	3	2	8	6	1
5	1	7	9	4	8	6	3	2
9	4	3	5	2	6	1	8	7
2	8	6	3	1	7	9	4	5
8	7	1	2	5	3	4	9	6
3	5	9	6	7	4	2	1	8
4	6	2	1	8	9	5	7	3

Sudoku Puzzle 6

1	4	3	2	9	7	5	6	8
5	2	7	4	8	6	9	3	1
6	9	8	1	5	3	4	7	2
7	5	9	3	2	1	8	4	6
4	3	1	5	6	8	2	9	7
8	6	2	9	7	4	3	1	5
9	1	5	6	4	2	7	8	3
3	7	4	8	1	5	6	2	9
2	8	6	7	3	9	1	5	4

Sudoku Puzzle 7

3	7	4	9	5	6	2	8	1
2	9	5	1	3	8	6	7	4
1	6	8	4	7	2	5	9	3
8	1	2	7	9	4	3	5	6
6	4	3	8	1	5	9	2	7
9	5	7	2	6	3	4	1	8
4	8	9	3	2	7	1	6	5
5	3	1	6	8	9	7	4	2
7	2	6	5	4	1	8	3	9

Sudoku Puzzle 8

8	4	7	1	6	2	5	9	3
5	6	1	3	7	9	2	4	8
9	3	2	4	8	5	7	1	6
6	7	3	8	2	4	9	5	1
1	5	9	7	3	6	4	8	2
2	8	4	5	9	1	6	3	7
7	1	6	9	5	3	8	2	4
4	2	5	6	1	8	3	7	9
3	9	8	2	4	7	1	6	5

Sudoku Puzzle 9

3	2	5	7	4	1	8	6	9
1	9	7	2	8	6	3	4	5
8	4	6	9	3	5	7	2	1
2	5	1	8	6	7	9	3	4
6	7	8	4	9	3	1	5	2
9	3	4	5	1	2	6	7	8
7	8	9	6	2	4	5	1	3
5	1	2	3	7	9	4	8	6
4	6	3	1	5	8	2	9	7

Sudoku Puzzle 10

6	4	2	8	1	9	7	3	5
7	5	1	3	6	2	8	4	9
9	3	8	5	4	7	6	1	2
8	6	9	7	3	5	1	2	4
5	2	4	1	9	8	3	7	6
3	1	7	4	2	6	9	5	8
1	7	5	9	8	4	2	6	3
2	8	3	6	5	1	4	9	7
4	9	6	2	7	3	5	8	1

Sudoku Puzzle 11

6	9	5	3	1	8	7	4	2
4	7	8	2	6	9	5	3	1
1	3	2	7	5	4	8	6	9
2	4	7	9	8	1	6	5	3
8	1	6	5	4	3	2	9	7
3	5	9	6	2	7	1	8	4
5	6	4	1	9	2	3	7	8
9	2	3	8	7	5	4	1	6
7	8	1	4	3	6	9	2	5

Sudoku Puzzle 12

9	1	3	8	6	4	5	7	2
7	5	8	3	2	9	6	1	4
2	6	4	5	1	7	3	8	9
4	3	5	7	8	2	1	9	6
8	7	9	1	5	6	4	2	3
6	2	1	9	4	3	8	5	7
5	4	2	6	7	8	9	3	1
1	9	7	4	3	5	2	6	8
3	8	6	2	9	1	7	4	5

Sudoku Puzzle 13

8	1	6	5	7	4	9	3	2
2	3	4	8	1	9	7	6	5
7	9	5	6	3	2	1	4	8
5	6	7	2	4	1	8	9	3
3	4	1	9	8	6	2	5	7
9	2	8	7	5	3	6	1	4
1	7	9	3	2	5	4	8	6
6	8	3	4	9	7	5	2	1
4	5	2	1	6	8	3	7	9

Sudoku Puzzle 14

4	6	1	7	3	2	5	8	9
5	3	2	8	9	4	7	6	1
8	9	7	5	1	6	4	2	3
1	2	9	4	8	3	6	7	5
6	7	8	9	2	5	3	1	4
3	5	4	6	7	1	8	9	2
2	1	5	3	6	7	9	4	8
9	4	6	2	5	8	1	3	7
7	8	3	1	4	9	2	5	6

Sudoku Puzzle 15

1	5	7	3	8	2	9	4	6
8	9	6	4	5	1	7	2	3
2	4	3	6	7	9	1	8	5
5	2	9	1	3	8	4	6	7
7	3	1	2	4	6	8	5	9
4	6	8	7	9	5	2	3	1
3	8	5	9	1	4	6	7	2
9	7	2	8	6	3	5	1	4
6	1	4	5	2	7	3	9	8

Sudoku Puzzle 16

3	7	6	8	2	5	4	1	9
4	8	1	7	3	9	5	6	2
2	5	9	1	6	4	8	7	3
8	9	5	4	1	2	6	3	7
6	2	4	9	7	3	1	5	8
7	1	3	6	5	8	9	2	4
1	4	7	2	8	6	3	9	5
9	3	2	5	4	1	7	8	6
5	6	8	3	9	7	2	4	1

Sudoku Puzzle 17

2	3	1	4	9	8	5	7	6
8	4	5	2	7	6	1	9	3
9	6	7	5	1	3	4	2	8
5	7	2	9	6	4	3	8	1
6	1	4	3	8	7	9	5	2
3	8	9	1	5	2	6	4	7
4	5	8	7	3	1	2	6	9
1	2	6	8	4	9	7	3	5
7	9	3	6	2	5	8	1	4

Sudoku Puzzle 18

7	6	2	3	5	9	1	4	8
1	3	9	4	6	8	2	5	7
5	8	4	2	1	7	3	9	6
3	1	7	6	4	2	9	8	5
2	9	6	5	8	1	4	7	3
4	5	8	9	7	3	6	1	2
6	4	1	8	2	5	7	3	9
9	7	5	1	3	6	8	2	4
8	2	3	7	9	4	5	6	1

Sudoku Puzzle 19

7	3	8	9	2	5	1	4	6
1	5	6	8	3	4	9	2	7
4	9	2	6	1	7	3	5	8
2	1	3	4	7	8	6	9	5
9	6	7	2	5	3	4	8	1
8	4	5	1	6	9	2	7	3
5	2	9	3	8	1	7	6	4
6	7	1	5	4	2	8	3	9
3	8	4	7	9	6	5	1	2

Sudoku Puzzle 20

3	5	8	1	6	7	4	2	9
4	7	9	8	2	5	3	1	6
2	1	6	4	9	3	7	8	5
8	3	4	9	5	1	6	7	2
1	9	5	2	7	6	8	3	4
6	2	7	3	8	4	5	9	1
7	6	1	5	3	2	9	4	8
5	8	2	7	4	9	1	6	3
9	4	3	6	1	8	2	5	7

Sudoku Puzzle 21

8	1	3	7	6	2	5	9	4
4	5	6	3	1	9	7	2	8
9	7	2	4	8	5	3	1	6
3	4	1	9	5	7	6	8	2
2	6	5	8	4	3	9	7	1
7	9	8	6	2	1	4	3	5
6	3	4	1	7	8	2	5	9
5	8	9	2	3	4	1	6	7
1	2	7	5	9	6	8	4	3

Sudoku Puzzle 22

4	3	5	6	7	2	9	1	8
7	8	1	9	3	4	6	2	5
6	2	9	5	8	1	4	7	3
3	5	7	4	2	6	1	8	9
2	1	6	7	9	8	5	3	4
8	9	4	1	5	3	7	6	2
5	7	8	2	6	9	3	4	1
9	4	3	8	1	7	2	5	6
1	6	2	3	4	5	8	9	7

Sudoku Puzzle 23

9	1	3	4	8	6	5	2	7
2	4	8	3	5	7	1	6	9
5	6	7	9	1	2	4	3	8
1	8	5	6	4	3	7	9	2
4	9	6	2	7	8	3	5	1
7	3	2	1	9	5	6	8	4
6	7	9	5	2	1	8	4	3
3	2	1	8	6	4	9	7	5
8	5	4	7	3	9	2	1	6

Sudoku Puzzle 24

7	9	1	2	5	3	6	4	8
4	6	2	8	7	9	1	5	3
3	8	5	1	6	4	2	7	9
5	7	6	4	9	2	8	3	1
1	4	3	7	8	6	9	2	5
9	2	8	3	1	5	4	6	7
8	1	4	6	3	7	5	9	2
6	3	9	5	2	8	7	1	4
2	5	7	9	4	1	3	8	6

Sudoku Puzzle 25

2	7	4	8	6	5	3	1	9
3	8	6	9	1	7	2	4	5
1	9	5	2	4	3	8	6	7
5	3	7	4	9	1	6	2	8
9	1	2	3	8	6	7	5	4
6	4	8	7	5	2	1	9	3
4	2	9	1	3	8	5	7	6
8	6	1	5	7	4	9	3	2
7	5	3	6	2	9	4	8	1

Sudoku Puzzle 26

4	8	7	6	9	2	1	3	5
3	2	9	4	5	1	7	8	6
1	6	5	3	8	7	9	2	4
5	3	8	2	4	9	6	7	1
2	1	4	7	6	5	8	9	3
9	7	6	1	3	8	4	5	2
6	9	2	8	1	3	5	4	7
8	4	3	5	7	6	2	1	9
7	5	1	9	2	4	3	6	8

Sudoku Puzzle 27

1	4	5	6	7	3	9	8	2
8	2	6	4	1	9	7	5	3
9	3	7	8	2	5	6	1	4
6	5	9	3	8	2	1	4	7
4	1	8	9	5	7	2	3	6
2	7	3	1	6	4	5	9	8
7	9	2	5	4	8	3	6	1
3	8	1	7	9	6	4	2	5
5	6	4	2	3	1	8	7	9

Sudoku Puzzle 28

1	2	5	4	6	8	3	9	7
7	3	4	9	1	2	8	6	5
8	6	9	3	7	5	4	2	1
5	7	3	8	2	6	9	1	4
6	4	8	1	9	7	2	5	3
9	1	2	5	3	4	7	8	6
2	8	7	6	4	1	5	3	9
3	5	6	7	8	9	1	4	2
4	9	1	2	5	3	6	7	8

Chapter 5: Lost and Found

Lost and Found 1

A	L	L			P	R	A	Y
R		I	T	S			R	
C	A	K	E		H	A	T	
H		E	N	T	E	R		
	E	L	D	E	S	T		
A		Y	E	A		I	L	L
R			N			S		A
C	O	N	C	E	P	T		V
			Y			S	E	A

Lost and Found 2

K	N	O	B		L	I	P	S
	O		I		A		I	
P	O	S	S	I	B	L	E	
	N		C		E	A	S	E
A		U	G	L	Y			A
L		I		S	E	W	S	
L	I	F	T			R		I
O		O		P	A	S	T	E
W	A	X						R

Lost and Found 3

M			C		T	U	B	
O		M	U	M			A	
D	R	I	P		C	A	S	H
E		R		W	O	R	E	
R		A	P	A	R	T		
A	C	C	O	R	D	I	N	G
T	A	L	E			S		O
E	L	E	M	E	N	T		E
	L							S

Lost and Found 4

	S		B	O	M	B		C
S	P	Y				E		A
	E		R		N	A	P	
A	C	H	I	E	V	E		
	I		A		F		S	
E	F	F	E	C	T	I	V	E
A	I	R		H	I	T		E
S	C	O	R	E	D			M
Y		G		D	E	A	L	S

Lost and Found 5

A	C	T		H			W	
	H			I		P	E	N
P	R	E	S	S	U	R	E	
	I		A		O	D	D	
	S		V	E	R	B		I
	T	O	E			A	G	E
	I			O		B	U	S
F	A	R	E	W	E	L	L	
	N			N			E	L	F

Lost and Found 6

H	O	T	E	L		Z	I	P
E				A	R	E		E
R		A		P	E	R		A
O		B			S	O	N	
E		S	I	T	E		A	
S	E	E			M	I	S	S
	A	N	D			B		T
A	C	T	U	A	L	L	Y	
	H		E		E			

Lost and Found 7

M	A	R	S			S	
I		U		G	L	A	D
D	I	G		R		C	
D			E		R		
A	L	P	H	A	B	E	T
Y		H	A	T	E	D	S
	J	O	B		A		I
		T	I	C	K		Z
	H	O	T		S	A	K	E

Lost and Found 8

	D		E	F	F	O	R	T
D	I	D		O			I	
R	A	I	L	R	O	A	D	
A	L	S	O				C	
G		T	O	R	C	H		R
	G	A	S	O	L	I	N	E
R		N	E	W	E	R		W
I		C		R	E	D	S	
M	E	E	T		K			

Lost and Found 9

H	A	D		U		A	D	D
E			U	S	E		E	
L			U		O	N	E	
P	R	O	B	A	B	L	Y	
	A			L	E	D		
	F		F	L	Y		S	
A	T	E		Y	O	L	K	
N		A			N		I	
Y	E	T			D	U	M	P

Lost and Found 10

		B		D		P		H
T	H	E	R	E	F	O	R	E
E		L		V	A	P	O	R
X		O	M	I	T		B	
T	O	W		L	A	B	O	R
B			T		L	A	T	E
O	A	S	I	S		I		D
O			L	I	S	T	S	
K	N	E	L	T				

Lost and Found 11

		L		B		D	
	I	S	O	L	A	T	E	D
M		O	V	E	R		C	
I		M	E	T		B	I	T
S	H	E		S		S		
T		T			A	X	I	S
S	A	I	L	O	R		O	
		M		A	M	O	N	G
	L	E	A	K				

Lost and Found 12

	R			C	R	E	P	T
H	E	M				L		
	S			F	O	U	R	
S	U	N	S		U		M	
	L		E	U	R	O	P	E
O	T	H	E	R	S			A
U	S	I	N	G		D		G
R		P		E	Q	U	A	L
S		S				G		E

Lost and Found 13

```
E . . . . P L O T
C U B I C . I . O
H . A . O . P A W
O C C U R S . . E
. H O S P I T A L
H O N E S T . W .
. I . F . S E A S
G R O U P . . R .
. . . L . H I D .
```

Lost and Found 14

```
S . . . U P S E T
C O I L . . T . U
A . N . S A I L S
R . T O O . T . K
. . E . F O C U S
B E N E A T H . .
A . D . . H E A D
L . E D G E S . A
L A D . . R . . D
```

Lost and Found 15

```
J A Z Z . K I L L
. . . I N N . A .
S I G N . E . W .
. D E C R E A S E
B E T . . . I . V
. A . A . E D G E
B L O W . A . . N
. S W E E T E S T
. . E . . S . . .
```

Lost and Found 16

```
E . . A F F A I R
X . M O . . . . A
A G I N G . W . I
M . X . . M I N D
I . . . C A N E .
N . P . L I K E S
E A R N E D . D .
. . E . A . P E G
A N Y O N E . D .
```

Lost and Found 17

```
. I N C R E A S E
B . U . . . R . .
E V I L . T E A R
D . S . G R A B .
. D A I L Y . L .
P I N . A . W E T
. S C A R C E . A
S C E N E . B I G
. O . T . . . . .
```

Lost and Found 18

```
O W L . . . . L .
. H O P . L E A F
N O W A D A Y S .
A . . J . N E T .
T . B A N G . E .
U . . M O U N D .
R . D A T A . . T
E Y E S . G . . W
. . W . T E M P O
```

Lost and Found 19

```
B U I L D S . E .
U . O . C R Y . .
L E S S . D . O .
B L O S S O M S .
. S M E L T . I .
G E E S E . T O Y
. . D . E A R N .
G R A S P . E . .
. Y . Y I E L D .
```

Lost and Found 20

```
. H E R O I N E S
. E . . . . E . E
O R G A N . W O N
. I . G U Y . . D
S T I R R E D . S
. A . E S S A Y .
A G R E E . M A T
. E . D R Y . R .
. . . . Y . E N D
```

Lost and Found 21

```
C H I N A . C U T
A . . N . I . O .
R . B . A N G R Y
. H O W L . A . S
G O D . Y A R D .
. R I B S . . R .
. R E L I G I O N
N O S E S . . W .
. R . W . F A N .
```

Lost and Found 22

```
S H R I L L . P .
. I . . O . . L .
. S O F T . J A W
. T . E . P E T .
. O P E R A T E D
. R E L A Y . A .
D Y E . I S S U E
. . L . L . I . .
F I S H . O X E N
```

Lost and Found 23

```
. G A P . . . R .
R A G . M A K E S
. S O L O . . A .
. . A V O I D . .
. H I K E . V E T
R E M E M B E R .
E R A . E . . . .
L E G . N . . . .
Y . E I T H E R .
```

Lost and Found 24

```
H . . . R . O . .
I . A P P E A R S
M O M . . L I D .
. . E . A I M E D
. W R O N G . R .
S . I . K I T . A
O . C . L O A D S
A M A T E U R . K
K . N . . S . S .
```

Lost and Found 25

O	U	T	P	U	T		G	
U					H	A	L	L
N	I	B		R		U		
C		E	X	C	U	S	E	
E		G		A	S	K		E
	F	U	N	C	T	I	O	N
		N	U	T				D
			T	U	R	T	L	E
	B	O	S	S				D

Lost and Found 26

A	S	H		C	U	B		O
	E		U		O	U	R	
E	V	E	N			R		A
	E	X	T	E	R	N	A	L
I	N	C	O	M	E		P	
C		E		P	A	I	R	S
E		S	E	T	S		O	
		S		Y	O	U	N	G
				N		S		

Lost and Found 27

C	O	N	C	E	P	T	S	
	A		O		R		C	
	T		P	O	O	R	E	R
	H	A	Y		G	O	N	E
C		C			R	A	T	S
R		C		B	A	D		P
I	D	E	A		M			O
E		S		S	O	O	N	
D	U	S	T	Y				D

Lost and Found 28

			C					
A		N	E	E	D	L	E	S
U		E	R					O
G	U	I	D	E		C		N
U		T		A	T	O	M	S
S	C	H	O	L	A	R		
T	I	E	D		S	K	I	P
	T	R	O	U	T			A
	Y		R		E	X	I	T

Chapter 6: Double Scrambles

Will They Come Out Tonight?

- SHEEP
- SKILL
- TEARS
- APRIL
- RELAX

STARS

Yes or No

- YOUNG
- BEARS
- EXACT
- ALLOW
- MONEY

MAYBE

Makes a Boat Go

- LEDGE
- SWORD
- ADULT
- SEVEN
- INDEX

SAILS

Out of This World

- RADIO
- TEACH
- IDEAS
- OATHS
- BADGE

ORBIT

Take Away

- NORTH
- SPILL
- IRONS
- URBAN
- MARRY

MINUS

Abracadabra

- COULD
- GRADE
- AGREE
- MOTOR
- IDEAL

MAGIC

How to Get an A

- SCRAP
- DRAIN
- UNCLE
- THUMB
- YOUTH

STUDY

Made with Bread

- STUNT
- TOWER
- TIMID
- AGENT
- OASIS

TOAST

Dry Off

- OCEAN
- LIGHT
- EMPTY
- WORRY
- TRICK

TOWEL

Black and White All Over

- ROOTS
- ZIPPY
- ESSAY
- AWARE
- BORED

ZEBRA

Room at the Top

- CRISP
- TABLE
- ARGUE
- TORCH
- IMAGE

ATTIC

Pioneer Vehicle

- WIDOW
- OWNER
- GRAPH
- NAMES
- ACTOR

WAGON

Slow Mover

- AMUSE
- LABEL
- INPUT
- NANNY
- SWAMP

SNAIL

Not Once, Not Three Times

- COLOR
- WITCH
- IRONY
- ENEMY
- TEASE

TWICE

Why Are You So Sour?

- MERRY
- LINEN
- EVERY
- OPERA
- NOISE

LEMON

One Hump or Two?

- LOVER
- MAYOR
- CHOIR
- EVENT
- ANKLE

CAMEL

A Wake-Up Call

- RANCH
- ANNOY
- AWOKE
- LAUGH
- MOOSE

ALARM

Owns a Pitchfork

- DISCO
- LARGE
- ERROR
- ISSUE
- VOCAL

DEVIL

That's Funny

- HOBBY
- OLIVE
- RAPID
- UNTIL
- MUSIC

HUMOR

A Thousand

- NAVAL
- RHYME
- GEESE
- ARRAY
- DREAM

GRAND

You Like

- YIELD
- OUNCE
- JUICY
- ELBOW
- NINTH

ENJOY

Would You Like a Burger with Those?

- ITEMS
- FANCY
- SHIRT
- RIGHT
- ELVES

FRIES

Neigh Sayer

- OFTEN
- EAGLE
- REACH
- HABIT
- SHARP

HORSE

Nonsense

- LIMIT
- YOURS
- INNER
- SHINE
- LEVER

SILLY

It May Be Wild

- EARLY
- SANDY
- SCORE
- GIANT
- UNION

GUESS

See It in a Parade

- AVOID
- FRESH
- LUCKY
- TEETH
- ORDER

FLOAT

They Are Open or Shut

- RANGE
- DIARY
- SALAD
- OTHER
- ORGAN

DOORS

Purchase at a Nursery

- LUNAR
- ABOUT
- NOVEL
- THEME
- POINT

PLANT

Tie the Knot

- ROAST
- MAYBE
- YOUTH
- AGAIN
- ROBIN

MARRY

Surgeon's Assistant

- EARLY
- NOBLE
- RURAL
- UNCLE
- SLEEP

NURSE

Charlie Chaplin Persona

- PITCH
- ANGEL
- MAJOR
- REACH
- TIMID

TRAMP

Rocker Site

- READY
- OCCUR
- HOUSE
- POINT
- CHAIR

PORCH

Grown-Up Kids

- GREAT
- ALIEN
- OTHER
- THIEF
- STEEP

GOATS

Fable Finale

- AGENT
- RIVER
- MOVIE
- OPERA
- LARGE

MORAL

Pasta Topper

- UNTIL
- CHEEK
- SCORE
- AFTER
- ENTER

SAUCE

Classroom or Poolroom Item

- KNELT
- HAUNT
- LODGE
- ARISE
- CHOIR

CHALK

It's Stuck in the Corner

- MINOR
- ARRAY
- PANEL
- TEASE
- SPILL

STAMP

Three, They Say

- RAZOR
- DREAM
- WRECK
- COMIC
- OFTEN

CROWD

Give a Hoot

- SHAPE
- OLIVE
- TIGER
- USUAL
- HONEY

SHOUT

Prepare for Surgery

- RHYME
- UPPER
- COLOR
- BACON
- SEVEN

SCRUB

Tot Watcher

- ADDED
- NOVEL
- YIELD
- NOISE
- NEVER

NANNY

Cold Covering

- SUPER
- RATIO
- TEMPO
- FLOOR
- ORBIT

FROST

Syrup Source

- LABOR
- ALARM
- EXACT
- PANIC
- MAGIC

MAPLE

Toward Santa's Pole

- NIGHT
- OUNCE
- TEACH
- HAPPY
- RELAX

NORTH

First Anniversary Gift

- PILOT
- ALOUD
- ROYAL
- PEACE
- ELDER

PAPER

Out of Practice

- RAPID
- SIGHT
- TASTE
- YACHT
- UNION

RUSTY

One of the Deadly Sins

- RIGID
- DOZEN
- EVENT
- PULSE
- IDEAL

PRIDE

Cheese Choice

- STAFF
- SCARE
- IMAGE
- WORRY
- STEAK

SWISS

Uncle Sam Feature

- APRON
- BERRY
- DIRTY
- RADIO
- EQUAL

BEARD

'70s Hot Spot

- IDEAS
- SILKY
- DOLLY
- ORGAN
- CRAFT

DISCO

Diametrically Opposite

- ONION
- ALIVE
- LASSO
- PLANT
- RANCH

POLAR

Dining Room Staple

- TORCH
- LEVEL
- ESSAY
- BLEND
- ANKLE

TABLE

Worthless Wheels

- MERCY
- LAUGH
- EMPTY
- NERVE
- OASIS

LEMON

Conversation Starter

- LIGHT
- HANDY
- LEARN
- ENEMY
- OCEAN

HELLO

Some Canines

- HOTEL
- THINK
- ENJOY
- THANK
- EAGLE

TEETH

Rosetta Stone Language

- GRACE
- EATEN
- KNIFE
- EIGHT
- ROMAN

GREEK

Chapter 7: Crosswords

Crossword Puzzle 1

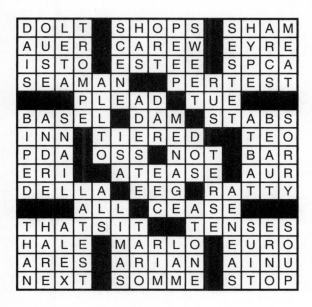

Crossword Puzzle 2

Crossword Puzzle 3

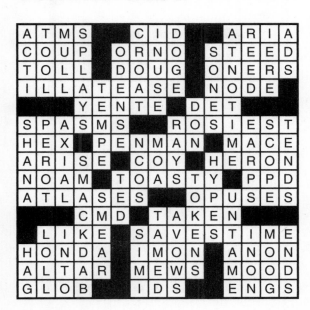

Crossword Puzzle 4

Crossword Puzzle 5

Crossword Puzzle 6

Crossword Puzzle 7

Crossword Puzzle 8

Crossword Puzzle 9

H	A	T	S		A	B	A	B	A		M	A	R	G
A	W	H	O		R	A	V	E	L		D	A	B	A
N	A	I	L		S	H	I	R	E		S	H	I	M
D	Y	N	A	M	O		D	E	P	R	E	S	S	
			C	I	N	C		F	H	A				
M	O	D	E	S		H	A	T		Y	A	L	U	
T	H	O		T	H	A	N		D	E	L	A	N	O
S	Y	N	S		O	T	E	R	I		G	U	S	T
T	E	N	A	N	T		N	U	N	S		R	E	T
	S	E	G	O		S	T	E		Y	E	A	R	S
		M	O	E		D	E	N	S					
	A	D	H	E	R	E	S		L	E	T	H	A	L
O	H	I	O		C	O	R	N	Y		H	E	M	I
P	O	O	P		A	U	T	O	S		E	X	A	M
T	Y	R	E		S	T	A	G	E		R	A	J	A

Crossword Puzzle 10

Y	S	E	R		D	E	B	I			T	U	M	
M	O	L	E	S		E	S	A	U		A	O	N	E
C	O	A	T	I		N	T	H	D	E	G	R	E	E
A	N	S		L	I	T	E	S		A	R	E	A	S
			T	O	O	L	E	R		C	R	E	A	S	E
N	O	I	D	E	A			D	E	L	E	T	E	
R	I	C	E	D		F	O	A	L	E	D			
C	D	S			B	O	R	I	S			W	E	S
			E	M	E	N	D	S		G	L	I	N	T
	A	R	D	E	N	T			T	H	E	R	O	D
G	O	E	S	A	T		O	T	I	O	S	E		
A	R	C	E	D		F	A	R	M	S		H	E	S
S	T	A	L	E	M	A	T	E		T	I	A	R	A
P	I	N	S		T	M	E	N		S	C	I	O	N
E	C	T		V	E	N	D			U	R	S	A	

Crossword Puzzle 11

O	R	A	L		A	R	A	T		R	A	S	T	A
M	I	N	E		T	A	C	O		A	S	E	A	T
B	A	I	N		A	C	E	R		T	A	N	T	O
	S	L	O	A	N	E		A	M	E		D	I	M
			R	E	E	D	S		O	R	S			
	S	T	E	R	N		T	I	S		A	L	E	F
I	T	O		A	D	M	E	N		S	M	E	A	R
S	E	E	I	T		A	R	R		C	E	A	S	E
A	L	I	N	E		R	E	E	S	E		S	T	D
K	E	N	T		S	L	O		I	N	S	T	S	
		O	N	S		S	A	N	T	A				
L	A	D		O	A	T		L	A	S	S	I	E	
A	L	E	R	O		A	S	I	T		S	O	S	O
M	I	L	A	N		B	R	E	R		E	N	T	O
S	E	I	N	E		S	A	N	A		D	E	A	F

Crossword Puzzle 12

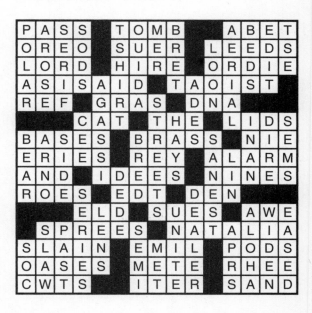

P	A	S	S		T	O	M	B			A	B	E	T
O	R	E	O		S	U	E	R		L	E	E	D	S
L	O	R	D		H	I	R	E		O	R	D	I	E
A	S	I	S	A	I	D		T	A	O	I	S	T	
R	E	F		G	R	A	S		D	N	A			
			C	A	T		T	H	E		L	I	D	S
B	A	S	E	S		B	R	A	S	S		N	I	E
E	R	I	E	S		R	E	Y		A	L	A	R	M
A	N	D		I	D	E	E	S		N	I	N	E	S
R	O	E	S		E	D	T		D	E	N			
			E	L	D		S	U	E	S		A	W	E
	S	P	R	E	E	S		N	A	T	A	L	I	A
S	L	A	I	N		E	M	I	L		P	O	D	S
O	A	S	E	S		M	E	T	E		R	H	E	E
C	W	T	S		I	T	E	R		S	A	N	D	

Crossword Puzzle 13

F	I	B	S		E	D	G	E	R		H	A	I	L
L	O	R	I		T	O	I	L	E		Y	V	E	S
A	N	A	T		H	A	L	O	S		D	I	R	T
K	A	S	E	M		D	I	O	C	E	S	E		
		D	I	P	S		S	D	I					
M	C	A		T	O	T	I	E		A	R	P	S	
A	R	M		T	I	E	D		R	O	I	L	E	D
D	I	E	M		S	T	E	N	O		G	A	G	A
D	E	B	O	N	E		N	U	M	B		T	A	N
	D	A	D	O		F	T	L	E	E		E	R	G
		G	P	O		L	O	T	S					
	S	E	N	S	O	R	Y		H	A	C	K	S	
D	E	W	Y		L	O	O	P	Y		C	H	E	R
A	M	O	S		A	N	G	I	E		K	I	R	I
M	I	K	E		R	E	A	C	T		S	A	N	S

Crossword Puzzle 14

E	G	G	A	R		C	U	P	S		O	S	S	O
S	O	A	V	E		A	G	R	I		C	H	A	P
P	A	G	E	S		R	O	O	F		H	A	R	T
	D	E	N	I	S		S	T	O	O	L	I	E	
		U	N	I	T		E	E	C		L	S	D	
H	Y	P	E		S	O	L		R	E	W			
I	A	L		T	I	T	A	N		A	B	O	I	L
T	R	E	V	I		E	C	O		N	A	N	C	E
E	D	D	I	E		M	E	A	L	S		N	A	V
			S	U	B		S	H	O		T	O	N	I
I	R	V		P	E	T		S	A	K	E			
D	E	E	P	S	E	A		D	E	E	P	S		
T	U	T	U		T	M	E	N		A	H	A	L	F
A	S	T	R		L	I	K	E		T	E	N	O	R
G	E	E	R		E	L	E	V		S	E	T	G	O

Chapter 8: Diagramless

Diagramless 1

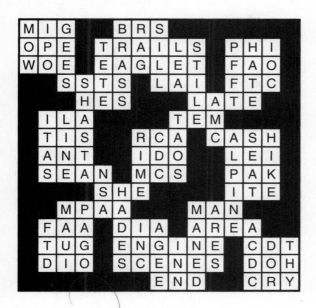

Diagramless 2

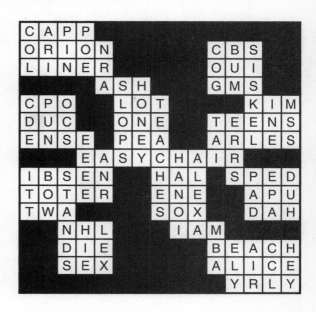

Diagramless 3

Diagramless 4

Diagramless 5

Diagramless 6

Diagramless 7

Diagramless 8

Diagramless 9

Diagramless 10

Diagramless 11

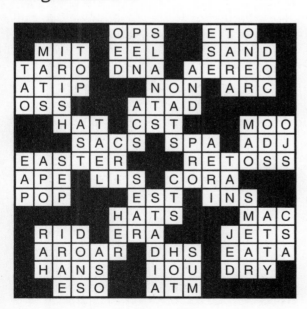

Diagramless 12

Diagramless 13

Diagramless 14

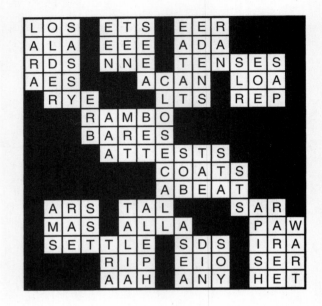

Chapter 9: Word Ladders

These puzzles have many possible solutions. Here are some answers; yours might be different.

Word Ladder 1

PUP, PUG, DUG, DOG

Word Ladder 2

PRO, BRO, BOO, COO, CON

Word Ladder 3

ONE, OWE, OWL, OIL, TIL, TIN, TEN

Word Ladder 4

MOM, MOD, MAD, DAD

Word Ladder 5

BOY, BAY, MAY, MAN

Word Ladder 6

TEE, BEE, BET, BAT, OAT, OFT, OFF

Word Ladder 7

BELL, SELL, SILL, SILK, SINK, RINK, RING

Word Ladder 8

WILD, MILD, MILE, TILE, TALE, TAME

Word Ladder 9

GIVE, HIVE, HIKE, TIKE, TAKE

Word Ladder 10

DRAG, BRAG, BRAD, BEAD, BEAK, BECK, BACK, RACK, RACE

Word Ladder 11

YEAR, BEAR, BOAR, BOOR, BOOK

Word Ladder 12

WORK, CORK, CORE, CARE, CASE, CASH

Word Ladder 13

SHIFT, SHIRT, SHIRK, SHARK, SPARK, SPARS, SEARS, GEARS

Word Ladder 14

WORDS, CORDS, CORKS, COOKS, BOOKS

Word Ladder 15

WALK, WALE, PALE, PATE, PATH

Word Ladder 16

HEAD, HEED, TEED, TOED, TOES

Word Ladder 17

PUSH, HUSH, HUSK, HULK, HULL, PULL

Word Ladder 18

FAIR, FAIL, FOIL, FOOL, FOOD, GOOD

Word Ladder 19

TREE, TREY, GREY, GRAY, GRAD, GOAD, GOOD, WOOD

Word Ladder 20

TRICK, CRICK, CROCK, CROAK, CREAK, BREAK, BREAD, TREAD, TREAT

Word Ladder 21

RISE, RILE, FILE, FILL, FALL

Word Ladder 22

PIG, BIG, BAG, HAG, HAM

Word Ladder 23

RATE, BATE, BITE, BIKE, HIKE

Word Ladder 24

SWEET, SHEET, SHEER, SHIER, SHIES, STIES, STIRS, STARS, SEARS, HEARS, HEART

Word Ladder 25

DOC, DOE, JOE, JOY, SOY, SLY, FLY, FLU

Word Ladder 26

PLAY, CLAY, CLOY, CLOP, COOP, COMP, CAMP, CAME, GAME

Word Ladder 27

FARM, FORM, FORD, FOOD

Word Ladder 28

MIXED, MIRED, WIRED, WIRES, WARES, WARNS, WAINS, PAINS, PAINT, PRINT, PRINK, DRINK

Word Ladder 29

LOG, LAG, TAG, TAR, OAR

Word Ladder 30

TIME, TILE, TILL, TELL, BELL

Word Ladder 31

SEND, SAND, SANE, SAME, SOME, HOME

Word Ladder 32

KISS, KIDS, AIDS, AIDE, TIDE, TILE, TILL, TELL

Word Ladder 33

BEE, WEE, WED, WAD, WAX

Word Ladder 34

PLAY, CLAY, CLAW, FLAW, FLOW, GLOW, GROW

Word Ladder 35

TOWN, TORN, CORN, CORE, CURE, CUTE, CITE, CITY

Word Ladder 36

OUTER, CUTER, CURER, CURED, CARED, CAKED, BAKED

Word Ladder 37

TIGER, TIMER, TIMES, TILES, MILES, MALES, MATES, MATED

Word Ladder 38

SIREN, SIRES, FIRES, FARES, FADES

Word Ladder 39

PAPER, TAPER, TAMER, GAMER, GAMES

Word Ladder 40

POND, BOND, BAND, LAND, LANE, LAKE

Word Ladder 41

BOOK, COOK, CORK, FORK, FORM, FIRM, FILM

Word Ladder 42

ZERO, HERO, HERD, HEED, FEED, FEET, FRET, FREE

Word Ladder 43

FOX, FAX, FAN, PAN, PEN, DEN

Word Ladder 44

EASY, EAST, CAST, CART, CARD, HARD

Word Ladder 45

EAT, BAT, BET, BEE, BYE, AYE, ATE

Word Ladder 46

AIR, AIM, ARM, ART

Word Ladder 47

CAR, BAR, BAY, BOY, TOY

Word Ladder 48

EGG, EGO, AGO, AGE, AYE, BYE, BEE, TEE, TEN, HEN

Word Ladder 49

SING, DING, DINE, DONE, TONE

Word Ladder 50

MOUSE, HOUSE, HORSE, WORSE, WORST

Word Ladder 51

COAT, BOAT, BOOT, SOOT, SHOT, SHOE

Word Ladder 52

CLUMP, CLAMP, CLASP, CLASH, CRASH, TRASH

Word Ladder 53

START, STARE, STORE, STONE, SHONE, PHONE

Word Ladder 54

MORE, LORE, LOSE, LOSS, LESS

Word Ladder 55

SAD, SOD, SOY, JOY

Word Ladder 56

ICE, ACE, AYE, DYE, DOE, HOE, HOT

Word Ladder 57

JET, PET, PAT, PAY, PLY, FLY

Word Ladder 58

FOUR, FOUL, FOOL, FOOT, FORT, FORE, FIRE, FIVE

Word Ladder 59

SOUP, SOUL, FOUL, FOWL, BOWL

Word Ladder 60

FOOL, POOL, POLL, PILL, WILL, WILE, WISE

Word Ladder 61

WARM, WORM, WORD, CORD, COLD

Word Ladder 62

BORN, TORN, TERN, TEEN, THEN, THEE, TREE, FREE

Word Ladder 63

WHEAT, CHEAT, CLEAT, BLEAT, BLEAK, BREAK, BREAD

Word Ladder 64

NORTH, FORTH, FORTS, SORTS, SOOTS, SOOTH, SOUTH

Word Ladder 65

PAWN, PAWS, PANS, PINS, PING, KING

Word Ladder 66

SNACK, STACK, STARK, STARS, SEARS, SEALS, MEALS

Word Ladder 67

FOG, BOG, BUG, BUN, SUN

Word Ladder 68

OWL, OIL, NIL, NIX, FIX, FOX

Word Ladder 69

TOP, BOP, BOD, BID, AID, AND, END

Word Ladder 70

DRY, PRY, PAY, PAT, PET, WET

Word Ladder 71

FLESH, FLASH, FLASK, FLANK, BLANK, BLAND, BLOND, BLOOD

Word Ladder 72

SEED, SEES, SEWS, SAWS, LAWS, LAWN

Word Ladder 73

TEARS, SEARS, STARS, STARE, STALE, STILE, SMILE

Word Ladder 74

HAND, BAND, BOND, FOND, FOOD, FOOT

Word Ladder 75

OLD, ODD, ADD, AID, BID, BED, FED, FEW, NEW

Word Ladder 76

JOG, JUG, RUG, RUN

Word Ladder 77

SMILE, SMITE, SPITE, SPITS, SLITS, SLOTS, SLOWS, FLOWS, FLOWN, FROWN

Word Ladder 78

PAL, PAR, FAR, FOR, FOE

Word Ladder 79

SLEEP, BLEEP, BLEED, BREED, BREAD, DREAD, DREAM

Word Ladder 80

FRESH, FLESH, FLASH, FLASK, FLACK, SLACK, STACK, STALK, STALE

Word Ladder 81

WORD, CORD, CARD, CARE, CAME, GAME

Word Ladder 82

DAYS, BAYS, BOYS, BOAS, BOAR, BEAR, YEAR

Word Ladder 83

SEED, FEED, FLED, FLEE, FREE, TREE

Word Ladder 84

SHARP, SHARE, SPARE, SPARS, SPURS, SLURS, BLURS, BLURT, BLUNT

Chapter 10: Dropouts

Theodore Roosevelt

The only man who never makes a mistake is the man who never does anything.

Keith Richards

If you're going to kick authority in the teeth, you might as well use two feet.

Will Rogers

Even if you're on the right track, you'll get run over if you just sit there.

Groucho Marx

I don't care to belong to a club that accepts people like me as members.

William Shakespeare

Life is a tale told by an idiot—full of sound and fury, signifying nothing.

Oscar Wilde

The only thing worse than being talked about is not being talked about.

John F. Kennedy

Let us never negotiate out of fear. But let us never fear to negotiate.

Bill Cosby

A word to the wise ain't necessary—it's the stupid ones that need the advice.

Anne Frank

Think of all the beauty that's still left in and around you, and be happy.

Jesus

Greater love has no one than this, that one lay down his life for his friends.

Martin Luther King, Jr.

We must learn to live together as brothers or perish together as fools.

George Bernard Shaw

Without art, the crudeness of reality would make the world unbearable.

Marvin Gaye

If you cannot find peace within yourself, you will never find it anywhere else.

Claude Monet

The richness I achieve comes from Nature, the source of my inspiration.

Lily Tomlin

The trouble with the rat race is that even if you win, you're still a rat.

Steve Martin

Chaos in the midst of chaos isn't funny, but chaos in the midst of order is.

Raymond Chandler

When in doubt, have a man come through the door with a gun in his hand.

Forrest Gump

Life is like a box of chocolates . . . you never know what you're gonna get.

Abraham Lincoln

No matter how much the cats fight, there always seem to be plenty of kittens.

Mahatma Gandhi

Whatever you do will be insignificant, but it is very important that you do it.

St. Francis of Assisi

All the darkness in the world cannot extinguish the light of a single candle.

Albert Einstein

A happy man is too satisfied with the present to dwell too much on the future.

Jimi Hendrix

When the power of love overcomes the love of power the world will know peace.

Harry S. Truman

It is amazing what you can accomplish if you do not care who gets the credit.

Mae West

Whenever I'm caught between two evils, I take the one I've never tried.

Basho

Do not seek to follow in the footsteps of the men of old; seek what they sought.

Galileo Galilei

I have never met a man so ignorant that I couldn't learn something from him.

Victor Hugo

An invasion of armies can be resisted, but not an idea whose time has come.

Ann Landers

Television has proved that people will look at anything rather than each other.

Edith Wharton

If only we'd stop trying to be happy we could have a pretty good time.

F. Scott Fitzgerald

Vitality shows in not only the ability to persist but the ability to start over.

John Rushkin

There is no such thing as bad weather, only different kinds of good weather.

Henry Adams

A teacher affects eternity; he can never tell where his influence stops.

Eleanor Roosevelt

The future belongs to those who believe in the beauty of their dreams.

Jean Giraudoux

The secret of success is sincerity. Once you can fake that you've got it made.

Thomas Edison

Genius is one percent inspiration and ninety-nine percent perspiration.

Kurt Vonnegut

We are what we pretend to be, but we better be very careful what we pretend.

George Burns

Retire? I'm going to stay in show business until I'm the only one left.

Douglas Adams

I love deadlines. I like the whooshing sound they make as they fly by.

Henry Miller

Every moment is a golden one for him who has the vision to recognize it as such.

St. Thomas Aquinas

There is nothing on this earth more to be prized than true friendship.

Robert Frost

In three words I can sum up everything I've learned about life: it goes on.

Chapter 11: Brain Teasers

Answer to Language Teaser #1

1. Mortimer was a tax collector.
2. Dirk was a lumberjack who died because he didn't hear his partner yell "Timber!"
3. Suzy was a comedian.
4. Ethel was a maid, always fighting dust.

Answer to Language Teaser #2

1. The FUNCTION of a stoplight is to make a road JUNCTION safer.
2. Like the saying goes, you can't FORCE a HORSE to drink. He'll do it in due COURSE.
3. The JOCKEY was terrible at HOCKEY because he was much too short and kept slipping on the ice.

Answer to Language Teaser #3

1. The cut on his HEEL won't HEAL in time for the race, so HE'LL have to drop out.
2. The man was so upset about being BALD that he regularly BALLED himself up on the bed and BAWLED his eyes out.
3. I couldn't SENSE any of the SCENTS in the flower shop, because for some strange reason I had 50 CENTS crammed up my nose.
4. A pirate will wander the SEAS and essentially SEIZE everything he SEES.

Answer to Language Teaser #4

My FATHER, the BATHER, would RATHER LATHER with soap than with body wash.

Answer to Language Teaser #5

1. MANACLES
2. MANATEE
3. MANDATE
4. MANNEQUIN
5. MANUAL

Answer to Language Teaser #6

1. Intent
2. Inmate
3. Invent
4. Intern
5. Inspire

Answer to Language Teaser #7

1. under + stand = understand
2. short + cut = short cut
3. horse + shoe = horseshoe
4. tea + spoon = teaspoon
5. honey + moon = honeymoon

Answer to Language Teaser #8

1. water + fall = waterfall
2. book + case = bookcase
3. star + fish = starfish
4. hair + dresser = hairdresser
5. butter + scotch = butterscotch

Answer to Language Teaser #9

1. DISADVANTAGE (staged)
2. SOMERSAULT (slates)
3. PENITENTIARY (pretty)
4. RETAINERS (strain)
5. SCARCITIES (access)

Answer to Language Teaser #10

1. BEEF for a THIEF
2. A JESTER with a FESTER
3. Don't IMPEDE the STEED
4. A SHREW with a CLUE

Answer to Language Teaser #11

1. Grip gripe
2. Ant rant
3. Irate pirate
4. Latter platter
5. Thin thing

Answer to Language Teaser #12

The words, when combined with the correct placement letter, form new words.

1. Corn (acorn)
2. Leaf (belief)
3. Saw (see-saw)
4. Part (depart)
5. Mitt (emit)

Answer to Language Teaser #13

Each word can be changed into a new word by adding a letter of the alphabet to either the beginning or the end. These new words fit the definitions.

1. Treaty (TREE-T)
2. Esquire (S-CHOIR)
3. Elfin (L-FIN)
4. Unite (U-KNIGHT)
5. Piccolo (PICKLE-O)
6. Pansy (PAN-Z)
7. Entire (N-TIRE)

Answer to Language Teaser #14

1. Below elbow
2. Mentors monster
3. Hectare cheater
4. Alps pals
5. West stew

Answer to Logic Teaser #1

Bobby could draw a straight line from between 9 and 10 on the left side of the clock face to the right side between 3 and 4. The sum of the numbers on both sides of the line equals 39.

Answer to Logic Teaser #2

The statement is "I always lie." If Bobby always lies, then that statement would be the truth, so he couldn't say it. If he always tells the truth, then he obviously couldn't say it because it would be a lie.

Answer to Logic Teaser #3

You could make a circular chain with all the links using only three cuts and mends. Completely separate one of the four chains by cutting all three of its links. Use these three open links to connect the remaining three chains into a circle.

Answer to Logic Teaser #4

In every game there is one loser. Since every person must lose once, except for the champ, there are 127 losers and therefore 127 games.

Answer to Logic Teaser #5

Western Florida is on Central Standard Time and eastern Oregon is on Mountain Standard Time. This means Florida is normally one hour ahead. Twice a year, when Daylight Saving Time begins and ends, the time changes by one hour. During the transition, there is one hour when the time in both places is the same.

Answer to Logic Teaser #6

He can do it in one. Of the 10 barrels being shipped to the French fry factory, one contains heavy potatoes that weigh 1.1 pounds. Pete should take one potato from the first barrel, two from the second, three from the third, and so on, until he has taken 10 potatoes from the last barrel. Then he should weigh all these potatoes together. His digital scale will give him a reading ending in a certain number of tenths of a pound. If the total weight ends in a .4, for instance, Pete will know that four of the potatoes are heavy. Since he knows that the only group of four potatoes came from the fourth barrel, he knows which barrel contains the heavy potatoes.

Answer to Logic Teaser #7

There would be 4,950 handshakes. All 100 people at the fundraiser shake 99 hands. That's 9,900 when you multiply it, but two people participate in each handshake. Divide 9,900 by 2, and you have your answer.

Answer to Logic Teaser #8

Since the alien in the #4 jersey doesn't have four limbs, it must have either two or three limbs. The three-limbed alien replies, so we know that #4 cannot have three limbs. The alien who is #4 must therefore have two limbs. This leaves #2 with three limbs and #3 with four limbs.

Answer to Logic Teaser #9

From the fourth clue, we know that the cheeseburger had extra ketchup.

From the fifth clue, we know that the fish had mustard.

From the seventh clue, we know that the salad doesn't have mayo and that salad was not the first or last thing ordered. Combine these facts with the second clue, and we find that the salad had ranch dressing.

From the sixth clue, we know that Derek was third.

From the third clue, we know that Candy had chicken, and because of the first and fourth clues, we know she was second in line.

Therefore John was first in line, Rose was last, and Steve was fourth. The third and fifth now mean that neither Candy nor John had mustard; therefore, it must have been Steve. Since we know that the chicken was ordered second, the salad must have been ordered third by Derek, based on the first and seventh clues. This leaves Rose with the mayo hamburger. The only remaining option is for Candy to have ordered barbeque sauce and for John to have ketchup. In summary:

John was first in line and ordered a cheeseburger with extra ketchup.

Candy was second and ordered the chicken sandwich with barbeque sauce.

Derek was third and had a salad with ranch dressing.

Steve was fourth and ate a fish sandwich with mustard.

Rose was last in line and ate a hamburger with mayo.

Answer to Logic Teaser #10

The rook needs a minimum of 16 moves to pass over all the squares and return to the original position.

Answer to Logic Teaser #11

You should drink both vials. The answer cannot be determined from the clues, and if you think about it too long the poison will kill you. Even though you are sure to drink more poison, you are also sure to drink the antidote.

Answer to Logic Teaser #12

From the second clue, we know that Cabin 5 is assigned to Miss D. Werk.

From the fourth clue, we know that Mr. Lastrain, Mr. Buss, and Mr. Meaner can only occupy cabin numbers 1, 2, and 3, although not particularly in that order. This leaves Miss Fortune and Mr. Allot with cabins 4 and 6, although not necessarily in that order.

From the third clue, we know that Mr. Buss (a smoker) must be in Cabin 3 and Mr. Allot (a nonsmoker), must be in Cabin 4. Thus, Miss Fortune is in Cabin 6.

From the fifth clue, we know that Mr. Meaner must be in Cabin 1, to give him the silence he needs during work. Hence, Mr. Lastrain is in Cabin 2.

Thus, the cabin numbers are:

1. Mr. Meaner
2. Mr. Lastrain
3. Mr. Buss
4. Mr. Allot
5. Miss D. Werk
6. Miss Fortune

Answer to Logic Teaser #13

Four colors. In fact four colors will suffice for any map, real or fabricated. This famous theory was proposed in 1853, but it was not proven until 1977, when computers became available that could handle much of the number-crunching.

Answer to Logic Teaser #14

From the first clue, we know that Bobby is the right fielder.

From the fourth clue, we know that Isaac is the catcher.

From the second clue, we know that the shortstop is female.

From the third clue, we know that Isabel got five runs as the shortstop.

From the first and third clues, we now know that Shane is the first baseman and Mimi is the pitcher. Going back to the third clue, we can now also solve for the remaining hits:

Bobby is the right fielder, and he got four hits.

Isaac is the catcher, and he got one hit.

Isabel is the shortstop, and she got five hits.

Mimi is the pitcher, and she got two hits.

Shane is the first baseman, and he got three hits.

Answer to Math Teaser #1

Rod does. At the point Rod reaches the Puzzle Shop, Wally is only halfway there. By the time Rod has run home again, Wally will have just made it to the shop.

Answer to Math Teaser #2

520. There are 26 letters and 10 digits, for 260 possible combinations with the letter first and 260 more when the letter is last. That's a total of 520 possible horses.

Answer to Math Teaser #3

Hyde carried the heavy backpack 2 miles longer than Bobby did. It doesn't matter how long the actual hike was. On the way there, Hyde carried it for x miles, and on the way home he carried it for 5 miles, for a total of $x + 5$ miles. Bobby carried it for 4 miles on the way there and for $x - 1$ miles on the way back (due to the extra mile Hyde carried it) for a total of $x + 3$ miles. If you subtract $(x + 3)$ from $(x + 5)$ you get 2, which is the answer.

Answer to Math Teaser #4

It broke at least 18 seconds ago.

With 18 seconds between every donut, the age difference between the oldest and freshest is 144 seconds, so Old = Fresh + 144. We also know that Old = Fresh × 5. Plug the second equation into the first: Fresh × 5 = Fresh + 144, which solves to Fresh = 36. The age of the freshest donut is 36 seconds. Since the next donut was not produced on schedule 18 seconds later, the machine must have been broken for at least 18 seconds.

Answer to Math Teaser #5

There are 51 steps. The first thing the monk does is meditate on the middle step, which means the number of steps above him is equal to the number below. The easiest way to picture this is on a number line, with the middle step at 0. The monk's various rituals move his position up and down the number line like so: 0 + 8 − 12 + 1 + 2(14) = 25. This final value tells us how many steps the monk had to climb from the middle point to reach the top. Add the equal number that were below him, plus the middle step itself, for a total of 51.

Answer to Math Teaser #6

The ones digit will be 0. Both 2 and 5 are prime numbers. Anything multiplied by 2 and 5 will have a 0 in the ones place.

Answer to Math Teaser #7

36 pennies can make a square and triangle.

Write down the number of pennies that can make a triangle (3, 6, 10, 15, 21, 28, 36, etc.) and the number that can make a square (4, 9, 16, 25, 36, etc.). The first number both sets have in common is 36.

Answer to Math Teaser #8

Going uphill for 10 miles, Bobby burns 0.286 gallons of gas. On the 5 miles of level land, Bobby burns 0.1 gallon each way. Going downhill the 10 miles back home, his car only consumes 0.125 gallons. That's a total of 0.611 gallons for the 30-mile trip. 30 divided by 0.611 is 49.1 mpg for the complete trip.

Answer to Math Teaser #9

140 pogo sticks. The equation that defines this problem is $x + (x + 30) + (x + 60) + (x + 90) + (x + 120) = 1,000$. Solve this equation to get $x = 140$.

Answer to Math Teaser #10

The dog can run in a 6-foot radius circle.

To get the answer, first draw a right triangle. The long side (hypotenuse) is the length of the rope when fully stretched by the dog, 10 feet. The medium side is the distance from the ceiling to the dog's collar, 8 feet. The short side is the radius of the circle. Using the Pythagorean theorem, $a^2 + b^2 = c^2$, we get $a^2 + 64 = 100$ or $a = 6$.

Answer to Math Teaser #11

Because Santa started with trains, the 108th train will occur during his fifth batch of toys, for a total of 208. At 2 minutes a toy, he will complete his 108th train 416 minutes after he starts work, at 2:56 p.m.

Answer to Math Teaser #12

On a normal watch, the minute and hour hands should meet 11 times in 12 hours, at 12:00, 1:05, 2:11, 3:16, 4:22, 5:27, 6:33, 7:38, 8:44, 9:49, and 10:55. To figure out how much time this leaves between each meeting of the hands, multiply 12 (the number of hours) by 60 (the number of minutes in an hour) and divide by 11 (the number of times the hands meet).$(12 \times 60) \div 11 = 65.45$ minutes, or 65 minutes and 27.27 seconds.

In Bobby's case, the hands meet after every 65 minutes, which means the watch is gaining 27.27 seconds per hour.

Answer to Math Teaser #13

$2.85 \times 1.60 \times 1.25 = 5.70$

$2.85 + 1.60 + 1.25 = 5.70$

You can simplify this to 3 equations that can be solved using algebra. $A + B + C = 5.70$, $A \times B \times C = 5.7$, and $A + B + C = A \times B \times C$.

Answer to Math Teaser #14

There are 6 contestants who ate a total of 42 bunnies.

From what the first contestant says, we know that Bunnies = 7 × Contestants. From the second contestant we know that $2 \times (2/3)$Bunnies $= 10 \times$ Contestants $- 4$. Just plug the first equation into the second equation and you can solve for Contestants, of which there are 6. Plug this back into the first equation to determine that there are 42 bunnies.

Answer to Trivia Teaser #1

The nickel wasn't invented until 1866, so this was clearly a fake.

Answer to Trivia Teaser #2

Hawaii.

Answer to Trivia Teaser #3

Utah, Colorado, Arizona, and New Mexico come together at the same point, so someone could run through all four states in under a minute.

Answer to Trivia Teaser #4

Stephen Hawking was only thirteen when Albert Einstein died, so this meeting never could have taken place.

Answer to Trivia Teaser #5

Christmas in the Southern Hemisphere occurs in the summer; therefore, he couldn't have been building a snowman.

Answer to Trivia Teaser #6

It wasn't until 1969 that women could be declared "incorrigible." Thus, no women could ever have been sent to Alcatraz.

Answer to Trivia Teaser #7

In official golf rules, you are allowed to lift your ball to determine if it's yours, but you can only do this if your ball is not in a hazard. Since Bobby's ball is in a hazard, he is not allowed to touch it. Fortunately, another rule states that there is no penalty for playing the wrong ball from a hazard. Bobby should pick one ball and play it. If he then finds out it's not his, he can play the other ball.

Answer to Trivia Teaser #8

Since each name refers to a coin, we can set up the following equation: Lincoln(0.01) + Jefferson(0.05) + Roosevelt(0.10) + Washington (0.25) + Kennedy(0.50) = $0.91.

Answer to Trivia Teaser #9

The letter Q.

Answer to Trivia Teaser #10

Alligators only live in the southeastern United States. Crocodiles live in the Amazon.

Answer to Trivia Teaser #11

When Queen Elizabeth was born on April 21, 1926, no one could have possibly known she would have been the heir to the throne. Her father wasn't crowned king until his brother, King Edward VIII, abdicated some ten years later.

Answer to Trivia Teaser #12

Hamate. These are the bones in your hand, not including the fingers.

Answer to Trivia Teaser #13

In a blackjack game. In blackjack, the ace can represent 11 or 1. In this case, although the ace started out being worth 11, it is now counted as 1 to keep the total from going over 21.

Answer to Trivia Teaser #14

1. A bunch of buzzards is a wake.
2. A bunch of cobras is a quiver.
3. A bunch of turtles is a bale.
4. A bunch of sharks is a shiver.

Chapter 12: Groupies

Groupie 1

Groupie 2

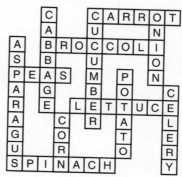

Groupie 3

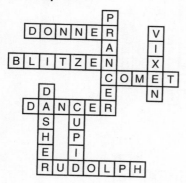

Groupie 4

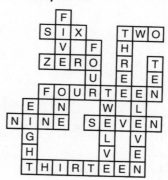

Groupie 5

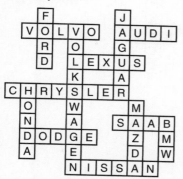

Groupie 6

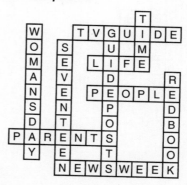

Groupie 7

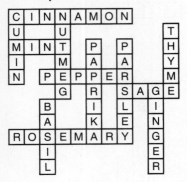

Groupie 8

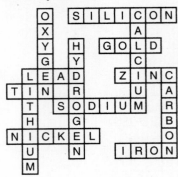

Groupie 9

Groupie 10

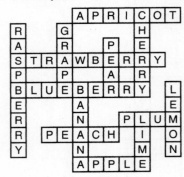

Groupie 11

Groupie 12

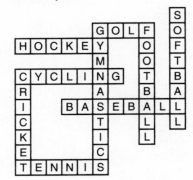

Groupie 13

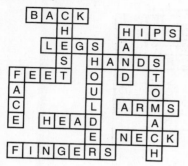

Groupie 14

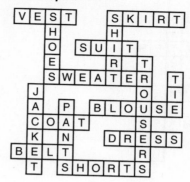

Groupie 15

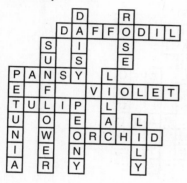

Groupie 16

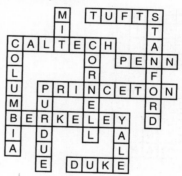

Groupie 17

Groupie 18

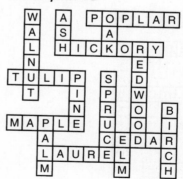

Groupie 19

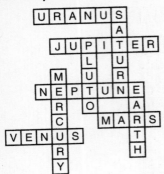

Groupie 20

Groupie 21

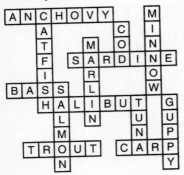

Groupie 22

Groupie 23

Groupie 24

Groupie 25

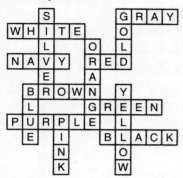

Groupie 26

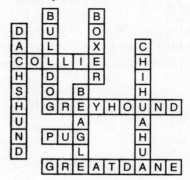

Groupie 27

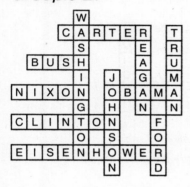

Groupie 28

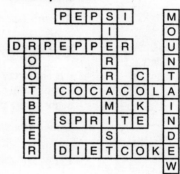

Chapter 13: Cryptograms

Cryptogram 1

If you hear a voice within you say "You cannot paint," then by all means paint, and that voice will be silenced.

Vincent Van Gogh

Cryptogram 2

Power without principle is barren, but principle without power is futile. This is a party of government, and I will lead it as a party of government.

Tony Blair

Cryptogram 3

Use what talent you possess: the woods would be very silent if no birds sang except those that sang best.

Henry Van Dyke

Cryptogram 4

We're all capable of mistakes, but I do not care to enlighten you on the mistakes we may or may not have made.

George W. Bush

Cryptogram 5

No more tears now; I will think upon revenge.

Mary Queen of Scots

Cryptogram 6

When we got into office, the thing that surprised me the most was that things were as bad as we'd been saying they were.

John F. Kennedy

Cryptogram 7

Only those who will risk going too far can possibly find out how far one can go.

T. S. Eliot

Cryptogram 8

The journey of a thousand miles must begin with a single step.

Lao Tzu

Cryptogtam 9

Here is a test to find out whether your mission in life is complete. If you're alive, it isn't.

Richard Bach

Cryptogram 10

It is necessary to try to surpass oneself always; this occupation ought to last as long as life.

Queen Christina

Cryptogram 11

Sure, there are dishonest men in local government. But there are dishonest men in national government, too.

Richard Nixon

Cryptogram 12

After silence, that which comes nearest to expressing the inexpressible is music.

Aldous Huxley

Cryptogram 13

Government is not reason; it is not eloquent; it is force. Like fire, it is a dangerous servant and a fearful master.

George Washington

Cryptogram 14

Be bold. If you're going to make an error, make a doozy, and don't be afraid to hit the ball.

Billie Jean King

Cryptogram 15

The best and most beautiful things in the world cannot be seen or even touched. They must be felt within the heart.

Helen Keller

Cryptogram 16

I have stepped out upon this platform that I may see you and that you may see me, and in the arrangement I have the best of the bargain.

Abraham Lincoln

Cryptogram 17

Every artist dips his brush in his own soul, and paints his own nature into his pictures.

Henry Ward Beecher

Cryptogram 18

Politics is not a bad profession. If you succeed there are many rewards, if you disgrace yourself you can always write a book.

Ronald Reagan

Cryptogram 19

Supreme excellence consists in breaking the enemy's resistance without fighting.

Sun-Tzu

Cryptogram 20

There is real magic in enthusiasm. It spells the difference between mediocrity and accomplishment.

Norman Vincent Peale

Cryptogram 21

The policy of the American government is to leave their citizens free, neither restraining nor aiding them in their pursuits.

Thomas Jefferson

Cryptogram 22

It's amazing that the amount of news that happens in the world every day always just exactly fits the newspaper.

Jerry Seinfeld

Cryptogram 23

America is not anything if it consists of each of us. It is something only if it consists of all of us.

Woodrow Wilson

Cryptogram 24

Courage is doing what you are afraid to do. There can be no courage unless you're scared.

Eddie Rickenbacher

Cryptogram 25

What lies behind us and what lies before us are tiny matters compared to what lies within us.

Ralph Waldo Emerson

Cryptogram 26

The first human who hurled an insult instead of a stone was the founder of civilization.

Sigmund Freud

Cryptogram 27

O how small a portion of earth will hold us when we are dead, who ambitiously seek after the whole world while we are living.

Philip II

Cryptogram 28

All strange and terrible events are welcome, but comforts we despise.

Cleopatra

Cryptogram 29

The whole world is in revolt. Soon there will be only five Kings left—the King of England, the King of Spades, The King of Clubs, the King of Hearts, and the King of Diamonds.

King Farouk

Cryptogram 30

And so, my fellow Americans: ask not what your country can do for you—ask what you can do for your country.

John F. Kennedy

Cryptogram 31

I have found it impossible to carry the heavy burden of responsibility . . .

King Edward VIII

Cryprogram 32

Democratic nations must try to find ways to starve the terrorist and the hijacker of the oxygen of publicity on which they depend.

Margaret Thatcher

Cryptogram 33

You can't influence Europe's future from the terraces. You have to be on the pitch and playing hard.

John Major

Cryptogram 34

The main essentials of a successful prime minister [are] sleep and a sense of history.

Harold Wilson

Cryptogram 35

Government must keep pace with the changing needs of our state and its people to be sure that government can fulfill its legitimate obligations.

Ronald Reagan

Cryptogram 36

America did not invent human rights. In a very real sense human rights invented America.

Jimmy Carter

Cryptogram 37

I always turn to the sports pages first, which records people's accomplishments. The front page has nothing but man's failures.

Chief Justice Earl Warren

Cryptogram 38

Computers make it easier to do a lot of things, but most of the things they make it easier to do don't need to be done.

Andy Rooney

Cryptogram 39

Men can only be happy when they do not assume that the object of life is happiness.

George Orwell

Provider Puzzle 1

Provider Puzzle 2

Provider Puzzle 3

Provider Puzzle 4

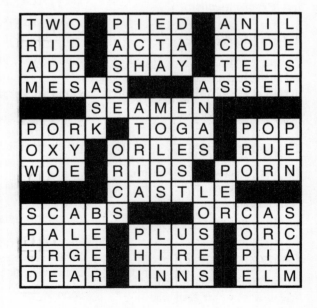

Provider Puzzle 5

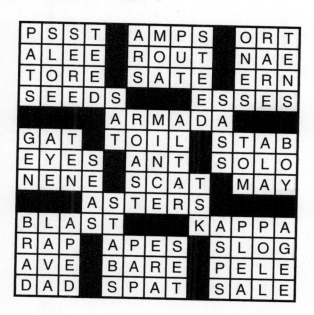

R	U	S	E		B	E	G	S		C	H	I	
U	S	E	S		A	G	H	A		Y	A	R	
T	E	X	T		L	O	I	N		S	K	I	
		E	L	L			T	A	T	E	S		
M	A	D	R	E		I	D	O	L				
I	V	Y		D	O	O	R		T	O	Y	S	
L	E	N	T		G	N	U		O	R	A	L	
T	R	E	E		L	I	M	B		T	W	A	
	A	L	E	C		R	A	S	P	Y			
S	A	B	R	A		S	O	L					
C	U	E		M	Y	N	A		P	H	E	W	
U	T	A		B	O	I	L		H	E	A	R	
M	O	M		S	U	P	S		A	W	R	Y	

Provider Puzzle 6

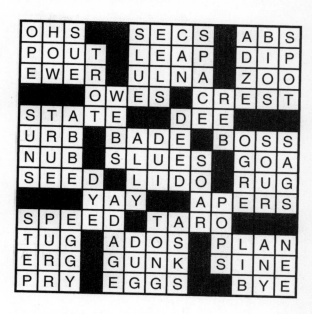

O	H	S		S	E	C	S		A	B	S
P	O	U	T		L	E	A	P		D	I	P
E	W	E	R		U	L	N	A		Z	O	O
	O	W	E	S		C	R	E	S	T
S	T	A	T	E		D	E	E	
U	R	B		B	A	D	E		B	O	S	S
N	U	B		S	L	U	E	S		G	O	A
S	E	E	D		L	I	D	O		R	U	G
	Y	A	Y		A	P	E	R	S
S	P	E	E	D		T	A	R	O	
T	U	G		A	D	O	S		P	L	A	N
E	R	G		G	U	N	K		S	I	N	E
P	R	Y		E	G	G	S		B	Y	E

Provider Puzzle 7

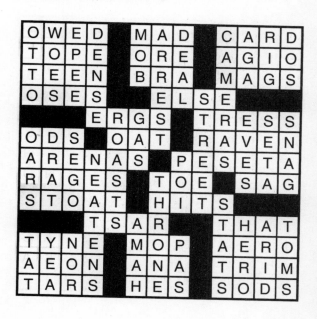

P	S	S	T		A	M	P	S		O	R	T
A	L	E	E		R	O	U	T		N	A	E
T	O	R	E		S	A	T	E		E	R	N
S	E	E	D	S		E	S	S	E	S
	A	R	M	A	D	A	
G	A	T		T	O	I	L		S	T	A	B
E	Y	E	S		A	N	T		S	O	L	O
N	E	N	E		S	C	A	T		M	A	Y
	A	S	T	E	R	S	
B	L	A	S	T		K	A	P	P	A
R	A	P		A	P	E	S		S	L	O	G
A	V	E		B	A	R	E		P	E	L	E
D	A	D		S	P	A	T		S	A	L	E

Provider Puzzle 8

O	W	E	D		M	A	D		C	A	R	D
T	O	P	E		O	R	E		A	G	I	O
T	E	E	N		B	R	A		M	A	G	S
O	S	E	S		E	L	S	E	
	E	R	G	S		T	R	E	S	S
O	D	S		O	A	T		R	A	V	E	N
A	R	E	N	A	S		P	E	S	E	T	A
R	A	G	E	S		T	O	E		S	A	G
S	T	O	A	T		H	I	T	S	
	T	S	A	R		T	H	A	T
T	Y	N	E		M	O	P		A	E	R	O
A	E	O	N		A	N	A		T	R	I	M
T	A	R	S		H	E	S		S	O	D	S

Provider Puzzle 9

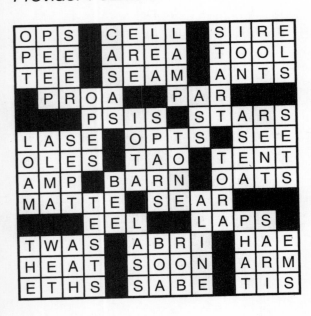

```
L A B   ■ B R A G ■ M A T ■
A G A R ■ R O T E ■ A G E ■
S O M A ■ O D E S ■ N U N ■
■ ■ T A S ■ ■ T R E E D ■
S A V E R ■ G L E E ■ ■ ■ ■
O B I ■ B R A E ■ S O T S ■
A L S ■ S A T E S ■ A H A ■
K E E L ■ C O R E ■ S E N ■
■ ■ A P E R ■ M A T E S ■
S L A T S ■ ■ M I L ■ ■ ■
E O N ■ A C H E ■ B R A S ■
A C T ■ L O O T ■ S A S H ■
L I E ■ M O P E ■ ■ S P Y ■
```

Provider Puzzle 10

```
T A E ■ T H E M ■ S L A M ■
A L L ■ A U R A ■ L A N E ■
P A L ■ S H A D ■ A G E D ■
A S S E S ■ S E A T ■ ■ ■ ■
■ ■ L E T ■ ■ B E S T S ■
S C A D ■ R O S E ■ H A Y ■
H O N ■ P I C O T ■ M E N ■
E R S ■ R O A N ■ T O L E ■
S N A R E ■ S P A ■ ■ ■ ■
■ ■ E P O S ■ A N G S T ■
B O W S ■ L A I N ■ O H O ■
A L I T ■ D I C E ■ B O O ■
Y E N S ■ S L E D ■ S O N ■
```

Provider Puzzle 11

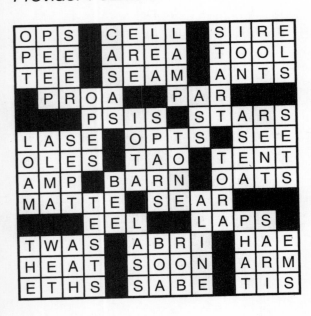

```
O P S ■ C E L L ■ S I R E ■
P E E ■ A R E A ■ T O O L ■
T E E ■ S E A M ■ A N T S ■
■ P R O A ■ ■ P A R ■ ■ ■
■ ■ P S I S ■ S T A R S ■
L A S E ■ O P T S ■ S E E ■
O L E S ■ T A O ■ T E N T ■
A M P ■ B A R N ■ O A T S ■
M A T T E ■ S E A R ■ ■ ■
■ ■ E E L ■ L A P S ■ ■ ■
T W A S ■ A B R I ■ H A E ■
H E A T ■ S O O N ■ A R M ■
E T H S ■ S A B E ■ T I S ■
```

Provider Puzzle 12

```
D A B ■ S L O T ■ M A N O ■
O W E ■ T U B E ■ A L A R ■
R E G A I N E D ■ S A V E ■
■ ■ C L A Y ■ T O N E S ■
A W A R E ■ E L A N ■ ■ ■
G A M E ■ T R O P ■ S I T ■
E N I S L E ■ P S E U D O ■
R E D ■ O R L E ■ C R E W ■
■ ■ S O N E ■ C R E S S ■
S P A T S ■ T H R U ■ ■ ■
C A K E ■ R H E O S T A T ■
U N I T ■ E A R N ■ A M I ■
P E N S ■ F L E E ■ M A N ■
```

Provider Puzzle 13

S	L	A	T		W	A	G		S	L	A	W
T	A	R	E		E	Y	E		P	A	P	A
A	C	E	S		B	E	N		A	W	E	D
R	E	S	T			S	E	T	T			
		Y	E	S			R	E	A	P	S	
A	R	C		M	O	C	H	A		R	A	H
W	O	O		B	R	O	O	D		F	R	O
L	U	V		R	E	S	E	E		S	A	W
S	E	E	P	Y			S	R	I			
		O	O	P	S			M	O	R	T	
T	O	D	S		F	I	B		A	M	I	E
H	O	O	T		F	L	U		M	I	L	S
O	H	M	S		T	O	Y		S	T	E	T

Provider Puzzle 14

C	A	P		P	E	P	S		S	H	A	G
H	I	E		A	L	S	O		H	O	B	O
I	D	S		S	K	I	P		R	E	A	D
S	E	T	A	E			S	H	E			
		L	O	S	S			A	D	A	P	T
B	Y	T	E		T	O	G	S		F	O	E
R	U	E	S		O	A	R		M	A	L	E
I	L	L		S	A	K	E		I	R	E	S
T	E	E	T	H		S	W	A	T			
		A	A	S			R	E	C	A	P	
A	L	L	S		E	A	V	E		O	V	A
N	E	A	T		I	L	I	A		N	O	T
D	I	M	E		S	P	A	S		E	W	E

Chapter 15: What's in a Name?

Conan O'Brien

abri, acne, acre, aeon, aero, airn, anon, arco, bane, bani, bare, barn, bean, bear, bice, bier, bine, boar, bone, boon, boor, bora, bore, born, brae, bran, bren, brie, brin, brio, broo, cain, cane, carb, care, carn, cero, ciao, cine, cion, cire, coin, coir, cone, coni, conn, coon, core, corn, crab, crib, earn, ebon, icon, inro, iron, nabe, naoi, narc, near, neon, nice, nine, noir, nona, none, noon, nori, obia, oboe, once, orca, race, rain, rani, rein, rice, roan, robe

Jimmy Carter

acme, acre, aery, airt, airy, amie, amir, army, arty, came, care, carr, cart, cate, cire, cite, city, cram, cyma, cyme, emic, emir, emit, etic, eyra, imam, immy, item, mace, maim, mair, marc, mare, mart, mate, meat, meta, mica, mice, mime, mire, miry, mite, mity, race, racy, rami, rare, rate, ream, rear, rice, rime, rimy, rite, tace, tame, tare, team, tear, term, tier, time, tire, tram, tray, trey, trim, tyer, tyre, yare, year, yeti, yirr

Henry Fonda

adore, adorn, afore, annoy, anode, deary, deray, donna, donne, doyen, drone, fader, faery, fanny, fanon, fared, fayed, fenny, ferny, foehn, foray, foyer, frena, frond, handy, hardy, hared, hayed, hayer, heady, heard, henna, henry, heron, hoard, hoary, honan, honda, honed, honer, honey, horde, horny, hydra, hydro, hyena, nerdy, oared, onery, oread, radon, randy, rayed, rayon, ready, redan, redon, yearn

Lauren Bacall

able, acne, acre, alae, alan, alar, alba, alec, anal, area, aura, baal, bale, ball, bane, bare, barn, bean, bear, beau, bell, blae, blue, blur, brae, bran, bren, bull, bura, burl, burn, call, cane, carb, care, carl, carn, caul, cell, clan, club, clue, crab, cube, cull, curb, cure, curl, curn, earl, earn, ecru, elan, lace, lall, lane, leal, lean, lear, lube, luce, lull, luna, lune, lure, nabe, narc, near, null, nurl, race, rale, real, rube, rule, rune, ulan, ulna, unbe, urea

Stephen King

egest, eight, eking, geeks, geest, genes, genet, genie, genip, gents, geste, ghees, ginks, heist, hents, hikes, hinge, hints, inept, inset, keens, keeps, keets, kepis, khets, kines, kings, kites, kithe, kiths, knees, knish, knits, neeps, neigh, neist, nighs, night, nines, ninth, nites, peeks, peens, peins, peise, pekes, pekin, penes, penis, penne, penni, pikes, pines, pings, pinks, pints, piste, piths, segni, seine, sengi, sente, senti, sheen, sheep, sheet, sheik, shent, shine, shtik, siege, sight, singe, skeen, skeet, skein, skene, skint, skite, snipe, spent, spike, spine, spite, steek, steep, stein, sting, stink, stipe, teens, tense, thegn, thein, thens, these, thine, thing, think, thins, tikes, tines, tinge, tings

Gene Wilder

deer, deil, dele, deli, dene, dere, diel, dine, ding, dire, dirl, dree, dreg, drew, edge, eger, eide, erne, ewer, geed, geld, gene, gied, gien, gild, gird, girl, girn, gled, glee, glen, gree, grew, grid, grin, idle, ired, leer, lend, lewd, lied, lien, lier, line, ling, lire, lwei, need, nerd, nide, rede, reed, reel, rein, rend, ride, riel, rile, rind, ring, weed, weel, ween,

weer, weir, weld, wend, were, wide, wild, wile, wind, wine, wing, wire, wren

Ross Perot

estop, pesos, pesto, pests, poets, pores, ports, poser, poses, posse, posts, press, prest, prose, proso, pross, prost, repos, repot, repro, rests, retro, roose, roost, roots, roper, ropes, roses, roset, rotes, rotor, rotos, septs, soots, sopor, sorer, sores, sorts, spoor, spore, sport, spots, steps, stoop, stope, stops, store, strep, strop, toper, topes, topos, tores, toros, torse, torso, tress, troop, trope

Farrah Fawcett

ache, acre, acta, afar, arch, area, cafe, caff, care, carr, cart, cate, char, chat, chaw, chef, chew, craw, crew, each, eath, etch, face, fact, fare, fart, fate, fear, feat, feta, frae, frat, fret, haaf, haar, haet, haft, hare, hart, hate, hear, heat, heft, race, raff, raft, rare, rate, rath, rear, reft, rhea, tace, tach, tact, tahr, tare, tart, tate, tear, teat, teff, teth, thae, that, thaw, thew, tref, tret, twae, twat, waff, waft, ware, wart, watt, wear, weft, wert, what, whet

John Malkovich

achoo, aloin, amino, amnic, anvil, avion, cajon, cavil, chain, chalk, chiao, china, chink, chino, cholo, chook, claim, clank, clavi, clink, cloak, clonk, colin, colon, comal, covin, hakim, havoc, hoick, hooch, hooka, jocko, kanji, laich, liman, linac, loach, macho, macon, malic, manic, mavin, milch, mocha, mooch, moola, nacho, nicol, nival, nomoi, ohmic, ovoli, vakil, vinal, vinca, viola, vocal, voila

Johnny Carson

achy, ahoy, anon, arch, arco, arcs, ashy, cans, carn, cars, cash, cays, chao, char, chay, chon, coho, conn, cons, cony, coon, coos, corn, cory, cosh, cosy, coys, cyan, hays, hoar, hons, hora, horn, hoya, hoys, jars, jays, john, josh, joys, nans, naos, narc, nary, nays, nona, noon, nosh, nosy, oars, ocas, oohs, orca, orcs, osar, racy, rash, rays, rhos, roan, rocs, rosy, ryas, scan, scar, scry, shay, shoo, soar, soja, soon, sora, sorn, soya, sync, yarn

Fred MacMurray

aced, acme, acre, aery, afar, area, army, arum, aura, cade, cafe, came, card, care, carr, cram, crud, cued, curd, cure, curf, curr, cyma, cyme, dace, dame, dare, deaf, dear, defy, demy, derm, dram, dray, drum, duce, duma, dura, dure, durr, dyer, ecru, emyd, eyra, face, fade, fame, fard, fare, farm, fear, feud, frae, fray, fume, fumy, fury, fyce, maar, mace, made, mama, marc, mare, maud, maya, mead, mura, mure, murr, race, racy, rare, raya, read, ream, rear, rude, rued, ruer, urea, yard, yare, yaud, year, yuca

Vincent Price

cerci, ceric, citer, civet, civic, civie, creep, crepe, crept, cripe, enter, erect, event, evert, evict, evite, icier, ictic, inept, inert, inner, inter, nerve, never, nicer, niece, nieve, niter, nitre, pence, penne, penni, peter, piece, preen, price, print, recce, recti, reive, renin, rente, repin, retie, revet, ricin, ripen, riven, rivet, terce, terne, treen, trice, trine, tripe, venin, vinic, viper

James Baker

abas, ajar, ajee, akee, amas, arak, arbs, area, ares, arks, arms, arse, asea, baas, bake, bams, bare, bark, barm, bars, base, bask, beak, beam, bear, beer, bees, bema, berm, brae, bras, bree, ears, ease, ekes, emes, eras, jabs, jake, jamb, jams, jars, jeer, jees, jerk, kaas, kabs, kaes, kame, kbar, keas, kerb, maar, mabe, maes, make, mare, mark, mars, mask, meek, mere, merk, mesa, raja, rake, rams, rase, ream, rebs, reek, rees, rems, sabe, sake, same, sark, seam, sear, seek, seem, seer, seme, sera, sere, skee

Pablo Picasso

abaci, aboil, albas, alias, appal, apsis, aspic, aspis, assai, baals, bails, balas, balsa, basal, basic, basil, basis, bassi, basso, blips, bliss, blocs, bloop, boils, bolas, bolos, cabal, capos, casas, cibol, claps, clasp, class, clips, clops, coala, coals, cobia, coils, colas, cools, coops, copal, isbas, labia, laics, lapis, lasso, lisps, lobos, locos, loops, oasis, obias, oboli, obols, olios, opals, ossia, pacas, pails, paisa, palpi, palps, papal, papas, pibal, pical, picas, pipal, pisco, pisos, plica, plops, polio, polis, polos, pools, poops, psoai, psoas, sails, salic, salpa, salps, salsa, scabs, scalp, scoop, scops, sials, silos, sisal, slabs, slaps, slips, slobs, sloop, slops, soaps, soils, solos, spail, spica, spics, spoil, spool

Meryl Streep

eels, eely, eery, elms, elmy, else, emes, epee, errs, erst, espy, eyer, eyes, eyre, leer, lees, leet, lept, lest, lets, leys, lyes, lyre, lyse, meet, mels, melt, mere, merl, mete, peel, peer, pees, pele, pelt, perm, pert, pest, pets, pree, prey, pyes, pyre, reel, rees, rely,

rems, reps, rest, rete, rets, ryes, seel, seem, seep, seer, seme, sept, sere, spry, stem, step, stey, stye, teel, teem, tees, tele, tels, temp, term, tree, trey, tyee, tyer, tyes, type, tyre, yelp, ylem

Petula Clark

aceta, acute, akela, alack, alate, alert, altar, alter, alula, apace, apart, apeak, apter, areal, areca, artal, artel, aurae, aural, calla, caper, caput, carat, caret, carle, carte, cater, caulk, cella, clapt, clear, cleat, clept, clerk, craal, crake, crape, crate, creak, crept, cruel, cruet, culet, culpa, cupel, curet, cuter, eclat, epact, eruct, erupt, kalpa, kaput, karat, kraal, kraut, kurta, lacer, laker, lapel, later, latke, laura, leapt, lepta, letup, lucre, lutea, pacer, palea, paler, palet, pareu, parka, parle, pater, pearl, peart, petal, place, plack, plate, pleat, pluck, prate, pruta, pucka, puler, ratal, ratel, react, reata, recap, recta, recut, taker, talar, taler, taluk, taper, taupe, tepal, trace, track, truce, truck, trull, tulle, ulcer, ultra, urate, ureal

Kurt Cobain

abort, about, acorn, actin, actor, antic, auric, bacon, bairn, banco, baric, baron, batik, baton, biont, biota, boart, boric, bourn, bract, brain, brank, brant, brick, brink, brock, bronc, bruin, bruit, brunt, bucko, bunco, bunko, buran, burin, burnt, cabin, cairn, canto, carbo, carob, coati, cobia, cobra, coria, cornu, cotan, count, court, crank, croak, cubit, curia, curio, cutin, incur, intro, kauri, knaur, knout, korai, korat, korun, krait, kraut, krona, krubi, kurta, narco, naric, nitro, noria, nubia, octan, ontic, orbit, orcin, rabic, racon, ratio, riant, robin, runic, rutin, tabor, tabun, takin, taroc, tarok, tonic, toric, track, traik, train, trank, triac, trick, troak, trock, trona, truck, trunk, tunic, turbo, unbar, uncia, urban, urbia

Dudley Moore

deedy, deled, demur, doled, dolor, domed, dooly, doomy, dormy, dreed, drool, duomo, dured, elder, elude, emery, emyde, erode, leery, lemur, looed, looey, loury, lured, merde, merle, model, moldy, moody, mooed, moory, morel, mould, muddy, muled, muley, mured, odder, oddly, odeum, odour, odyle, older, oleum, reded, redly, redye, reedy, rodeo, romeo, roomy, ruddy, ruled, udder, uredo, yodel, yodle

Van Morrison

aims, ains, airn, airs, amin, amir, amis, anis, anon, arms, arvo, avos, inns, inro, ions, iron, main, mair, mano, mans, mars, mina, mirs, miso, moan, moas, mono, mons, moon, moor, moos, mora, morn, mors, nans, naoi, naos, nims, noir, noma, noms, nona, noon, nori, norm, nova, oars, orra, osar, rain, rami, rams, rani, rias, rims, rins, roam, roan, roar, roms, room, sain, sari, sima, soar, soma, soon, sora, sori, sorn, vain, vair, vans, vars, vims, vina, vino, vins, visa

Milton Berle

belie, belle, beret, berme, betel, beton, biome, biont, birle, biter, blent, blite, boite, boner, borne, botel, brent, brill, brine, broil, brome, elemi, elint, elite, eloin, ember, emote, enorm, enrol, enter, inert, inlet, inter, intro, irone, leben, lemon, lento, leone, libel, liber, limbo, limen, liner, lirot, liter, litre, loner, melon, merit, merle, meter, metre, metro, miler, mille, miner, minor, miter, mitre, moire, monie, monte, morel, motel, nerol, niter, nitre, nitro, noble, noter, obeli, oiler, olein,

omber, ombre, orbit, oriel, rebel, relet, relit, remet, remit, rente, reoil, retem, retie, rille, robin, roble, teloi, tenor, terne, tiler, timer, toile, toner, treen, tribe, trill, trine, triol, troll, trone

George C. Scott

cees, cere, cero, cete, coco, cogs, coos, coot, core, cost, cote, cots, croc, eger, eggs, egos, ergo, ergs, eros, erst, gees, gest, gets, goer, goes, gogo, goos, gore, gree, grog, grot, ogee, ogre, oots, orcs, ores, orts, otto, recs, rees, regs, rest, rete, rets, rocs, roes, root, rose, rote, roto, rots, scot, sect, seer, sego, sere, sett, soot, sore, sort, stet, tees, tegs, test, tets, toes, togs, toot, torc, tore, toro, tors, tort, tost, tote, tots, tree, tret, trot

Willem Dafoe

adeem, ailed, aimed, aldol, allee, allod, allow, amide, amido, amole, dolma, domal, dowel, dowie, dwell, edema, edile, elemi, elide, famed, felid, fella, field, filed, fille, fillo, flail, flame, fleam, flied, folia, ideal, ileal, ladle, lamed, lawed, limed, lowed, maile, maill, mawed, medal, media, mewed, miaow, mille, modal, model, molal, mowed, oiled, oldie, waled, weald, wedel, wield, wifed, wiled, woald

Margaret Thatcher

aargh, aceta, agama, agate, agree, ameer, areae, areca, arete, arhat, armer, armet, attar, cager, carat, carer, caret, carte, cater, chare, charm, charr, chart, cheat, cheer, chert, cheth, crate, cream, creme, eager, eagre, earth, eater, egret, erect, ether, gamer, garth, gerah, grace, grama, grate, great, greet, harem, hatch, hater, heart, heath, herma, macer, mache, march, marge,

match, mater, matte, merer, merge, meter, metre, racer, ragee, ramee, ramet, rarer, ratch, rater, rathe, reach, react, rearm, reata, recta, regma, rehem, remet, retag, retch, retem, tacet, tache, tamer, targe, tarre, tatar, tater, teach, tecta, teeth, terce, terga, terra, tetra, tharm, theca, theme, there, therm, theta, three, trace, tract, treat

Bing Crosby

bingo, bison, boing, bongs, boric, brigs, bring, brins, briny, brios, bronc, brosy, cions, cobbs, cobby, coign, coins, coirs, corby, corgi, corns, corny, cribs, crony, girns, giron, giros, gorsy, grins, groin, gyron, gyros, icons, incog, irons, irony, nobby, noirs, noisy, noris, orcin, orgic, ornis, ribby, rings, robin, rosin, scion, scorn, sonic, yogic, yogin, yogis, yonic, yonis

J. Edgar Hoover

aero, aged, agee, ager, ajee, arvo, aver, dago, dare, dear, deer, dere, deva, doer, doge, dojo, door, dore, dorr, dove, drag, dree, dreg, eave, edge, egad, eger, ergo, ever, gaed, gave, gear, geed, ghee, goad, goer, good, gore, grad, gree, hade, hadj, haed, hard, hare, have, head, hear, heed, herd, here, hero, hoar, hoed, hoer, hood, hora, hove, jade, jeed, jeer, odea, odor, ogee, ogre, ohed, orad, ordo, orra, over, rage, rare, rave, read, rear, rede, redo, reed, rhea, road, roar, rode, rood, rove, veer, vera

Quincy Jones

cine, coin, cone, cons, cues, eons, ices, icon, inns, ions, jinn, joey, join, joys, neon, nice, nine, none, nose, nosy, noun, nuns, once, ones, onus, sine, sync, yens

Arthur Ashe

areas, arhat, arras, aster, aurae, aurar, auras, aures, earth, haars, haets, hahas, hares, harsh, harts, haste, hater, hates, haute, hears, heart, heath, heats, heths, hurst, hurts, rares, raser, rater, rates, rathe, rears, reata, rheas, ruers, ruths, saute, share, shear, shute, stare, surah, surer, surra, sutra, tahrs, tares, tarre, tears, terra, trash, truer, trues, urare, urase, urate, ureas, ursae, usher

Ansel Adams

aals, alae, alan, alas, ales, alma, alme, alms, amas, amen, anal, anas, ands, anes, ansa, asea, dale, dals, dame, damn, dams, deal, dean, dels, dens, elan, elds, elms, ends, lade, lads, lama, lame, lams, land, lane, lase, lass, lead, lean, leas, lend, lens, less, made, mads, maes, male, mana, mane, mans, mass, mead, meal, mean, meld, mels, mend, mesa, mess, nada, name, nema, ness, sade, sale, sals, same, sand, sane, sans, seal, seam, seas, sels, send, slam, sled, sned

Chris Evert

cees, cere, cete, chis, chit, cire, cist, cite, cris, eche, errs, erst, etch, eths, etic, ever, eves, heir, here, hers, hest, hets, hies, hire, hist, hits, hive, ices, ichs, ires, itch, recs, rees, reis, resh, rest, rete, rets, revs, rice, rich, rise, rite, rive, sect, seer, sere, shiv, shri, sice, sire, site, sith, stir, tees, thee, thir, this, tics, tier, ties, tire, tree, veer, vees, vert, vest, vets, vice, vier, vies, vise

Ginger Rogers

eger, eggs, egis, egos, engs, eons, ergo, ergs, erne, erns, eros, errs, gees, gene, gens, gien, gies, gigs, gins, girn, giro,

goer, goes, gone, gong, gore, gree, grig, grin, grog, inro, ions, ires, iron, noes, nogg, nogs, noir, nori, nose, ogee, ogre, ones, ores, rees, regs, rein, reis, rigs, ring, rins, rise, roes, rose, seen, seer, sego, sene, sere, sign, sine, sing, sire, snog, sone, song, sore, sori, sorn

Jack Nicklaus

aals, ails, ains, akin, alan, alas, anal, anas, anil, anis, ansa, anus, asci, auks, caca, cain, calk, cans, casa, cask, caul, clan, cusk, ilka, ilks, inks, jack, jail, jauk, jink, jins, junk, kaas, kail, kain, kaka, kaki, kana, kick, kiln, kina, kink, kins, lack, lacs, laic, lain, lank, lick, link, lins, luck, luna, lunk, nail, nick, nils, sack, sail, sain, saki, sank, saul, scan, sial, sick, silk, sink, skin, skua, suck, sulk, sunk, ulan, ulna, unai, unci

Federico Fellini

ceder, celli, cello, ceorl, cered, cider, cliff, cline, clone, coden, coder, coled, colin, coned, cored, credo, creed, creel, cried, crone, decor, defer, deice, dicer, diene, diner, dolce, dolci, donee, drill, droll, drone, edile, eerie, eider, elder, elfin, elide, eloin, ender, enrol, erode, felid, felon, fence, ficin, field, fiend, fifed, fifer, filed, filer, fille, fillo, fined, finer, fiord, fired, fleer, flied, flier, force, freed, fried, frill, frond, icier, idler, indie, indol, indri, infer, iodic, iodin, ionic, irone, leone, lifer, lined, liner, loden, loner, nerol, nicer, nicol, niece, offed, offer, oiled, oiler, olden, older, oldie, oleic, olein, orcin, oriel, recon, redon, refed, refel, relic, reoil, riced, ricin, rifle, riled, rille

Goldie Hawn

adown, agile, aglow, agone, ahold, ailed, algid, algin, alien, align, aline, aloin,

alone, along, angel, angle, anile, anode, anole, awing, awned, danio, dawen, deign, dewan, dhole, dinge, dingo, diwan, dogie, doing, donga, dowel, dowie, dwine, elain, eland, eloin, endow, gelid, genoa, geoid, glade, gland, glean, glide, gonad, gonia, gowan, haled, halid, haole, hawed, helio, hinge, hogan, holed, honda, honed, ideal, indol, indow, ingle, laden, laigh, lawed, liane, liang, ligan, lined, linga, lingo, loden, lodge, logan, logia, longe, lowed, naled, neigh, nidal, nodal, ogled, ohing, oiled, olden, oldie, olein, owing, owned, waged, wagon, waled, waned, weald, weigh, whale, whang, wheal, while, whine, whole, widen, wield, wigan, wiled, wined, woald, wodge

Lionel Richie

ceil, cell, cere, cero, chin, chon, cine, cion, cire, clon, coil, coin, coir, cole, cone, coni, core, corn, eche, echo, elhi, enol, erne, heel, heil, heir, hell, helo, here, herl, hern, hero, hili, hill, hire, hoer, hole, hone, horn, icon, inch, inro, iron, lech, leer, lehr, leno, lice, lich, lien, lier, line, lino, lion, lire, liri, loch, loci, loin, lone, lore, lorn, nice, nill, noel, noil, noir, nori, once, orle, reel, rein, rice, rich, riel, rile, rill, roil, role, roll

Amelia Earhart

aerie, aimer, airer, airth, alarm, alate, alert, almah, almeh, altar, alter, ameer, areae, areal, arete, arhat, ariel, armer, armet, artal, artel, atria, earth, eater, elate, elemi, elite, ether, haler, halma, hamal, harem, hater, heart, hemal, herma, hilar, hirer, ihram, irate, ither, laari, lahar, laith, lamer, lamia, laree, later, lathe, lathi, lethe, liter, lithe, litre, maile, malar, maria, mater, merer, merit, merle, metal, meter, metre, miler, mirth, miter, mitre, ramee, ramet, ramie, ratal, ratel, rater, rathe, realm, rearm, reata, rehem, relet, relit, remet, remit, retem, retia, retie, riata, rimer, talar, taler, tamal, tamer, tarre, telae, telia, terai, terra, tharm, their, theme, there, therm, thirl, three, tiara, tiler, timer, trail, trial, trier

Will Rogers

egis, egos, ells, ergo, ergs, eros, errs, gels, gies, gill, girl, giro, glow, goer, goes, gore, grew, grow, ills, ires, isle, legs, leis, lier, lies, lire, loge, logs, lore, lose, lowe, lows, lwei, ogle, ogre, oils, oles, ores, orle, owes, owls, owse, regs, reis, riel, rigs, rile, rill, rise, roes, roil, role, roll, rose, rows, sego, sell, sill, silo, sire, slew, sloe, slog, slow, soil, sole, soli, sore, sori, swig, weir, well, wigs, wile, will, wire, wise, woes, wogs, wore

Regis Philbin

begin, being, bergs, biers, biles, bilge, bines, binge, birle, birls, birse, blini, blips, brens, bries, brigs, brine, bring, brins, genii, genip, giber, gibes, girls, girns, girsh, glens, grins, gripe, grips, heils, heirs, helps, herbs, herls, herns, hinge, hires, ingle, iring, lehrs, lenis, liber, libri, liens, liers, liger, liner, lines, lings, lipin, neigh, nighs, nihil, nisei, peins, penis, peril, peris, piers, piing, pilei, piles, pilis, pines, pings, pirns, plebs, plier, plies, pries, prigs, prise, reign, reins, renig, repin, resin, ribes, riels, riles, rings, rinse, ripen, ripes, risen, rishi, segni, sengi, serin, shiel, shier, shine, shire, shlep, sigil, singe, siren, slier, sling, slipe, snipe, speil, speir, spiel, spier, spile, spine, spire, sprig

Greg LeMond

deem, deer, dele, deme, demo, dene, dere, derm, doer, doge, dole, dome, done, dong, dore, dorm, dree, dreg, edge, eger, enol, ergo, erne, geed, geld, gene, germ, gled, glee, gleg, glen, glom, goer, gold, gone, gong, gore, gree, grog, leer, lend, leno, lode, loge, lone, long, lord, lore, lorn, meed, meld, mend, meno, mere, merl, mode, mold, mole, more, morn, need, neem, nerd, node, noel, nogg, nome, norm, ogee, ogle, ogre, omen, omer, orle, rede, redo, reed, reel, rend, rode, role

Glen Campbell

abele, agene, aglee, allee, amble, ample, anele, angel, angle, bagel, becap, began, belga, belle, blame, bleep, cable, camel, celeb, cella, clamp, clang, clean, clepe, eagle, enema, gable, gambe, glace, gleam, glean, gleba, glebe, label, lance, lapel, leben, legal, leman, macle, mange, maple, panel, peace, peage, pecan, penal, pence, place, plage, plane, plebe, plena

Gerard Depardieu

adage, added, adder, adieu, aerie, agape, agree, agria, aided, aider, aired, airer, areae, argue, audad, auger, aurae, aurar, aurei, dared, darer, deair, direr, dirge, drape, dread, drear, dreed, dried, drier, druid, drupe, duded, duped, duper, dured, durra, eager, eagre, eared, edged, edger, eerie, eider, erred, gaddi, gadid, gaped, gaper, grade, grape, greed, gride, gripe, guard, guide, irade, padre, padri, paged, pager, pardi, pared, parer, pareu, parge, peage, perdu, perea, preed, pride, pried, prier, prude, purda, puree, purer, purge, radar, raged, ragee, raped, raper, rapid, rared, rarer, readd, reded, redia,

redid, redip, repeg, rerig, rider, ridge, riped, riper, ruder, rugae, rupee, udder, uraei, urare, urari, urged, urger

Dianne Feinstein

adits, aedes, aides, anent, anise, anted, antes, antis, aside, dates, deans, deets, defat, defis, deist, denes, dense, dents, diene, diets, dines, dints, ditas, dites, eased, eaten, edits, enate, entia, etnas, fades, faint, fanes, fated, fates, fease, feast, feats, feeds, feint, feist, fends, fetas, feted, fetes, fetid, fiats, fiend, finds, fined, fines, finis, ideas, inane, indie, inned, inset, intis, naifs, nates, neats, needs, neifs, neist, nides, nines, nisei, nites, nitid, saint, saned, sated, satin, sedan, seine, senna, sente, senti, setae, sited, snide, stade, staid, stain, stand, stane, stead, steed, stein, stied, tains, tease, teens, teiid, teind, tends, tenia, tense, tides, tinea, tined, tines, tsade, tsadi

Keanu Reeves

akee, anes, anus, ares, arks, arse, auks, aver, aves, earn, ears, ease, eave, ekes, eras, erne, erns, even, ever, eves, kaes, kane, karn, keas, keen, kens, kern, knar, knee, knur, kues, kvas, nark, nave, near, neuk, neve, nuke, rake, rank, rase, rave, reek, rees, revs, rues, rune, runs, ruse, rusk, sake, sane, sank, sark, save, sear, seek, seen, seer, sene, sera, sere, skee, skua, suer, sunk, sura, sure, ukes, urea, urns, ursa, user, uvea, vane, vans, vars, vase, vaus, veer, vees, vena, vera

Jason Robards

abas, abos, ados, ajar, anas, ands, anoa, ansa, arbs, baas, bads, band, bans, bard, barn, bars, bass, boar, boas, bods, bond, boon, boor, boos, bora, born, boss, brad, bran, bras, broo, bros, dabs, darb, darn, dojo, dona, dons, door, dorr, dors, doss, drab, jabs, jars, jobs, joss, nabs, nada, naos, nard, nobs, nods, oars, odor, orad, orbs, ordo, orra, osar, ossa, rads, raja, rand, road, roan, roar, robs, rods, rood, sabs, sand, sans, sard, snob, soar, sobs, soda, sods, soja, sons, soon, sora, sorb, sord, sorn

Cat Stevens

aces, acne, acts, anes, ante, ants, ates, aves, cane, cans, cant, case, cast, cate, cats, cave, cees, cent, cess, cete, ease, east, eats, eave, eses, etas, etna, even, eves, nave, neat, ness, nest, nets, nett, neve, sacs, sane, sans, sate, save, scan, scat, seas, seat, secs, sect, seen, sees, sene, sent, seta, sets, sett, stat, stet, tace, tact, tans, tass, tate, tats, tavs, teas, teat, teen, tees, tens, tent, test, tets, vacs, vane, vans, vase, vast, vats, vees, vena, vent, vest, vets

Sam Donaldson

aals, adds, ados, alan, alas, alma, alms, also, amas, anal, anas, ands, anna, anoa, anon, ansa, dada, dado, dads, dals, damn, dams, dodo, dols, doms, dona, dons, doom, doss, lads, lama, lams, land, lass, load, loam, loan, loom, loon, loos, loss, mads, mana, mano, mans, mass, moan, moas, mods, mola, mold, mols, mono, mons, mood, mool, moon, moos, moss, naan, nada, nana, nans, naos, nods, nolo, noma, noms, nona, noon, odds, olds, ossa, sals, sand, sans, slam, soda, sods, sola, sold, solo, sols, soma, sons, soon

Richard Gere

aced, ache, acid, acre, aged, agee, ager, aide, arch, arid, cade, cadi, cage, caid, card, care, carr, cede, cedi, cere,

chad, char, chia, chid, cire, crag, dace, dare, dear, deer, dere, dice, dire, drag, dree, dreg, each, eche, edge, egad, eger, eide, gadi, gaed, gear, geed, ghee, gied, gird, grad, gree, grid, hade, haed, hair, hard, hare, head, hear, heed, heir, herd, here, hide, hied, hire, iced, idea, ired, race, rage, ragi, raid, rare, read, rear, rede, reed, rhea, rice, rich, ride

Art Linkletter

aerie, airer, akene, alert, alien, alike, aline, allee, alter, anele, anile, ankle, antre, arete, ariel, artel, atilt, eaten, eater, elain, elate, elint, elite, enate, enter, entia, ileal, inert, inker, inkle, inlet, inter, irate, kerne, kiter, kneel, knell, knelt, krait, krill, laker, laree, laten, later, latke, leant, learn, liane, liken, liker, liner, liter, litre, niter, nitre, rakee, raker, ranee, ratel, rater, reink, relet, relit, renal, rente, reran, retia, retie, riant, rille, taint, taken, taker, takin, taler, tarre, tater, telae, telia, tenet, tenia, terai, terne, terra, tetra, tilak, tiler, tinea, titan, titer, title, titre, traik, trail, train, trait, trank, treat, treen, trial, trier, trike, trill, trine, trite

Barry Manilow

aboil, aboma, alamo, alarm, alary, aliya, aloin, alway, amain, ambry, amino, amnia, anima, anomy, arbor, armor, aroma, array, arrow, bairn, balmy, banal, barmy, barny, baron, bialy, binal, blain, blawn, blimy, blown, blowy, bolar, boral, boyar, boyla, brail, brain, brawl, brawn, briar, briny, broil, brown, bwana, bylaw, inarm, inlay, irony, laari, labia, labor, labra, lamby, lamia, lanai, lawny, liana, libra, liman, limba, limbo, limby, loamy, lobar, loran, lorry, malar, mania, manly, manor, maria, marly, marry, mayan, mayor, mbira, miaow, minor, moira, molar, moral, moray,

naira, nawab, nobly, noily, noria, noway, nyala, rainy, rawin, rawly, rayon, riyal, robin, roily, roman, rowan, royal, wanly, wirra, woman, womby, wormy, worry

Carrie Fisher

aches, acres, aerie, afire, airer, areic, arise, arris, cafes, carer, cares, carrs, carse, cease, ceres, ceria, chafe, chair, chare, charr, chars, chase, cheer, chefs, chias, chief, chirr, cires, cirri, crash, crier, cries, eches, erase, erica, escar, facer, faces, fairs, farce, farci, farer, fares, fears, fease, feces, feres, feria, fiars, fices, fiche, firer, fires, freer, frees, frere, fresh, friar, frier, fries, frise, hafis, hairs, hares, hears, heirs, heres, hirer, hires, icier, racer, races, raise, rarer, rares, raser, reach, rears, reefs, refer, reifs, rheas, ricer, rices, rifer, riser, rishi, safer, saice, saree, scare, scarf, scree, serac, serai, serer, serif, share, sheaf, shear, sheer, shier, shire, shirr, siree, sirra

Golda Meir

adore, agile, aider, ailed, aimed, aimer, aired, alder, algid, algor, amide, amido, amigo, amole, argil, argle, argol, ariel, armed, aroid, deair, derma, dimer, dirge, dogie, dogma, dolma, domal, drail, dream, gamed, gamer, gelid, geoid, gimel, glade, glair, glare, gleam, glide, glime, gloam, golem, goral, gored, grade, grail, gride, grime, ideal, idler, image, imago, irade, lader, lager, laird, lamed, lamer, large, largo, liard, lidar, liger, limed, lodge, logia, madre, maile, marge, medal, media, midge, miler, mired, modal, model, moira, moire, molar, morae, moral, morel, oared, ogled, ogler, oiled, oiler, older, oldie, omega, oread, oriel, radio, raged, ramie, realm, redia, regal, regma, reoil, ridge, riled, rimed

Dean Martin

adman, admen, admit, aider, aimed,
aimer, aired, amain, amend, ament,
amide, amine, amnia, anear, anent,
anima, anime, antae, anted, antra,
antre, arena, armed, armet, atman,
atria, daman, damar, dater, deair,
demit, denim, derat, derma, dimer,
dinar, diner, drain, drama, dream,
entia, inane, inarm, inert, inned, inner,
inter, irade, irate, madre, maned,
mania, manna, manta, maria, mated,
mater, matin, meant, media, menad,
menta, merit, minae, mined, miner,
mired, miter, mitre, nadir, naiad,
naira, named, namer, niter, nitre,
ramet, ramie, ranid, ratan, rated,
reata, redan, redia, reman, remit,
renin, retia, riant, riata, rimed, tamed,
tamer, tared, teind, tenia, terai, tiara,
timed, timer, tinea, tined, tired, trade,
train, tread, trend, triad, tried, trine

Anton Chekhov

achoo, ancon, anent, atone, canoe,
canon, canto, cento, chant, cheat,
cheth, choke, chook, conte, conto,
cotan, coven, covet, enact, hacek,
hance, hatch, haven, havoc, heath,
henna, honan, hooch, hooka,
hotch, kench, ketch, kheth, knave,
nacho, nance, natch, neath, nonce,
nonet, notch, novae, oaken, oaten,
ocean, octan, ovate, tache, taken,
teach, tench, tenon, thack, thane,
thank, theca, token, tonne, vetch

Jacques Cousteau

aces, acta, acts, ajee, aqua, asea, ates,
auto, caca, casa, case, cast, cate, cats,
ceca, cees, cess, cete, coat, coca,
coss, cost, cote, cots, cues, cuss,
cute, cuts, ease, east, eats, ecus, eses,
etas, jato, jees, jess, jest, jete, jets,
joes, joss, jota, jots, just, jute, juts,
oast, oats, ocas, oses, ossa, oust,
outs, qats, sacs, sate, scat, scot, scut,
seas, seat, secs, sect, sees, seta, sets,
soja, sots, sous, stoa, sues, suet,
suqs, tace, taco, taos, tass, taus, teas,
tees, toea, toes, toss, uses, utas

Alfred Nobel

abele, abler, abode, adobe, adore,
adorn, afore, alder, aldol, allee, allod,
alone, anele, anode, anole, ardeb,
baled, baler, baned, barde, bared,
baron, beano, beard, bedel, belle,
blade, bland, blare, blear, bleed, blend,
blond, board, bolar, boned, boner,
boral, bored, borne, brand, bread,
brede, breed, broad, debar, defer, dobla,
dobra, donee, droll, drone, eared,
eland, elder, ender, enrol, erode, fable,
fader, fared, farle, fella, felon, feral,
flare, fleer, flora, freed, frena, frond,
label, labor, laden, lader, ladle, laree,
learn, leben, leone, llano, lobar, lobed,
loden, loner, loral, loran, naled, nerol,
noble, nodal, oared, olden, older, orbed,
oread, radon, ranee, rebel, redan,
redon, refed, refel, renal, robed, roble

Liam Neeson

aeons, aisle, alien, aline, almes, aloes,
aloin, alone, amens, amies, amine,
amino, amins, amole, anele, anile,
anils, anime, anion, anise, anole,
easel, elain, elans, elemi, eloin, enema,
enols, eosin, inane, lames, lanes,
leans, lease, leman, lemon, lenes,
lenis, lenos, lense, leone, liane, liens,
liman, limas, limen, limes, limns, limos,
linen, lines, linns, linos, lions, loams,
loans, loins, maile, mails, mains,
males, manes, manos, manse, mason,
meals, means, melon, mensa, mense,
mesne, meson, miens, miles, milos,
minae, minas, mines, moans, moils,
molas, moles, monas, monie, nails,
names, neems, nemas, neons, nines,
noels, noils, noise, nomas, nomen,
nomes, nonas, nones, olein, omens,
salmi, salon, seine, semen, senna,
slain, slime, smile, snail, solan, solei

Frankie Valli

aalii, afire, aiver, akela, alane, alien,
alike, aline, alive, anear, anile, ankle,
anvil, areal, arena, ariel, arval, avail,
avian, elain, elfin, ervil, faena, faker,
fakir, farle, fella, feral, feria, filar, filer,
fille, final, finer, fiver, flail, flair, flake,
flank, flare, flier, frail, frank, freak,
frena, frill, ileal, ilial, infer, infra, inker,
inkle, invar, kafir, kalif, kefir, kenaf,
kevil, knave, knell, knife, kraal, krill,
laari, laker, lanai, larva, laver, learn,
levin, liana, liane, lifer, liken, liker,
liner, liven, liver, livre, naevi, naira,
naive, naval, navar, navel, nival, ravel,
raven, ravin, reink, renal, rifle, rille,
rival, riven, vakil, varia, varna, velar,
venal, viler, villa, villi, vinal, viral

Chapter 16: Kakuro Puzzles

Kakuro Puzzle 1

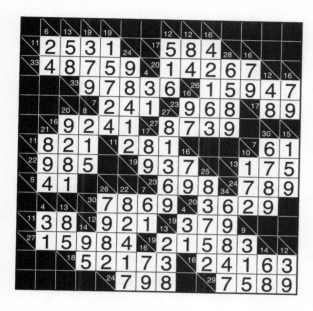

Kakuro Puzzle 2

Kakuro Puzzle 3

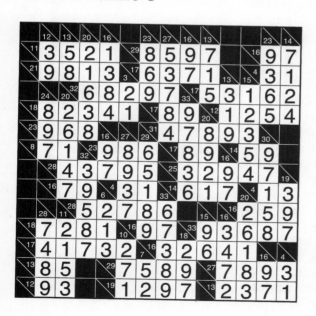

Kakuro Puzzle 4

Kakuro Puzzle 5

Kakuro Puzzle 6

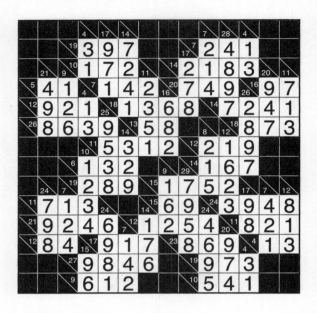

Kakuro Puzzle 7

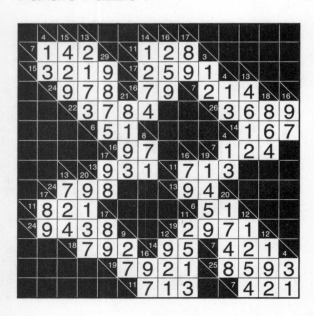

Kakuro Puzzle 8

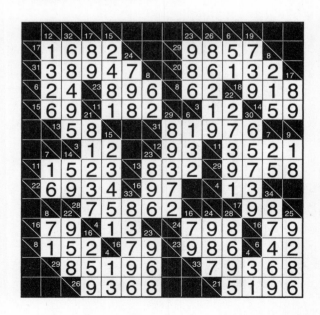

Kakuro Puzzle 9

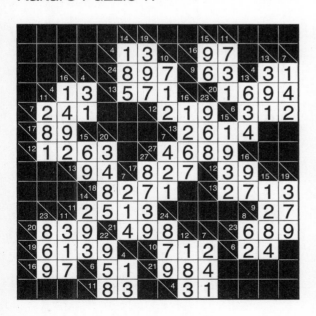

Kakuro Puzzle 10

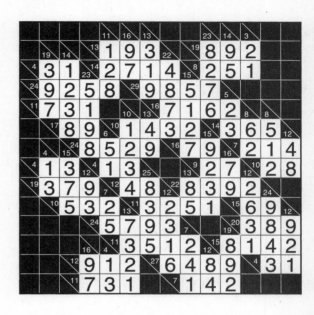

Kakuro Puzzle 11

Kakuro Puzzle 12

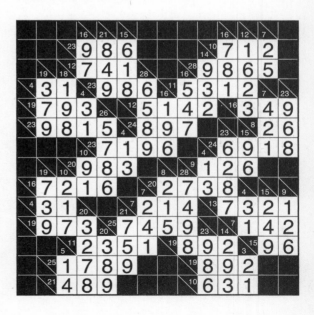

Kakuro Puzzle 13

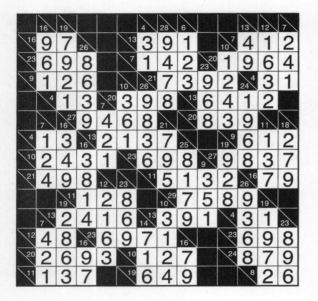

Kakuro Puzzle 14

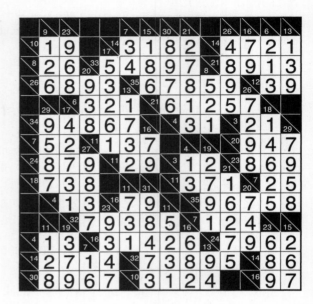

Chapter 17: Quotagrams

Stanley Kubrick

People can misinterpret almost anything so that it coincides with views they already hold. They take from art what they already believe.

- A. EARTHWORM
- B. TRY
- C. WHY
- D. ALPHABET
- E. DETAIL
- F. SALTINE
- G. STATEROOM
- H. YOSEMITE
- I. EIGHTY
- J. YACHT
- K. HEAVEN
- L. WITNESS
- M. HAYRIDE
- N. DVD
- O. ANTELOPE
- P. ARTICHOKE
- Q. CLIP
- R. FLINT

Albert Einstein

When you are courting a nice girl an hour seems like a second. When you sit on a red-hot cinder a second seems like an hour. That's relativity.

- A. TIKI
- B. WIT
- C. GREENHOUSE
- D. LARGE
- E. ODOMETER
- F. STAIRCASE
- G. HEY
- H. CONCRETE
- I. AVENUE
- J. SIT
- K. RHODEISLAND
- L. SAUNA

- M. ENRON
- N. YOUTH
- O. ALARMCLOCK
- P. SHINY
- Q. HOUDINI
- R. NEWS

Clint Eastwood

Respect your efforts, respect yourself. Self-respect leads to self-discipline. When you have both firmly under your belt, that's real power.

- A. ELEVATOR
- B. BICYCLE
- C. TRY
- D. TOMORROW
- E. NEEDLE
- F. BEETLE
- G. DESSERT
- H. REEFER
- I. FLOSS
- J. COPPERHEAD
- K. WHY
- L. ASSISTANT
- M. SYRUP
- N. THEORY
- O. SHUFFLE
- P. PULPFICTION
- Q. SULFUR

Mark Twain

There was never yet an uninteresting life. Such a thing is an impossibility. Inside of the dullest exterior there is a drama, a comedy and a tragedy.

- A. MANDARIN
- B. THIRD
- C. DESMOINES
- D. HALL
- E. WEAVE
- F. SUE

- G. REPAIRMAN
- H. CITY
- I. BIG
- J. OXIDE
- K. GADGET
- L. SHOUT
- M. ANNOY
- N. SISTER
- O. INFLATE
- P. FEET
- Q. TIS
- R. ITINERARY
- S. CELERY
- T. HAUNTED
- U. THESIS

Van Gogh

If one is master of one thing and understands one thing well, one has at the same time, insight into and understanding of many things.

- A. GEMINI
- B. TORNADO
- C. ANTENNA
- D. TUNNEL
- E. TENNIS
- F. GHOST
- G. SWING
- H. TINMAN
- I. SAUSAGE
- J. DENIM
- K. FAMILY
- L. RODEO
- M. OFFEND
- N. STONE
- O. NIGHT
- P. DISHES
- Q. HAND
- R. HITS
- S. THREAT

Abraham Lincoln

You can fool some of the people all of the time, and all of the people some of the time, but you can not fool all of the people all of the time.

A. LEMON
B. OUTLET
C. APOSTLE
D. OPIUM
E. HOME
F. OATMEAL
G. OFF
H. HE
I. ELLIOT
J. EMPLOY
K. ELOPE
L. COTTONCANDY
M. BUFFALO
N. TOFFEE
O. HEALTH
P. FLESH
Q. ANTELOPE
R. POLITE
S. HOOF

Amy Bloom

Love at first sight is easy to understand; it's when two people have been looking at each other for a lifetime that it becomes a miracle.

A. PROFIT
B. LAUGH
C. METHOD
D. AGAIN
E. CHOOSE
F. BROWSE
G. BLACKTIE
H. SHELF
I. ELEVATOR
J. EASY
K. IDIOT
L. STREETCAR
M. MITTEN
N. MOVIE
O. HOSPITAL

P. ANTENNA
Q. SWEET
R. THIEF

Dale Carnegie

Most of the important things in the world have been accomplished by people who have kept on trying when there seemed to be no hope at all.

A. LEMONDROP
B. BRAVEHEART
C. CHELSEA
D. CABINET
E. YOSEMITE
F. MOTOWN
G. WHOOPI
H. TENT
I. GHETTO
J. KITTEN
K. FRESHMEN
L. SHEEP
M. HOOD
N. BILL
O. HAPPY
P. PHONED
Q. WAVE
R. LENGTH

Nathaniel Hawthorne

Happiness is as a butterfly which when pursued is always beyond our grasp, but which if you will sit down quietly may alight upon you.

A. YACHT
B. DOUGH
C. ASPIRIN
D. WHIP
E. SHY
F. LAUNDRY
G. SWEATER
H. PUPIL
I. SUBURB
J. QUEEN

K. LIMIT
L. HAWAII
M. SNOOPY
N. SHOW
O. ESSAY
P. COYOTE
Q. WISH
R. FUN
S. WILL
T. LADYBUG
U. TUFT

Carl Jung

Even a happy life cannot be without a measure of darkness, and the word happy would lose its meaning if it were not balanced by sadness.

A. MEADOW
B. SEASON
C. TEAPOT
D. DESTINY
E. THOUSAND
F. SUNSET
G. FLOAT
H. NIECE
I. ANSWER
J. PELICAN
K. DOVE
L. HAMBURGER
M. ELEPHANT
N. SARDINE
O. KNOB
P. WHIFF
Q. BYWAY
R. PLAID

Alfred Hitchcock

Seeing a murder on television can help work off one's antagonisms. And if you haven't any antagonisms, the commercials will give you some.

A. AVOCADO
B. SNOW

C. FISH
D. SUMMIT
E. VIETNAM
F. PIONEER
G. GEYSER
H. DESMOINES
I. GECKO
J. MANSION
K. HONEY
L. CLOWN
M. TRIVIA
N. STATUE
O. SALARY
P. HOE
Q. FLAMINGO
R. FLANNEL
S. GUN

Ray Bradbury

Thinking is the enemy of creativity. It's self-conscious, and anything self-conscious is lousy. You can't try to do things. You simply must do things.

A. FIGHT
B. GHI
C. MINDY
D. YOYO
E. GASSTATION
F. DINOSAUR
G. UTENSIL
H. SILENT
I. OPOSSUM
J. TYCOON
K. COLONY
L. GLOSSY
M. MUTINY
N. THICK
O. SUNRISE
P. STUDENT
Q. IFFY
R. CATSTEVENS
S. CHICHI

Calvin Coolidge

Persistence and determination alone are omnipotent. The slogan "press on" has solved and always will solve the problems of the human race.

A. PISTACHIO
B. SOAPOPERA
C. PENTAGON
D. ANEMONE
E. SWEDEN
F. HEEL
G. REEVES
H. SEASHELL
I. LANDON
J. BESTMAN
K. ORNAMENT
L. STROLLER
M. SCOTTADAMS
N. IVORY
O. HULL
P. WITH
Q. FIND

Douglas Adams

A common mistake that people make when trying to design something completely foolproof is to underestimate the ingenuity of complete fools.

A. STOOGE
B. MOON
C. STREETCAR
D. SOURDOUGH
E. FIG
F. FILM
G. EIGHTEEN
H. NINETEEN
I. TOOTH
J. TOMMY
K. TEFLON
L. MEMO
M. MOTEL
N. FLY

O. POTATOSALAD
P. CHOPSTICKS
Q. PINEAPPLE
R. KIWI
S. ENEMY

Chapter 18: Transadditions

Transadd This Word: Rides
1. desire
2. rinsed
3. debris

Transadd This Word: Heart
1. threat
2. bather
3. wreath

Transadd This Word: Range
1. hanger
2. angler
3. gander

Transadd This Word: Scout
1. locust
2. stucco
3. courts

Transadd This Word: Miner
1. vermin
2. airmen
3. marine

Transadd This Word: Canoe
1. beacon
2. octane
3. cornea

Transadd This Word: Model
1. module
2. melody
3. seldom

Transadd This Word: Press
1. spears
2. passer
3. purses

Transadd This Word: Score
1. soccer
2. escort
3. source

Transadd This Word: Loser
1. morsel
2. lovers
3. solver

Transadd This Word: Skate
1. casket
2. basket
3. steaks

Transadd This Word: Noise
1. cosine
2. insole
3. ponies

Transadd This Word: Medal
1. damsel
2. flamed
3. bedlam

Transadd This Word: Ridge
1. glider
2. digger
3. ringed

Transadd This Word: North
1. throne
2. hornet
3. thorns

Transadd This Word: Purse
1. superb
2. supper
3. spruce

Transadd This Word: Snail
1. aliens
2. island
3. finals

Transadd This Word: Organ
1. groans
2. orange
3. jargon

Transadd This Word: Actor
1. costar
2. cantor
3. carrot

Transadd This Word: Nurse
1. prunes
2. reruns
3. unrest

Transadd This Word: Grand
1. danger
2. dragon
3. garden

Transadd This Word: Pride

1. spider
2. diaper
3. period

Transadd This Word: Panel

1. planes
2. planet
3. alpine

Transadd This Word: Raise

1. satire
2. rabies
3. sierra

Transadd This Word: Sharp

1. graphs
2. phrase
3. sherpa

Transadd This Word: Sight

1. lights
2. eights
3. fights

Transadd This Word: Horse

1. chores
2. shower
3. heroes

Transadd This Word: Moral

1. molars
2. normal
3. clamor

Transadd This Word: Naked

1. kneads
2. ranked
3. darken

Transadd This Word: Earth

1. halter
2. breath
3. father

Transadd This Word: React

1. crates
2. nectar
3. carpet

Transadd This Word: Relay

1. lawyer
2. argyle
3. yearly

Transadd This Word: Easel

1. please
2. asleep
3. leaves

Transadd This Word: Elder

1. leader
2. lender
3. dealer

Transadd This Word: Feast

1. faster
2. fiesta
3. facets

Transadd This Word: Ideal

1. ladies
2. derail
3. jailed

Transadd This Word: Later

1. antler
2. rattle
3. talker

Transadd This Word: Noted

1. docent
2. donate
3. rodent

Transadd This Word: Field

1. filmed
2. fiddle
3. filled

Transadd This Word: Point

1. pintos
2. option
3. piston

Transadd This Word: Slide

1. oldies
2. diesel
3. shield

Transadd This Word: Prime

1. empire
2. umpire
3. permit

Transadd This Word: Crisp

1. chirps
2. prices
3. script

Transadd This Word: Rates

1. starve
2. hearts
3. stream

Transadd This Word: Reach

1. archer
2. hacker
3. charge

Transadd This Word: Least

1. castle
2. plates
3. stable

Transadd This Word: Bread

1. adverb
2. balder
3. badger

Transadd This Word: Eager

1. reggae
2. grease
3. meager

Transadd This Word: Great

1. target
2. garret
3. garter

Transadd This Word: Price

1. copier
2. recipe
3. cipher

Transadd This Word: Scale

1. camels
2. cables
3. calves

Transadd This Word: Class

1. clasps
2. scales
3. slacks

Transadd This Word: Radio

1. hairdo
2. roadie
3. ordain

Transadd This Word: Scare

1. sacred
2. scream
3. racers

Transadd This Word: Pearl

1. parole
2. parcel
3. player

Transadd This Word: Loves

1. olives
2. shovel
3. novels